Taking the WATERS in Texas

SPRINGS, SPAS, AND FOUNTAINS OF YOUTH

Janet Mace Valenza

T0385977

UNIVERSITY OF TEXAS PRESS

AUSTIN

Requests for permission to reproduce material from this work should be sent to Permissions, University of Texas Press, P.O. Box 7819, Austin, TX 78713-7819.

∞ The paper used in this book meets the minimum requirements of ANSI / NISO Z39.48-1992 (R1997) (Permanence of Paper).

Library of Congress Cataloging-in-Publication Data

Valenza, Janet, 1947–
    Taking the waters in Texas : springs, spas, and fountains of youth / Janet Valenza.
        p.   cm.
    Includes bibliographical references and index.
    ISBN 978-0-292-78734-6
    1. Health resorts—Texas.   2. Hot springs—Texas.   3. Mineral waters—Texas.   I. Title.
RA807.T4V35   2000
613′.122′09764—dc21   99-23073

Parts of this work were previously published in " 'Taking the Waters' at Texas' Health Spas," *Southwestern Historical Quarterly* 98, no. 3 (January 1995): 427–456, and " 'Taking the Waters' at Texas Spas," *Journal of Cultural Geography* 11, no. 1 (Fall / Winter 1990): 57–70. The author gratefully acknowledges permission to reprint this material here.

For
my beloved daughter, Shonda,
my supportive husband, Michael,
and Tiger

Contents

Illustrations

Acknowledgments

I am indebted to Robin Doughty and Ian Manners for their numerous incisive and insightful readings of my manuscript. Their help, support, and editing clarified my thinking and shepherded me through some difficult junctures. My discussions with Robert Mugerauer also proved invaluable in understanding the nature of place.

After many hours of interviews, I discovered firsthand that these resorts were in truth "places of the heart." Frank Oltorf's colorful stories and Dr. Neil Buie Jr.'s firsthand medical experiences delighted and entertained while informing me about Marlin. I am also indebted to the following persons who provided interesting material about the watering experience in Marlin: Richard Peacock, Ruby Harris, Mrs. Hill Houston, and Virginia Torbett. For information on Mineral Wells, I thank Thelma Doss, Vernon Daniels, and Velva White. I also extend my heartfelt gratitude to Corine Talleson of Tioga and Pat Barton of Salado, who wrote to me about their experiences. Mary Lee of Fort Worth enthralled me for several hours about her years as the manager of Indian Hot Springs. Other folks who have helped include Jack and Bea Paul on Kingston Hot Springs; Willie Biggs of Luling; W. W. "Bill" Dennis of Jacksboro, Jim Davis and Martha Jones on Wizard Wells; Carlie Sego of Glen Rose; Martha Hand of Rosborough Springs; Mrs. R. M. Nugent and Leila LaGrone on Midyett; Rebecca Nickelson of Franklin; LaVerne Rutherford of Putnam; the men at Sour Lake's Texaco, who generously took me on a tour of the grounds of the old bathhouse; H. P. Cheatham of Tioga; Lillian Masters and Mrs. and Mr. Fred Anderson on Sutherland Springs; Dudley Staton and the Gonzales Warm Springs Foundation on Ottine; Judy King of Stovall Wells; and Jonathan de Vierville for the dip in Hot Wells' sulphurous brew. I extend special thanks to Susan

Dowell of Bremond, who so graciously let me examine and copy her scrapbook on Wootan Wells. For facilitating research on the mineral waters in smaller towns, I would like to thank the staff at the following libraries: Dr. James Conrad at East Texas State University, Darlene Mott of the Sam Houston Regional Library and Research Center, Lena Armstrong at the Belton City Library, Nancy Franklin of Mount Calm Library, the County-City Library in Sweetwater, the Tom Green County Library, Marilyn Alford of the Stephenville Public Library, Linda Fowler of the Sam Houston State University Archives, the Glen Rose Library, Inez Hatley Hughes of the Marshall Historical Museum Archives, Eastland's Centennial Memorial Library, Lesley Sandlin of the Mount Pleasant Library, the Archives of the Big Bend at Sul Ross University, and the San Antonio Conservation Society.

The Texas State Historical Commission's county chairmen and members who provided me with information are: Mrs. John Frank of Lee County, Lillie Gibson of Erath County, Chris Skelly of Hopkins County, Charlotte Teske of Gregg County, and Virginia Buchanan of the Smith County Historical Society. I am particularly grateful to the Lampasas County Historical Commission for letting me attend one of its meetings and giving me access to its files. Mrs. Jean Bruns, owner of the Anderson Bed and Breakfast in Warm Springs, Virginia, provided valuable material on the history of Virginia's springs. I also appreciate my conversations and subsequent leads from Gene Fowler, who researched the topic at the same time.

Finally, I owe my family for their support and sustenance throughout the research for my dissertation. My mother, Irene Creighton, and my husband, Michael Valenza, put up with many long hours of research, struggle, and frustration. Mostly I want to thank my daughter; if it had not been for her, I would never have attempted to hitch my wagon to this particular star. During her elementary years, I spent many hours away to do this research. Through loving her, I found places of strength and resolve I did not know I possessed. Those long years of graduate school resulted in my dissertation, and thereafter, with some revisions, this book.

INTRODUCTION

Vanishing Places

THE WATERS SYMBOLIZE the universal sum of virtualities; they are *fons et origo*, "spring and origin," the reservoir of all the possibilities of existence; they precede every form and support every creation.

—*Mircea Eliade*, The Sacred and the Profane

During the summer of 1992, I traveled to a remote location in West Texas to research hot springs. I was not sure what to expect. I had visited some of the country's most famous landmarks—Hot Springs, Arkansas; French Lick, Indiana; Warm Springs, Virginia—all noted health resorts. I knew that Indian Hot Springs, southeast of El Paso, was no longer open to the public, but the hot waters still attracted the locals, some of whom came across the river to take a dip. I thought the trip in my van would be simple and quick after I turned off I-10, and I planned to be back in El Paso for the night. Though the dirt road proved tediously crooked, after every turn I expected to see the old buildings loom ahead. Soon the twenty-some-mile trip had turned into a two-hour pilgrimage.

When I arrived, I saw right away that the sunset-streaked buildings no longer provided the focus of health-seeking journeys. They were all boarded up, including the main spring that led to the bathhouse. Yet there was a sense of expectancy—that the site still had something to offer. Indeed, the buildings appeared to be in good shape. As evening fell, I started to walk around the property, but clouds of mosquitoes immediately besieged me. I hurried back to the van and found that I had depleted my water supply. I knew I would be forced to leave the next morning to regroup, and now I settled in for a long and uncomfortable night in my van.

Around midnight the sky began to brighten with brilliant displays of lightning, preceding what I thought must be the storm to end all storms. I started to worry that if a deluge came, the dirt road might wash out, since the river ran parallel to it for miles. I perceived myself to be in a precarious position at best, so I decided that I should drive back to El Paso. As I tried to maneuver the hills and curves in the dark, my headlights started to flicker and fade. Of course, I was well aware that the desert was the least desirable place to become stranded on low ground during a cloudburst. Driving probably the worst road in Texas, with the wilderness on one side and the dark Rio Grande on the other, I prayed hard those few hours while I dodged legions of jackrabbits. With my rapidly fading lights, I could barely follow the road. Time dragged by as I took the hills and curves like a mad race driver in a broken car. I was in luck—the car lasted until I reached a truck stop. Then it conveniently died. I found out later that the alternator had gone out—not the easiest part of a vehicle to replace, especially in areas populated only by mosquitoes and jackrabbits.

While this episode could constitute a lesson on proper fieldwork preparation, I now understood why Olin Teague wrote in a 1968 *Congressional Record* that this was the most isolated spa in the country. I also discerned the essential nature of a pilgrimage—expectation fraught with difficulty. Although I had no chance to partake of these waters, I was baffled as to why this and other spas in the state were no longer going enterprises. Indian Hot Springs had a variety of strong mineral waters, a beautiful mountainous setting, and quaint cabins. It did not seem to differ much in circumstance from Ojo Caliente, a small, popular, and affordable spa still operating in northern New Mexico. Texas spas, on the contrary, have completely disappeared from the landscape. Yet they were influential in the history and settlement of the state. Indian Hot Springs, like most of the others, had seen both the rich and the poor mingle there for one purpose—health. It had been frequented by a Rockefeller and owned by a Hunt. Yet now it remained closed, with no foreseeable future as a public facility. Other mineral water spas in this country still operate; or, if they have closed, they are memorialized and preserved with their stories intact. Not much of the story of this spa remained; in fact, the stories of many spas in this state have disappeared.

This book tells the stories of these lost places—places that meant something to the settler, the homemaker, the town builder. In some cases, they symbolized a hope for relief from pain; in others, the chance for a new beginning in a place where others would also come to make a home. Each site had its own saga, often preserved only in old newspapers in dusty archives. While each is important in its own right, combined, they relay the sense of a force that shaped the way the state developed. That force essentially involved a belief in a nature cure—the power of the flowing waters.

In one respect these places became "sacred" to healthseekers; "taking the waters" embodied a basic and important but fleeting relationship with the natural environment. People searched for the healing powers of nature and found them in mineral springs. They sought companionship, leisure, and alleviation of bodily pain in an inspiring and comforting environment. Feelings of excitement and trepidation usually accompanied their pilgrimages. Participants left the security of their homes for alien and foreign places. Disabled people often endured considerable pain to travel to these spas. Others ventured forth to these unknown places and immediately felt at ease in their surroundings.

Once the visitors arrived at their chosen resorts, they became acquainted with the area, entered into daily routines, and grew familiar with life at the spa. In a new place, bodily routines often fostered a comfortable sense of at-homeness. Texas' mineral water resorts became homelike places that nurtured the bodies and the spirits of vacationers, healthseekers, and prospective settlers alike. These places were born from the collective memories and affections of inhabitants and spa-goers. They reflected the essence of human involvement, a creative spark that can make a place an enduring memory instead of merely a fleeting recollection.

Generally, the prized waters remained the nucleus of the activity at most of these watering places, and health more than pleasure was their raison d'être. As time passed, however, the idea of the spas as sacred places was supplanted by a transition at some places to a recreational and socializing role. With the emphasis more on secular pleasure than on health concerns, leisure activities became less place-specific, and the healing waters consequently attracted fewer visitors. Thus the importance of these sites diminished.

The Lone Star State once claimed hundreds of watering places, including some nationally famous ones. No comprehensive history has explored the meanings behind the establishment of these places. Today we know little of their pasts, for only a few scattered accounts in local or county histories memorialize them. Daily life in these towns revolved around the springs, and as the settlement of Texas progressed, the resorts changed. Some developed, and others declined. Yet these wells and springs facilitated Texas' settlement, influenced the state's transportation routes, and helped define people's attitudes toward the land and their own sense of health and well-being.

CHAPTER I

Taking the Waters

MUCH OF THE DISCUSSION to follow on the historical background of resort therapy will be concerned with the forces which at different periods have raised this therapy to the central feature of medical care, have reduced it to the status of a superstition, have diverted its main features into voluptuous cultural practices, have opposed its use on the puritanical background that its measures coddled the flesh that needed scourging for the sins of disease, have degraded it to a social fad, have allowed it to pass into the hands of the charlatan and enthusiast as a panacea, have obstructed it with the lack of economic provision for care and have brushed it aside with a disinterest that has come from attention fixed on only the novel in medicine.

> —*Howard W. Haggard, M.D.,* Journal of the
> American Medical Association, *1943*

A few years ago I somehow convinced my family that we needed to vacation in Virginia. I wanted to see the spas that figured in this country's history—those to which Jefferson, Washington, and Lee traveled for health and pleasure. When the time came to commence our road trip, however, I fell ill. My body ached, my throat burned, and the last thing I wanted to do was to travel halfway around the country to sightsee. But fearing that they might leave without me, I bundled up and decided to sleep my way to Virginia, hoping that in a few days my condition would improve. When we arrived in Warm Springs, though, I did not feel any better. In fact I felt worse.

After we checked into a lovely old cottage, a two-hundred-year-old tavern remodeled into a bed-and-breakfast, I grabbed my daughter and headed for the Warm Springs bathhouse. I certainly couldn't feel any worse, barring catching pneumonia, of course. I simply had to see where in the late 1700s the Virginia aristocracy began their fashionable tours of the various spas—

1. Author's daughter in front of Ladies' Bathhouse, Warm Springs, Virginia, 1992. Author photo.

first the Warm, then the Hot, the Sweet, the White, and so on, until a few months later they returned to the Warm.

We arrived at the bathhouses—the gentleman's pool house, standing since 1761, and the ladies' pool house, built in 1836—which were still open for business during the summer months (see fig. 1). The round women's pool had changing rooms scattered around the perimeter. About twenty-five feet in diameter and five feet deep, it had a natural sand and rock floor. The clear, 99°F water continually bubbled up from the bottom, tickling the bather who could swim, float, or stand in it for hours. One of the rooms surrounding the pool contained the chair used to dunk Mrs. Robert E. Lee into the water more than one hundred years ago. It still hung above the water, as if she would arrive to use it at any time (see fig. 2).

I had researched the history of the waters at spas in Texas and around the world, but I could not really identify with the bathers who flocked to these places. After all, how different could it be from sitting in a bathtub or a hot tub? To date, the personal stories of pilgrims seeking out various waters to heal their afflictions seemed remote and removed from me. This sophisticated age of modern medicine supposedly made age-old pilgrimages anachronistic.

So this was my first chance to experience one of these healing places as a participant and see if it worked. I was certainly sick enough to be a good test case. So my daughter and I took the waters for at least an hour. It even slightly rained upon us; the roof is open in places above the pool. After we got out, I felt somewhat better. We filled a jug with the water from the drinking fountain and returned to our lodgings, where I slept the rest of the afternoon. When I awoke in the evening, I felt alive again. I became a believer.

Still practiced in Europe, Japan, and many other regions of the world, bathing in mineral waters has largely disappeared from Texas and the rest of the United States. Nevertheless, Hot Springs, Arkansas, and Saratoga, New York, have attempted to resuscitate this tradition, and scattered other spas around the country still offer mineral baths in conjunction with health club

2. Mrs. Robert E. Lee's dunking chair, Ladies' Bathhouse, Warm Springs, Virginia, 1992. Author photo.

memberships. Although this tradition is emulated in modern-day hot tubs, its true spirit survives in the popular pastime of hot-springs bathing at natural sites, as in the Rocky Mountains and California, where the popularity of springs has resurged within the last ten or twenty years as a result of the environmental and New Age movements.

"Taking the waters" colloquially refers to bathing in mineral waters, a practice that has been employed since classical times. A healthseeker "takes the waters" at a spa, a facility that derives its name from the Belgian town of Spa, founded in 1326 by a Liége ironmaster whose health improved by using its iron-rich (traditionally called chalybeate) waters. Although technically a spa is any place with therapeutic waters, today's spas tend to emphasize weight loss or preventive health care and may or may not include mineral water baths.

A resort, on the other hand, is a place where people go for rest or relaxation; today's resorts are most associated with leisure and recreation. The term, however, also implies a place where one turns for help, for a final solution. One "resorted" to the waters when all else failed. This meaning predominated in the 1800s, when desperate people sought health as other medical therapies failed or were nonexistent. In 1879, Homer Thrall, a Methodist minister who recorded his travels around Texas, often used the phrase "resorted to by invalids" in reports about mineral springs in Texas. Other contemporary writers called even the smallest Texas spa a "resort," whether or not it had any organized recreational activities. Although the terms "resort" and "spa" once connoted different therapies, their meanings can be identical today. Therefore, the two words are used interchangeably in this text.

How did the idea of bathing in the country's medicinal waters become popular? Some medical thought in the nineteenth century emphasized harmony and equilibrium with the environment rather than disease-specific therapies. Hydrotherapy, in particular, emphasized the capacities of water to purify the body by wrapping an individual in a "wet" sheet or by mechanically applying water treatments, thereby restoring vital healing processes.

Many followers of hydrotherapy leaned to the crusading, progressive themes of William Alcott, Lucy Stone, Susan B. Anthony, and Horace Greeley. Water bathing became a type of nature religion, in which nature's laws became synonymous with God's laws. Some people sought to attune their bodies to natural forces and relied on no medical therapies other than water itself and its action on and within the body.

Similar to hydrotherapy is the science of *mineral* water bathing, or balneotherapy. Its modern-day equivalent is medical hydrology, which is still a thriving practice in parts of Europe. This practice emphasizes how minerals in the water exert a therapeutic effect on the body, whereas hydrotherapy, a more widely recognized regime, requires various dousings of plain water with no concern about mineral content. Although technically different, both movements involving bodily immersion were popular in the 1800s. While most medical practitioners minimized the differences, some doctors believed that the water's heat gave better results than did chemical properties (such as iron or sulphur). Others, however, stressed the differences between mineral water spas and hydropathic establishments. In Texas, there was little to distinguish them. Some mineral water establishments offered hydrotherapeutic techniques, such as wet packs or douches, but most clinics and bathhouses merely provided baths and massages. "Taking the waters" meant bathing in healing waters, more commonly without such elaborate techniques.

The therapeutic value of mineral waters depended upon the quantity of dissolved salts. Conceivably, all water that has not been distilled contains some minerals, but waters designated as "mineral" usually contained more than 500 milligrams per liter (mg/l) of combined salts. If the water was "unpotable," it usually registered more than 1,000 milligrams per liter, suitable for bathing but not drinking. Designation as "healthful" depended upon the ingredients, whether mineral, organic, or gaseous.

Classifications of water proliferated. Generally these defined water as nonthermal or thermal, meaning that it came from the ground warmer than the mean annual temperature of the surrounding air (or more commonly, any waters warmer than 70° F). Others elaborated on this widely accepted classification. In 1948, for example, Walter McClellan, medical director of the Saratoga Spa in New York, categorized water as thermal, saline (sulfate or chloride), gaseous (with carbon dioxide, hydrogen sulphide, or radon), or iron (containing at least 10 mg iron). Many Texas resorts compared their waters to more famous ones, particularly those of Carlsbad, Czechoslovakia (now the Czech Republic), which were thermal, carbonated, sodic sulphated, alkaline-saline.

Early classifications, however, required both a chemist's expertise to determine the water's composition and a specialist's knowledge to understand its therapeutic value. Most classifications rested upon chemical composition, but some included therapeutic effects, such as the American use of the term "purgative." The field was rife with undocumented claims about effectiveness, resulting in "cures" of almost any malady. By the 1940s, spa therapy was widely regarded as helpful for chronic diseases, especially rheumatism and arthritis, as well as gastrointestinal, mild cardiovascular, and skin ailments.

The complexity of analysis alone warranted a physician's referral to specific waters, although experts themselves wavered about which types of waters could bring about what results. Even in the 1960s, Hiroshi Nohara, a Japanese researcher, remarked that temperature, pressure, buoyancy, and chemical constituents complicated any designation of therapeutic water. He argued that substances could enter the body through the skin, a much-debated question. He stated that mineral water therapy was so complicated that

> if someone bathes in the same way in two different mineral waters containing the same amount of a certain constituent, its penetration must differ because electrolyte ions of other kinds may counteract or promote its penetration; hence the same efficacy would not be expected. These complexities create difficulty in deducing the therapeutic efficacy of any one spring from its analysis table alone. [1]

Because of the imprecise nature of balneotherapy, American scientists generally neglected it, leaving Europeans and the Japanese to push ahead with this medical regime.

Critics and even many spa enthusiasts believed that lasting effects came from the water's heat, a person's diet, the calming character of the place, or, more commonly, the psychological benefits of relaxation, rather than the water's mineral content. Many doctors theorized, however, that bathing and drinking could affect chemical and cellular metabolism. Throughout the history of the waters' use in Texas, physicians often attempted to explain their referrals to the waters by alluding to new scientific discoveries.

In the early decades of the twentieth century, a revolutionary new theory explained beneficial effects of taking the waters—radioactivity. The owner of Terrell Hot Well in San Antonio extolled this new discovery. He bragged that his hot well contained radium, declaring:

> Some scientists go so far as to say that it is life itself. . . . As the sun brings out trees and plants, so the radium brings out latent activities that bring health and life to the weak and sick body. . . . It is proven that the human body is particularly sensitive to radioactivity. Now if a body could be charged with radium, say once in five years, there is no reason why we

could not live forever. It seems that the Terrell Hot Well with its radio-activity is the much dreamed of fountain of youth.[2]

In 1910, C. W. Post, cereal manufacturer from Battle Creek, Michigan, spent six weeks in Mineral Wells, Texas. He noted: "The waters are radio-active in addition to having the properties that make them highly solvent for uric acid, [and] this shows that they pass over or near beds of radium, which gives them their wonderful medicinal properties."[3] Tioga (Grayson County) also advertised that its Radium Mineral Water contained 1.1 millimicrocuries of what was probably radon gas because it disappeared after several days.[4] Until the bathhouse recently burned down, Stovall Hot Wells continued to advertise its waters as containing 1,400 milligrams per liter of radium. In fact, some visitors there still considered radioactivity beneficial in minute amounts.

Despite many physicians' claims to the contrary, few scientific investigations confirmed therapeutic effects of certain waters on specific maladies. Nevertheless, resort publications extolled their benefits. Any water containing iron was thought to be most effective in treating anemia or blood diseases. Sulphur, obnoxious smelling in water, cured almost anything, according to the circulars, but was particularly helpful with skin afflictions. While these claims remained matters of speculation, the cleansing qualities of purgative salts were undisputed. In Mineral Wells, Texas, for example, well owners offered different strengths of water: "They used to say that if you ordered from the first one [the first well], it was OK. But if you ordered from the second, you better not go far from the hotel and if you ordered from the third, you'd better stay in your room."[5]

Yesterday's claims about the waters may not draw today's sophisticated consumer. One 1908 newspaper asserted that sore eyes and ulcers could be healed with poultices made from the mud and slime at the bottom of Burditt's (also spelled Burdette's) well. An 1877 article in the *Galveston Daily News* advised the reader to "drink Burditt's sour water that causes a man to throw physic to the dogs, get up an appetite by which he can barbecue an ox, and figuratively speaking, eat, digest and assimilate one-half of it at a single sitting, after which he is strong enough to pull down a house."[6]

Other claims, on the other hand, found a fertile market. Sour Lake's waters were touted as an antidote for morphine and opium addicts. The waters of Putnam, Marlin, and Sour Lake reportedly cured alcoholism.

One manager of the Marlin Sanitarium and Bath House remembered seeing heavy smokers wrapped in sheets turned brown from the nicotine that the bathers sweated out of their systems. Even in the late twentieth century, one Indian Springs manager contends that she knew a cancer-riddled woman from El Paso who had two weeks to live when she visited the springs a decade earlier. This woman, whose hands and feet were swollen on her arrival, was able to put on her shoes and rings and was up and around in four days.[7]

Many doctors ridiculed such extravagant claims. Others advised caution and instructed consumers to seek only those resorts with resident physicians. In 1884, Dr. J. M. Willis, the state health officer, also had reservations but acknowledged that the medical profession was "fast yielding to a better knowledge of their [waters'] therapeutic application." He remonstrated that "mineral waters are never indifferent remedies and either do good or ill to the patient using them." He himself in fact joined the chorus of testimonials: "I have visited Sour Lake, and believe that its waters are capable of relieving many diseases that defy the physician's art."[8]

When asked to write a testimonial for Mineral Wells, one physician produced an uncomplimentary letter, published in a 1907 *Texas State Journal of Medicine,* indicating that he had not "been favorably impressed by the results in numerous cases where they have been prescribed and used. I think that the policy of encouraging a universal and indiscriminate resort to any medicinal agent is productive of much and serious harm." A number of physicians, however, valued mineral waters as cures or palliatives for certain afflictions. Others praised the benefits of natural springs, especially after traditional medical therapies failed. Physicians also wrote testimonials, usually upon invitation. Upon the request of the Mineral Wells Commercial Club, fifteen doctors from Texas (fourteen of whom were registered in the 1906 *American Medical Directory*), two from Louisiana, two from Oklahoma, and one from Arkansas submitted favorable evaluations of this resort for ailments including rheumatism, insomnia, and malaria.[9] Although no clinician or researcher in the state could ascertain the exact mechanism by which relief came about, one Mineral Wells physician reasoned that "there is something which distinguishes the action of natural mineral water from the action of salts produced pharmaceutically."[10]

Balneotherapy and crounotherapy (the drinking cure) generated support from the public and from certain medical establishments for many years. That support gradually weakened until today the real spas are virtually gone, as are their slower, simpler lifestyles. In 1945, physician Richard Kovacs lamented the rapid disappearance of American spas. He noted that the 425 springs active in 1927 had dwindled to 34 by 1943. At that time there remained only 6 of the 17 "Great American Spas" chronicled in the 1927 book by his colleague W. E. Fitch, *Mineral Waters of the United States and American Spas.* Most physicians lamented losses in revenue, estimated at $100 million, which consumers paid at European spas in the early 1930s. Of the other spas recognized as competently staffed with physicians, Kovacs cited only one in Texas—Marlin, in Falls County.[11]

The number of spas dwindled as fewer and fewer physicians in the United States prescribed mineral baths, and then viewed them only as an adjunct to physical therapy. The practice diminished to such an extent that medical experts today are unfamiliar with its place in medical history, even though it has figured prominently throughout the world.

Modern medical technology has today displaced these special sites. Well-meaning but impersonal therapies have commandeered the bodies of tired and sick people. There is less reliance on the self, on the relaxing and health-promoting routine of spa life, and on the elusive qualities of an environmental cure. In the heyday of the spa, waters may or may not have cured anyone, but many patients certainly believed they did. They retreated to the waters, they respected these fountains of life, and they celebrated new vigor and youthfulness. If water cured them, no one ever explained why, nor did they need to. Today, there remains the perpetual hope that the Fountain of Youth exists and awaits discovery. We fear aging almost as much as dying. In that way we differ little from our predecessors of the nineteenth century. Because of my seemingly immediate cure at Warm Springs, I had certainly identified with them.

CHAPTER 2

Historic Watering Tradition

I AM AN OASIS in the busy world where the cosmopolite may find a fellow
from whatsoever clime or country. I possess the health-giving properties
which no modern scientist has been able to compound. I am the finisher
of all the ailments of the human economy. I am the builder of flesh and
bone. All but make the dead stand up and shout, "Oh thou fountain of
youth. . . ." Fate gave to the world but one of a kind. I am Tioga.

—*W. A. McDonald, 1919*

When I flew to England one summer, I expected to see the
spa tradition in full bloom. Instead, I saw relics of watering
days in museums of the once-famous resort towns of Harrogate, Chelten-
ham, Malvern, and Bath. An interesting and active corollary to these neglected resorts, however, is the still-honored place of holy wells throughout
the countryside.

During medieval times in Great Britain many wells considered sacred
to the Druids, or viewed as the abodes of nymphs or gods by the Romans,
were dedicated to Christian saints. Each spring or well gained a reputation
for healing certain afflictions. Saint Ann, for instance, became the patron
saint of the spring at Great Malvern, where women suffering from infertility
sought relief.

I visited the Binsey Church outside of Oxford. It is a simple country
church with surrounding graveyard. The last royal visitors were Henry VIII
and Catherine of Aragon. They must have visited because the well water was
said to restore fertility and to be good for the eyes and stomach. In the
middle of the cemetery were four steps carved into the ground with a concrete marker above denoting "St. Margaret's Well." I was sure that the setting
contributed to the mystery of the well. On a country road surrounded by

pastureland, this unassuming, ancient church conveyed a sense of tranquility and timeless secrets. I felt connected to the spirits of those who had come before, hoping for miracles, just as they followed in the footsteps of those who had come before them. This chain of expectations made the journey to the waters as important as the "taking" of the waters.

The one place where I had expected to take the waters—Bath—had closed its doors to bathers in the 1980s, although I could at least drink the mineralized water from a spigot in the museum (see fig. 3).

In the late 1700s, the city parents of Bath, the spa town immortalized in Jane Austen's *Northanger Abbey*, had rediscovered the old Roman baths that underlay Georgian and Victorian structures in the city. Much of the infra-structure—the heated floors, the lead pipes, and the foundations for the plunges, saunas, and Turkish baths—remained intact despite the neglect of the past 1,600 or so years. The hot mineral springs (the only ones in England) had been valued for 5,000 years before the Romans invaded, but the Romans fully developed the springs in about 60–70 A.D. and even incorporated the local deity, Sulis, in the name, Aquae Sulis. They built a large complex comprising a frigidarium (cold bath), tepidarium (warm bath), caldarium (hot bath), and exercise court. They also perfected the hypocaust, or cavity floor, through which hot air circulated.

The Sacred Spring supplied the baths with water. The Romans inge-niously built a reservoir to hold the water, and it subsequently became the site for offerings to the gods. Excavation revealed thousands of coins and votive offerings, including curses written on pewter to bring retribution to an enemy (and now displayed in the Roman Bath Museum), such as:

> May he who stole my cloak, whether he be man or woman, boy or girl, freedman or slave, become impotent and die. It may have been . . .

Although there seemed to be little acknowledgment of the waters' present-day value, there was a substantial interest in their cultural value, em-phasizing a tradition that began before the Romans. Archaeological discov-eries around many springs throughout the world, in fact, include pictographs denoting healing and other shamanistic practices. Recorded references of their influence in the history of Western civilization begins with the Greeks.

3. Roman baths and abbey, Bath, England, 1989. Author photo.

Europe

In classical Greece, waters with distinct tastes, smells, or colors often represented the abodes of gods and spirits. People erected altars near sacred springs where they celebrated recovery by placing crutches, bandages, and replicas of diseased organs around their edges. Coins or small objects thrown into the water served as tokens of supplication or gratitude. By the fifth century B.C. the cult of Asclepius established temples near springs, such as those at Epidaurus, Cos, Corinth, and Pergamum. The temples, or the Asclepia, housed spas, baths, and places for recreation and worship—the first holistic treatment centers. Later, Hippocrates classified waters as sulphur, salt, effervescent, alum, and bituminous, according to taste, smell, and appearance, a classification still largely in use today.[1]

The Romans also believed in the restorative powers of springs. Vitruvius, a Roman architect, observed that patients recovered more quickly if they frequented temples built near sacred water sources. In the first century A.D. the Romans founded more than one hundred bathing places throughout the Empire. Among the more famous were Bath and Buxton (Aquae Arnemetiae, the original Latin name) in England; Baden-Baden (Aurelia Aquensis) and Aachen (Aquae Grani) in Germany; Aix-les-Bains (Aquae Gratianae), Vichy (Aquae Calidae), and Bagnères de Luchon in France; and Baden (Vicus Aquarum) in Switzerland. Military hospitals for wounded soldiers sprang up at many bath sites. Luxurious baths in imperial Rome, such as Caracalla, accommodated more than three thousand people at a time. They were complex structures involving rooms with cold or tepid waters, some with hot air, areas for exercise, and a stadium and gardens.[2]

In Europe bathing rose and fell in social importance, depending on the century. From the thirteenth century onward, baths as places of entertainment figured prominently in the homes of prosperous citizens. Patients and guests spent two to twelve hours in mineral baths, snacking from floating tables and playing chess. They spent so much time bathing that they often fell asleep in the waters and occasionally drowned. From the fourteenth to the sixteenth centuries, with the spread of epidemics such as syphilis (carried in from the Americas) and the plague (from the Near East), more and more people became afraid of sharing baths. The communal tradition faded. Hygiene subsequently declined.

In the 1700s, spas resumed their earlier social role. Resorts in England figured importantly in the evolution of polite society, expressed in manners and behavior. Beau Nash, for example, a self-proclaimed social arbiter, dictated fashion at Bath, and any aspiring socialite spent a season there. Beginning in 1702, Queen Anne's visits to Bath spurred rapid urban development. Social life in that city revolved around the watering schedule. The daily routine began with a bath between 6:00 and 9:00 A.M., followed by breakfast and water consumption in the Pump Room until 11:00 A.M., morning service in the Abbey, dinner at 2:00 or 3:00 p.m., riding, walking, and window-shopping until returning to the Pump Room at 5:00 p.m. In the evening, a ball, concert, gambling, or the theater provided entertainment. Such routines varied little from what unfolded years later in North America.[3]

The United States

NEW ENGLAND

America's bathing tradition largely originated in England. Colonists knew about spas and consequently recognized the value of natural springs along the Atlantic coast. Pilgrims discovered Stafford Springs in Connecticut from a tribe of Indians, the Nipmucks, who used the springs in summer. Although many springs dotted the area, Stafford became the first resort in the Northeast. The late blossoming of northern resorts resulted from the Puritan influence in New England. Many immigrants came from the south and east of England, where the use of holy wells and springs had been suppressed during the Reformation. In 1771, John Adams wrote in his diary about Stafford Springs:

> The water is very clear, limpid, and transparent; the rock and stones and
> earth, at the bottom are tinged with a reddish yellow color, and so is the
> little wooden gutter, that is placed at the mouth of the spring to carry the
> water off; indeed the water communicates that color, which resembles
> that of the rust of iron, to whatever object it washes. . . . They have built a
> shed over a little reservoir, made of wood, about three feet deep, and into
> that have conveyed the water from the Spring; and there the people bathe,
> wash, and plunge, for which Child has eight pence a time. I plunged twice,
> but the second time was superfluous, and did me more hurt than good; it
> is very cold indeed.[4]

In the nineteenth century Saratoga, New York, one of the country's most celebrated watering places, grew famous among many Texans, who compared it to their resorts. Its history as a spa reportedly began in 1767 when Mohawk Indians carried Sir William Johnson, diplomat to the Iroquois, to Saratoga to cure his gout. Later, several physicians examined the medicinal benefits of its waters, debating the possible therapeutic value of the recent discovery of carbon dioxide—or fixed air, as it was called. When a hotel opened in 1803, Saratoga became the resort in vogue. From about 1820 "cards, billiards, and dancing, all terrible instruments of perdition, were introduced. . . . By 1835 Saratoga had become an acknowledged center of gambling."[5] Promenades, balls, and horse racing effectively elevated this site to a major social center in the mid-1800s. Transformation from an early religious retreat, where the first temperance society met in 1808, to a secular entertainment center was complete. The springs remained popular until the early 1900s when the elite in society headed off to beach resorts and bathing in the sea. During Franklin D. Roosevelt's administration, Saratoga became a federal reservation.[6]

Pennsylvania possessed many famous spas. Bedford Springs, James Buchanan's summer White House, attracted prominent Americans. Yellow Springs, later called Chester, near Philadelphia was an opulent establishment by colonial standards. In the 1770s, houses, thirty-five by eighteen feet, enclosed its three baths and contained drawing rooms, fireplaces, and sash windows. During the Revolution, this resort served as George Washington's headquarters, providing facilities for wounded soldiers. The value of Bristol's waters, near Philadelphia, was acknowledged by the medical profession after Dr. John De Normandie chemically analyzed them in 1768, found them to be diuretic, and studied case histories of patients who had benefited from the springs. Benjamin Rush, M.D., was impressed by the place and had written a paper titled "Experiments and Observations on the Mineral Waters of Philadelphia, Abington, and Bristol" in which he described diseases the water might alleviate. He was particularly impressed by the therapeutic value of water from one well—which was later found to be contaminated by sewage. Rush did warn, however, that "mineral water, like most of our medicines, are [sic] only substitutes for temperance and exercise in chronic diseases. An angel must descend from Heaven, and trouble these chalybeate pools, before we can expect any extraordinary effect from their use alone."[7]

Northern resorts were typified by the grandeur and opulence of such spas as Saratoga and later those in the Colorado Rockies and along the California coast. Primarily attracting an urban clientele, they exhibited an antebellum style, usually including a piazza surrounded by a colonnade several stories high in front of a tall structure. Buildings like the Catskill Mountain House, the Pavilion Hotel at Sharon Springs, New York, and several hotels at Saratoga reflected this Greek Revivalist style. Northern resorts also included tree-lined streets, promenades, and semipublic parks.[8]

THE SOUTH

Whereas northern resorts centered around cities and parks, antebellum southern resorts focused on western Virginia and emphasized outdoor recreation and a romantic attitude toward society and nature. The built landscape underwent several transformations. In early days spa facilities comprised simple log cabins or frame boardinghouses. Only when pleasure-seeking overwhelmed health concerns did the grand hotels emerge. Many southern springs offered only one hotel, fronting a park with surrounding cabins, in which clientele spent the summer partaking of the waters. This particular tradition exemplified architecture and site planning promoted by Thomas Jefferson. The model originated with Italy's Palladian style, adapted by Jefferson, who stressed the symmetrical placement of the main house with smaller cabins and springhouses. This southern tradition, simple and rural, also influenced American resort architecture after the Civil War.[9]

These spas played a large part in the lives of colonials, encouraged social mixing, and provided a venue for political maneuvers. In particular, they facilitated social contact between the planter aristocracy and backwoodsmen. By around 1760, when colonial gentry began a seasonal migration to spas, their families had accumulated extra funds and had more time to travel. City noise and a fear of summer fevers and unhealthful air also prompted this exodus to rural spas.

Most of Virginia's springs issued from the Allegheny Mountains, on the edge of the frontier in early colonial times. In 1748 George Washington visited Bath, the western Virginia resort named after its English counterpart, and bathed in its brush-surrounded springs. In 1761 he returned to it (by then it had been renamed Berkeley Warm Springs) to relieve pains from rheumatic fever. Thomas Jefferson likewise frequented springs and described some medicinal waters in Berkeley County. Jefferson even suggested that the state purchase White Sulphur Springs (now in West Virginia) for the "common good."[10]

It became customary to tour the springs. By the early 1800s, the rude accommodations of Berkeley and Warm Springs were replaced in spa-goers' affections by Virginia's opulent lodgings at White Sulphur Springs, Salt Springs, Sweet Springs, and Red Sulphur Springs. These frontier springs, a substantial distance from settlements, attracted several thousand visitors during July and August. The travelers would begin their journey at Warm Springs, the most northeastern resort in the cluster, and journey 170 miles to visit all the area's springs. Colonel Fry, the amiable host of Warm Springs, would tell his guests to "go, [said he,] and get well charged at the White Sulphur, well-salted at the Salt, well sweetened at the Sweet, well boiled at the Hot and then let them return to him and he would Fry them." Six weeks and many gallons of mineral water later, they would converge on the Warm by the last week of August.[11]

All these springs attracted both northerners and southerners, but some groups in particular. South Carolina's rice coast planters preferred the Salt Sulphur, while Tidewater Virginians preferred the Sweet. The Southern planters who repudiated Jacksonian Democracy railed against the government at the White Sulphur (see fig. 4). Wherever they went, social activities usually included billiards, boxing, gambling (particularly the card game of faro), horse racing, shooting, the occasional duel, and dancing. Dancing, in fact, became so popular that the master of ceremonies at White Sulphur's ballroom created the Billing, Wooing, and Cooing Society to make the proper introductions and promote dance etiquette. After the Civil War, even Robert E. Lee often escorted the young ladies to dances and parties and did the Treadmill, a type of parlor promenade of two or three people abreast.

In American resorts, at least until 1825, health was the primary concern of patrons, followed by religion, then gambling. Southern spas, in addition, became famous for their recreational pursuits. By the twentieth century, social activities were similar to those of the preceding century. Commentator Katharine Dos Passos described the annual ritual of "taking the waters:"

> Going away for the summer has always been an American habit and in the early nineteenth century "the young, the gay, the handsome and agreeable of both sexes" began seeking out these springs. An ancient sophisticated ritual of fun and fashion was set up like a little traveling theater in the flowering American wilderness.[12]

She further alluded to the opulence and grandeur of these resorts:

4. Springhouse, White Sulphur Springs, West Virginia, 1992. Most Southern resorts sported a circular Greek Revivalist–style springhouse, where patrons quaffed nourishing liquids. Author photo.

Stately hotels of brick and stone with white columns and Greek porticoes
rose among the freshly cleared forests. There were wood fires "big enough
to roast an ox" in the simple cabins of the guests, but there were Brussels
carpets too, and Paris fashions, European wines, music and dancing.

Harrison Rhodes, an observer of American holidays, described fellowship as "good-natured, well-bred, and idle, inclined to prefer Bourbon
whisky to the water from the spring, and apt to know a good poker hand
when it sees one." [13] He suggested that the resorts' prime historical function
was as a marriage mart—to find eligible gentlemen for unwed daughters.
The cult of the "Southern Belle" reigned at the springs even after the Civil
War and continued until the 1920s.

THE WEST

Whereas inaccessibility to Virginia's isolated resorts enhanced their attraction, the popularity of a spring site in the West depended to a great extent
on available transportation. In the 1880s, railroads built the great hotels of
the West as they strove to promote western spas: the Southern Pacific built
Del Monte in Monterey; the Atchison, Topeka, and Santa Fe constructed
the Montezuma Hotel in Las Vegas Hot Springs, New Mexico; the Denver
and Rio Grande developed the Antlers Hotel in Colorado Springs. [14]

Travel, reserved for the elite until the 1880s and 1890s, opened in the late
nineteenth century to more middle-class Americans who finally could afford
western travel. The popularity of the Pullman sleeping car and the rate wars
of the 1880s made mass travel possible. By that time also the central and
western areas sported fancy hotels, although the typical invalid could not
afford a long resort stay.

The medical establishment played an important role in promoting
Colorado as a health resort because of its mountains, considered particularly
health-promoting. Colorado Springs and Manitou Springs, called the Saratoga of the West, attracted 30,000 resort-goers by 1880 and 200,000 by 1890.
In Colorado's more remote watering places, however, visits of two or three
days sufficed as tour agencies arranged short stops for transcontinental passengers on their way to Southern California. Also around the turn of the
century California competed with Colorado for health-seekers. [15]

Although written documentation is sparse, there is enough evidence
to reveal that Native Americans considered California's springs to be sacred

environments. The Geysers in Sonoma County and Coso Hot Springs in Inyo County particularly attracted Native Americans from far away. Palm Springs Cahuila chief Patencio believed that hot springs, used by shamans in healing ceremonies, were doors to the underworld: "Now the Indian people know that all hot springs, everywhere, are joined together under the ground by passageways." The Wappo constructed scaffolding of willow and brush over the steam vents of the Geysers, and the Paiute supposedly buried their dead at a hot spring in the northeastern part of the state.[16]

California's resort towns with mineral or hot springs included Calistoga, Santa Barbara, Lake Arrowhead, Lake Elsinore, Palm Springs, and Desert Hot Springs, some of the earliest spas that became famous during the Health Rush, encompassing the thirty years after the Gold Rush of 1849. Because of poor transportation and a sparse population, California's springs generally remained unknown until later in the century.

Invalids, estimated as one fourth of all settlers in Southern California, brought more income into the state. It was largely healthseekers who tripled the state's population between 1870 and 1900. The opening of the transcontinental railroad in 1869 facilitated mass migration. Experts from Europe and the eastern U.S. then began to classify medicinal waters for the California State Board of Health.[17]

California attracted its share of healthseekers, and a building boom began that peaked by the 1890s. At that time Winslow Anderson, M.D., boasted of two hundred hot and cold mineral waters within the state. California's mineral waters and climate drew spa aficionados who also sought an arcadian ideal in the hills and valleys of the state. Many resorts sought to embody the romance of Southern California. They planted palm trees, emblematic of the ideal resort, and publicized past Indian and missionary use of the waters.[18]

A National Resort Tradition

Promoters continued to sell "romance" at their spas throughout the nineteenth century. As regional differences became indistinguishable, other commonalities among resorts after the Civil War included long verandas (typical at seaside hotels), rambling site plans, loosely connected wings, a greater integration of buildings with surrounding grounds, and an emphasis

on courtyards and connecting walkways. Much of this style and layout in the
South exemplified the Jeffersonian tradition with connecting walkways between cottages, similar to his campus plan of the University of Virginia.

Historian Cleveland Amory regards 1908 as the heyday of the big eastern
resorts. At that time a "Grand Tour" included the Berkshires in the fall, Hot
Springs, Arkansas, or White Sulphur Springs, Virginia, in the late fall or
spring, and Palm Beach, Florida, for the winter. To be sure, by the late 1940s
most eastern resorts appeared idle while western resorts such as Palm Springs,
Colorado Springs, and Reno prospered. The grand resort had changed into
a more recreation-oriented atmosphere where mineral waters held little value
for pleasure-seekers.

During World War II, one last hope for some health spas lay in military
plans for rehabilitation of wounded soldiers. According to the Committee
on Health Resorts of the American Medical Association, the chronic diseases most often treated at spas included heart and circulatory disorders
(31 percent), rheumatic conditions (24 percent), and gastrointestinal ailments
(18 percent). It was hoped that the health of wounded soldiers, who also
suffered from these ailments, might improve with water therapy. Though
many spa facilities were considered (including reports on seventeen spas in
Texas), the United States Army Medical Corps established only two water-
therapy hospitals: at White Sulphur Springs, West Virginia, and at Hot
Springs, Arkansas. Meanwhile, the U.S. Navy founded a hospital at Glen-
wood Springs, Colorado, where its doctors utilized what was supposedly the
world's largest mineral water swimming pool and set up natural fever therapy rooms over mountainside caves where warm water circulated through
troughs in the floor. Finally, the Veterans Administration planned to develop treatment facilities at Saratoga Springs, New York; Hot Springs, South
Dakota; Mineral Springs (Wells), Texas; Hot Springs, Utah; and Excelsior
Springs, Missouri. Many of the plans, however, either were never executed
or failed to ensure the continued prosperity of these resorts.[19]

Not every locality could afford a massive infusion of capital to build in
a grand style. Every state (except North Dakota) boasted mineral springs, but
not all of these water sources featured the "improvements" of shelter or facilities. Most facilities at the estimated one thousand improved springs and
wells in the United States (and its territories) in the 1880s likely included
only a modest hotel, boardinghouse, or bathhouse.[20] Some were improved
with merely a canvas to cover their waters. Nevertheless, with modest build-

ings, resorts could still meet the needs of a water-seeking public who wanted simple, inexpensive access to medical therapy.

Compilations of spas never agreed on numbers, much less the tally of improved springs. In the early 1880s, the American Medical Association, for example, noted 500 spa localities, while A. Peale tabulated 2,822 localities with 634 spas. By contrast, more than 900 improved mineral springs existed in France, 1,200 in Spain, 300 in Italy, 100 in England, and 2,500 in Germany, Austria, and Switzerland.[21] Though the United States possessed several thousand springs, few waters received the medical acknowledgment that those in Europe did. Most, in fact, remained unknown except to a loyal local contingent of healthseekers.

Texas' Spas

As inland watering places in the eastern part of the nation declined in number and popularity, those in Texas blossomed. Most early listings of American spas recorded only a handful in Texas. An 1880 report to the American Medical Association on mineral springs listed only Burdette, Kellum, Piedmont, and Cardwell Springs in the state. Yet by that time more than forty Texas springs had been "improved." The resorts that drew the most visitors—Lampasas, Sour Lake, and Hynson Springs—received no listing whatsoever.

Most observers disagreed on the number of spas in Texas. In 1892 physician G. Walton recorded 67 spas in the northeastern United States, 30 in the Midwest, 38 in the West, and 89 in the South, with only three in Texas (Piedmont, Fairview, and White Sulphur). That same year, another physician, W. Anderson, noted 206 important watering places in the West, 24 in the Midwest, 47 in the South, and 29 in the Northeast. Although this was a peak time in Texas for spas, he found none. In 1893, the United States Geological Survey (USGS) *Mineral Resources of the U.S.* provided a more accurate count. It recognized the value of many mineral springs:

> Both for commercial purposes and as places of resort . . . there is scarcely
> a State in the country which is without its mineral-spring resorts of recog-
> nized medicinal value, which are sources of profit to the owners of the
> springs and, therefore, indirectly, an addition to the wealth of their
> localities.[22]

Thereafter, the author listed thirty resorts in Texas.

By 1927, in the United States as a whole, W. E. Fitch, M.D., reported 425 flowing spring areas, 240 of which had been popular resorts fifty years earlier and then abandoned. Fitch further reported that only 25 spring areas in Texas qualified as resorts. He named 17 "Great American Health Resorts," which offered "all the comforts of a home, all the service of the best hotel and all the advantages of the best sanitarium, with every comfort, convenience and luxury to be had at any spa in the world." There were three in Virginia and in West Virginia; two in Indiana and in New York; one each in Arkansas, Colorado, Maine, Missouri, North Carolina, Pennsylvania, and South Dakota—but none in Texas.

Most chroniclers of watering traditions operated under the misconception that Texas had few spas. In 1942 medical historian Henry Sigerist noted that Texas was second in the nation in the number of medicinal springs (Wyoming was first), although he failed to list the number of improved resorts. Geographer James Vance incorrectly drew the boundaries of "Arcadia," where nineteenth-century healthseekers fled to the western countryside, around parts of California, Arizona, New Mexico, and Colorado, with no consideration given to their "bucolic search for health" in Texas. Historian Billy Jones, however, documented the immigration of a large number of healthseekers to the Lone Star State after the Civil War. He noted that Texas almost equaled California and Colorado for its reputation as a healthful location. His work, however, covered tubercular patients, many of whom did not visit Texas after 1900. Many of these omissions can be attributed to the state's frontier image and to the lack of development in the grand style.

Many Texas resorts exhibited some regional and some national characteristics in their morphology and style. Hot Wells (Bexar County) and Hynson Springs (Harrison County) displayed long verandas and connecting walkways, indicative of national resort design. Generally, spas lacked an integrated plan (with the exception of Wootan Wells, which was a completely planned resort). Resort owners picked what worked for them. Simplicity seemed the key.

Few hotels embodied the Greek Revivalist style, but some included promenades or boardwalks, as did the northern spas. More informal in nature, lovers' lanes along scenic vistas (particularly Mineral Wells in Palo Pinto County and Lampasas in Lampasas County) expressed the spirit of the more elegant northern equivalents. One aspect of the southern resort style survived in Texas' early spas where cabins surrounded a hotel—at Sour Lake, for example, or at Lampasas' Hancock Springs and at Piedmont. Simple sheds or more elaborate pavilions also replaced southern springhouses.

Wealthier folk usually visited a resort in its early years, before the general populace caught on. This "mass follows class" phenomenon held true for most resorts in this country, although many remained the domain of the well-to-do. In Texas, the prosperity of the southern planter contributed to the popularity of a few early-day resorts (notably Piedmont, in Grimes County). Although seasonal migrations played less of a role in the social life, some spas higher in elevation (notably Hynson Springs in Marshall) became retreats as summer fevers decimated the populace of lower-lying towns. Generally, both the rich and the poor met at Texas spas, where less-opulent architecture and routines assured greater social interaction. After the Civil War, when more people could afford to travel, Texas' watering places attracted a wide range of people, from the poorer, who could camp at any spring, to the rich, cattle barons who stayed at hotels, such as the Baker Hotel in Mineral Wells. Often their social activities converged, either through normal intercourse in commerce or the service sectors or, just as likely, through sharing social routines.

Resort-goers in Texas led less elaborate routines, although Mineral Wells' activities involved aspects reminiscent of southeastern resort life. Many visitors traveled to Texas to pass a season at Mineral Wells, often following an agenda of morning "calling," afternoon "drives," and evening "balls." [23]

Texas' spa enthusiasts characterized the landscape around many springs as romantic and picturesque. They made daily excursions into the countryside to picnic or ride, emulating Arkansas's Hot Springs to some extent. Visitors rode burros up Mineral Wells' mountains as they did at Hot Springs' Happy Hollow. Similarly, San Antonio's Hot Wells boasted an alligator farm and an ostrich farm. Mineral Wells also emulated the Arkansas resort in its many bathhouses, which were named after several in that state's Hot Springs. Mineral Wells' Baker Hotel dominated the city's skyline, as did the Arlington Hotel in Hot Springs; both, in fact, were designed by the same architect. Also sharing the names of Hot Springs' landmarks were the Majestic and Arlington Hotels of Mineral Wells, the Bethesda Bathhouse of Marlin, the Park Hotel of Lampasas, and the Lamar Bathhouse in Mineral Wells.

If Texas spas lacked the grand style of the East, the society of the South, and the widespread, natural hot springs of the West, they did not lack the ingenuity and adaptability required to meet the needs of a demanding public. From the frontier years of the Republic to the postwar years of the twentieth century, people flocked to the state's mineral waters primarily for one reason—health. In that sense, Texas springs were resorts in the truest sense, despite their relative anonymity to the rest of the nation.

CHAPTER 3

Texas' Resorts

HAVING PLEASURE AS WELL as health in view after "doing" Sour Lake, we extended our trip westward in order to fully inform ourselves as to the comparative merits of the various watering places that are becoming of so much importance to our State—becoming more so as they have heretofore been but little known.

—Galveston Daily News, *August 14, 1877*

Few traces remain of many resorts. At some places I found only a rusted pipe or a rotting foundation. At others, buildings lay in ruins, awaiting either a bulldozer or a massive infusion of capital. At Sour Lake, Texaco officials personally escorted me to the old site, where only the rudiments of the bathhouse remain. They evidently did not want me wandering around their property, for the site was close to an oily lake where a sinkhole had swallowed up acres of land in the 1920s. In Tioga, the old sites had either burned down or been refashioned for other uses. One old fountain remained, but it was overgrown with weeds. In San Antonio, one of the owners of the Hot Wells Bathhouse showed me where Teddy Roosevelt had signed one of the walls and guided me around the dilapidated, and oftentimes dangerous, openings in what was left of the run-down structure. I swam in one of the two pools where warm, sulphurous water still continually pours from the bank above the San Antonio River. The water was so strong that I could smell its residue on my skin for hours after the swim. At Wizard Wells, some old tubs were hidden away in a defunct restaurant and motel complex, and the only outside signs of its heyday were a covered well and a disappearing wall sign that hailed the baths. As the last vestiges of these sites pass away, we also lose sight of their stories.

Identification of Mineral Springs and Wells

Texas is blessed with an abundance of hot and cold mineral waters. More than one hundred recognized springs and wells with varying characteristics, including temperature, mineral composition, and volume, occur in different terrains around the state. Despite the differences in landscapes and waters, settlers created an identifiable resort tradition centered around wells and springs.

People consumed well and spring waters because of their clarity and freshness. They deemed water that contained substantial dissolved salts to be healthful, or health-promoting. Commonly, a pungent taste, smell, or unusual color indicated that the water cured a range of human ailments. Many waters seemed to qualify, and numerous physicians and governmental agencies documented their existence. The United States Geological Survey (USGS) listed watering places as commercial springs, primarily by the criterion of whether liquids were bottled and sold. The Texas Agriculture Department and other state publications also recorded medicinal waters in various counties. Physicians, newspapers, geologists, chemists, and commercial clubs or chambers of commerce described additional springs and wells.

Developed wells and springs spanned most of the state, except the Panhandle and South Texas. Although some large springs, such as San Solomon Springs and Comanche Springs, flowed in West Texas, most people did not regard them as especially therapeutic.

ANATOMY OF TEXAS' SPRINGS

Since the basis of any spa is its "healing waters," it is useful to understand the source of these waters. Springs occur as a more or less continual flow of water from the point where the water table intersects the surface of the ground. Surface water from rainfall, for example, generally percolates downward until it reaches an impenetrable layer of rock or fine-grained soil. At that point, the water moves laterally, sometimes for many miles, until it emerges from the ground as a spring. Springs exist in all of the physiographic regions of Texas, although they predominate in East Texas, where rainfall is most abundant.

In 1919, geologist K. Bryan compiled an extensive classification of springs based on the rock structure from which they emerged.[1] Other scientists' classifications took into account the amount of dissolved minerals, such as sulphur or iron, and the volume of discharge. Yet another category detailed the physical forces that caused springs to emerge. Gravity springs issue from the contact of a permeable rock layer with an impervious rock bed. In the Central Texas Hill Country many gravity springs lie at the heads of streams in the Edwards Plateau and along slopes where water-bearing strata meet the surface.

Springs in which the water-bearing strata do not break out at the surface but are deeply buried and rise under hydrostatic pressure through fissures are called artesian springs. Typical artesian springs are those lying at the edge of the Coastal Plain and the Balcones Escarpment. They funnel upward from Edwards and related Cretaceous limestones and include San Marcos Springs, Barton Springs, and Comal Springs. Because of their large size, they tend to be less mineralized than smaller springs, principally because the water has less contact with surrounding rock units and thereby less opportunity to dissolve minerals from those rocks.

The Gulf Coastal Plain is the continuation of the Atlantic Plain from the East Coast to the Texas coast. Here formations dip to the southeast or toward the Gulf, and salt domes such as the famous Spindletop in Jefferson County are common in the western coastal section. Waters laden with different mineral salts occur nearer to the surface than in the surrounding strata and emerge as gravity springs. The springs near Sour Lake and High Island were once believed to be the only artesian springs in the coastal region.[2]

Most springs in the northern part of the area, in Cherokee, Rusk, and Harrison Counties, for example, occurred at the edges of perched water tables, or where the groundwater is separated from the main water table by an impermeable zone. Water percolating through these beds tended to be iron-charged or "chalybeate." In Nacogdoches, Angelina, and Gregg Counties, many springs contained sulphur compounds as the waters passed through lignite beds.

Underground waters often pool in large reservoirs called aquifers. Water from resorts in particular clusters usually came from the same deposits. The waters from southeast of San Antonio, such as Sutherland Springs and the Gonzales Warm Springs Foundation (Ottine), as well as others from Karnes and Gonzales Counties, came from the Carrizo-Wilcox Aquifer. The natural springs from Sutherland Springs emerged cold, while the well at Ottine brought up water at 102° F from a depth of 3,398 feet. The water at Hot Wells and Terrell Hot Well (also called Terrell Wells) resorts in San Antonio (as well as the highly mineralized—10,500 milligrams per liter—well in Thorndale from which, reportedly, many of Mineral Wells' famous Crazy Water Crystals were made) came from the "bad water" zone of the Edwards Aquifer. The old wells in Austin at the state capitol and the Austin Natatorium dipped into the Cretaceous Hosston Sand. Marlin's, Waco's, and Hubbard's water came from the Hosston/Trinity Aquifer, but from different depths depending upon the dip of the aquifer. The Pennsylvanian Aquifer supplied Mineral Wells and Lampasas, while in West Texas the spas lay above the Basin and Range Undifferentiated Aquifers.

As a rule, the deeper the source, the hotter the water tends to be. Depth thus accounts for the hot water from wells in the central part of the state. Natural hot springs, however, emerge on the state's western border. One geologist proposed that the heat from the western hot springs—Indian Hot Springs, Kingston Hot Springs, and the Boquillas Springs—came from the abnormally high thermal gradient in this area that occurs because of a suspected thinning of the earth's crust.[3]

RESORT IDENTIFICATION

Appendix A lists the 109 of Texas' 254 counties that boasted of some medicinal mineral waters, although it is probable that almost all counties had at least one small, locally used mineral well or spring.[4] Compiled from governmental reports, early maps, and emigrant guides, this list identifies some sites as "resorts" while others may only have been sources for bottled water. Since most bottlers in Texas marketed waters for medicinal purposes, however, it is assumed that healthseekers also "resorted to" these localities. Names also may refer to the same well or spring under different ownership at a later date. Bell's Mineral Wells, Blossom Wells, and Beauchamp Wells (Lamar County), for example, may have designated the same place at different times.

Histories of watering places recount stories of Texas' settlement. For instance, according to one newspaper editor, Hubbard's Hot Well "was undoubtedly the one facility that brought the most people to the area during the early 1900s and was responsible for Hubbard's early reputation throughout the State."[5] Development companies formed to activate plans in the hopes that the waters would provide the nucleus for prosperity. Some succeeded; most did not. New towns withered. Others enjoyed but little prosperity, then died when spa waters no longer seemed important. Among these former resorts are Bath, Wootan Wells, New Birmingham, Burditt's Wells, New Sutherland Springs, Tuscaloosa or Wyser's, White Sulphur Springs, Viola, Trinity Mills, Elkhart, Dalby Springs, Mangum, Myrtle Springs, Midyett, and Hynson Springs. Other once-functioning towns, built around the waters, are no longer active, bustling communities: Piedmont, Putnam, Wizard Wells, Saratoga, and Tioga. Still other towns hold few reminders of their watering days: Sulphur Springs (Hopkins County), Franklin, Mount Pleasant, Sour Lake, Salado, Georgetown, Hubbard, Waco, Sweetwater, Arlington, and Thorp Spring.[6] Nevertheless, one might imagine these towns in their heyday, when the "healing waters" drew visitors from far and wide.

RESORT ESTABLISHMENT

There were early periods in the state's history when springs were the focus of development, notably before and immediately after the Civil War. The 1890s, however, was the peak era for resort establishment (see fig. 5). During that decade, fifty-four new places sprang up. In the first decades of the twentieth century, the establishment of resorts declined, and no new watering places appeared in the 1920s. The 1930s ushered in the final and fleeting phase of new establishments with sporadic developments of springs and wells in West and North Central Texas.

Resort establishment thus occurred in major phases: 1830–1889, 1890–1919, 1920–1949. From the late 1830s to the 1850s springs in Southeast Texas, the region closest to the coastal ports, gained prominence (see fig. 6). After the Civil War, more watering places became popular in the northeastern part of the state and in Central Texas. The focus next shifted to mineral waters farther west in drier, upland sites, characterized by some as a more healthful area. Finally, from 1920 to 1950 a few sites on this western periphery and in the north central part of Texas sprang up. In this sense the watering tradition in Texas followed the same pattern as Anglo-American settlement, moving west with the frontier.

Incipient Growth: 1830–1889 Settlers and Native Americans probably informally used the more mineralized waters earlier than 1830. Unusual physical features engendered multiple meanings. Salt domes dotted coastal areas in southeastern Texas. The land around Sour Lake exuded different

RESORT ESTABLISHMENT IN TEXAS

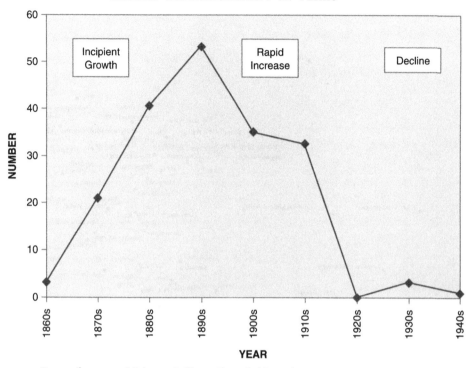

5. Stages of resort establishment in Texas. Compiled by author.

varieties of water, as well as petroleum seepages. Indians from Texas and Louisiana visited Sour Lake—or Medicine Lake, as they called it—to use the water and the black pitch seeping out of the ground to heal sores on their ponies' backs. Consequently, from such local therapies, bathers later applied petroleum and mud to alleviate skin problems, rheumatism, and venereal diseases. Some Native Americans also believed that there had been a violent eruption in the immense mound, which had filled the lake with sour water when it subsided. In 1897 Sour Lake's black therapist, Dr. Mud, related another version of its origin: At one time Indians started a fire to roast venison while camping in an area that would later be the lake. The earth subsequently caught fire around them and burned a shallow hole until rain filled the lake with medicinal waters. Such examples accounted for the appearance of landscape features and the consequent Native American reverence for them.[7]

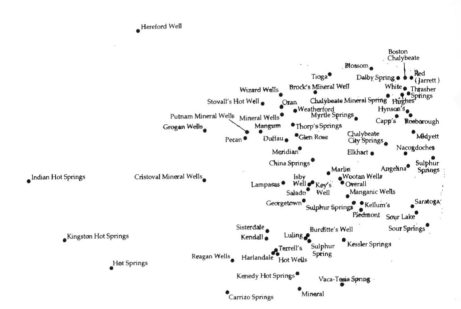

6. Resort establishment in Texas. Source: research by author.

Several legends depicted supernatural guidance in the discovery of healing waters. One accounted for the mythical qualities of Sour Lake's waters. An Indian chief's daughter, who had died from a disease that plagued the tribe, appeared to her father in a dream. She told him that when she appeared in a different form, he should follow her and drink from the waters. Thereafter, a white doe led the chief and his tribe to a lake fed by springs, and sickness disappeared.[8]

Native Indian occupation of some springs was more than anecdotal. Physical evidence confirms the use of certain water sites. The Mimbres band of Apaches frequented Indian Hot Springs and probably carved the depres-

sions in rocks around the springs. Numerous archaeological sites affirm pre-
historic settlement. Crude tubs carved out of rock at Brewster County's
Hot Springs also originally served as bathing reservoirs until J. O. Langford
built his bathhouse over them. Pictographs and artifacts have also been found
there. Langford's daughter, Lovie, even remembers Indians at her father's
place in the 1920s when the Kickapoos from Nacimiento frequented the
springs during the winter.[9]

The historical phase of initial resort establishment involved springs in
areas close to immigration entry points—the Gulf Coast and northeastern
counties. The Civil War interrupted a growth trend that saw nineteen new
springs develop in the 1850s.

Many emigrant guides and maps of Texas during the 1840s and 1850s
mentioned medicinal springs. Descriptions recognized some sites as poten-
tially important resorts. Chronicler George Bonnell, for example, noted a
white sulphur spring in Montgomery County (probably later called Kellum's
Sulphur Springs in Grimes County), where the surroundings were "pleasant
and healthy," and he suggested that it could become a "fashionable resort
during the summer season."

Such recognition often reflected knowledge of famous springs beyond
the borders of the Lone Star State. Bonnell recalled that the town of Carolina, originally named Bath after the English spa, had "red, white sulphur
and calibeat [iron-rich]" springs.[10] As with many other settlements in this
early period, the town disappeared a few years later. Other mineral springs
that attracted interest in this phase of development included Saratoga in Har-
din County (named after the New York resort), Sulphur Springs in Tyler
County, Salinilla Springs on the Brazos River (location unknown), Piedmont
in Grimes County, and several sites named White Sulphur Springs, probably
after Virginia's resort with that name. In an 1866 map of Texas, cartographer
J. H. Colton located one White Sulphur Springs in Bexar County (eventually
called Sutherland Springs) and another in Walker County. There was also a
White Sulphur Springs in Cass County. Toward the end of the century, the
name of White Sulphur Springs fell from usage, perhaps as settlers tried less
to emulate distant places.

The first resorts generally featured crude accommodations. Town developers set aside grounds for tents or boardinghouses. Entrepreneurs sometimes put in concrete or wooden curbs around the edge of a spring and a
brush arbor shelter or shed that covered the spring site. Other facilities for

visitors included cottages, such as those at Sour Lake, one of the earliest resorts in southeast Texas. In 1857, Frederick Law Olmsted described how its owners had built barracks and crude bathhouses for visitors. That same year, the *Galveston Daily News* reported on the status of the developing Sour Lake:

> Over the pool in the centre of the Lake there is a frame building, which, after some repairing, is to used [*sic*] as a bath house for ladies, and a dry path to this structure is now being thrown up for their use. On the line of this path, near the margin of the pool, is a spring of pure sulphur water with a wooden curb around it, but owing to its hitherto isolated position, and the occasional overflowing of the Lake into it, there has been but little attention paid to it, and it is in rather a dilapidated condition. The same may be said of a Chalybeate Spring still nearer to the centre of the Lake. These, together with a number of [springs of] various descriptions on the outer circle of the Lake, some of them hidden under the bushes and trees, will all be resuscitated in due time, and made accessible and useful in the medicinal jurisprudence of the place.[11]

Establishment of resorts sometimes lagged behind settlement because of the time necessary for developers to recognize the medicinal value of their waters, evidenced either through chemical analysis or through improvement in someone's health. At other times these valuable waters promoted the area's settlement. However, accessibility posed an obstacle to resort development. Not all places had the good fortune of being located on a stagecoach line, as was Piedmont Sulphur Springs, on the line between Hempstead and Waco. In 1859 it advertised that "attentive ostlers and good Carriage Houses will secure to beast and vehicle that care and attention so much wanting at many of the public houses of Texas."[12] However, the popularity of some waters surpassed their inconvenient location. F. M. Cross wrote that "as much as 20 acres of ground [was] solidly covered at one time with tents in the day of their [Lampasas' springs] discovery [in the 1850s], especially during the summer season."[13]

Finally, the Civil War contributed to the demand for well-known therapeutic waters, even though no new resorts sprang up at this time. In 1865 Walker's Texas Division camped at Piedmont near Navasota and drank the waters for their healthful "benefit." Colonel Hynson tanned leather for the Confederate Army at his springs near Marshall, and a Confederate pharmaceutical laboratory utilized Tyler's Headache Springs' water for bottled medicines.[14]

Rapid Increase: 1890–1919 With the establishment of more than one hundred new watering places, this period was the "Golden Age" for resorts in Texas. The attraction of new and different sites, however, posed major problems for already established places. Resort-goers abandoned some earlier resorts and headed farther west. Commentators recognized the trend. A county historian in 1895, for example, noted that Thorp Spring declined because of "the development of western Texas, opening up so many great watering resorts, that the single handed little sulphur spring began to grow less important."[15] In addition, visitors likely abandoned some of the other spas because of their poor accommodations. One editorial in an 1882 *Texas Medical and Surgical Record* called average resorts in Texas a "first-class fraud" because "their little medicinal virtues are entirely offset by the rude accommodations and rougher fare generally encountered by the deluded health-seeker, when he reaches them." The article further noted:

> It is time that proprietors should know, that the majority of their visitors do not honor them with their presence merely for the sake of a first-class purge, or a sweat, or a good, old, healthy diuresis, for all these can be easier procured through a druggist's apprentice, right at home, by means of salts, or nitre, and at far less cost, but such health seekers go more for the trip, the change and the recreation than they do for the waters. They expect pleasure as well as physicing [*sic*]. . . . In many localities the temperature of these places ranges very high, and ice is a dream of the past. Again, rooms are small and disagreeable, and not unfrequently the reflections of a melancholy subject are enlivened by the sudden appearance of a scorpion or a viper in his bedroom.[16]

The newer resorts tended to cluster around particular waters, though some areas were more popular than others. One group centered around San Antonio. With the exception of San Antonio's Hot Wells, these sour or sulphurous waters never became overly popular with spa-goers. A second cluster, in the Blacklands, included many highly mineralized, occasionally sulphurous, artesian wells. Except for the nationally famous wells at Marlin, these sites drew only a local or, at most, a regional following. The growth of a third cluster of resorts in northeastern Texas around Marshall had begun earlier. These spas featured more variety in the waters, including rarer iron-bearing or chalybeate springs, and as a result they were more successful in attracting resort-goers. Resorts in the fourth group, in North Central Texas, also varied in the mineral constituents of their waters and gained an excellent reputation, including a national clientele.

In the era of expansion, the railroad guaranteed success for certain resorts. Illustrated brochures advertised the aesthetic and healthful features of towns along their routes. Tioga, for instance, grew up around a watering hole for railroad workers. Railroad promoters developed Hancock Springs in Lampasas, a small cattle town famous for its waters before the town's settlement. Lampasas flourished as the western terminus of the Gulf, Colorado, and Santa Fe. The Houston and Texas Central Railway boosted one route that included Lampasas, Marlin, and Wootan Wells as "points of interest to tired people."[17]

Despite the expansion of the railroad network, no "Grand Tour" existed in Texas. It was never fashionable to visit the resorts in succession as it had been in the eastern United States. With the exception of the growing fame of Marlin and Mineral Wells (and later, to a certain extent, Sutherland Springs) with facilities to satisfy out-of-state visitors, the majority of resorts relied on a more local clientele.

The establishment of new resorts peaked in the 1890s. After the turn of the century, fewer new resorts were established and many smaller ones closed as larger ones, particularly Mineral Wells, monopolized the market. In the early 1900s, visitors to Mineral Wells, a town of 8,000 inhabitants, numbered 150,000 annually; in one twelve-month period (from 1902 to 1903), the railroad sold 45,000 tickets to Mineral Wells. Twenty years later, 80,000 to 100,000 people a year visited Marlin, a town of merely 5,000 residents. Texas' more famous establishments thus enjoyed a heyday during the first decades of the current century.[18]

Mineral Wells in particular attracted new settlers and became the model for new resort towns. In 1907, the town's *Daily Index* noted: "A very large percentage of our business and professional men and capitalists came here for their health or that of their families."[19] The *Texas and Pacific Quarterly* regularly featured articles about towns on its routes, but it eulogized Mineral Wells. As a veritable North American "Carlsbad" and "Fountain of Youth," it was "utterly impossible for one to drink the mineral water [there] and attempt to drink liquor at the same time." If Mineral Wells was not the Fountain of Youth, at least one article suggested that "miracles are performed here every week." A Fort Worth attorney, "almost restored to [my] former vigor and good health," advised others to visit Mineral Wells rather than more expensive, out-of-state resorts.[20]

Most Texas spas hoped to emulate the success of Mineral Wells. When Lampasas' popularity waned, some local citizens hoped to regain it. Mineral Wells provided the standard:

> I was struck by the amount of enterprise by the people here [in Mineral Wells] and the lack of anything of the sort in Lampasas. Every owner of a well has a large pavilion, musicians and everything to entertain their guests. Every house, nearly every residence, has the sign, "Rooms to Rent." We could outshine Mineral Wells 10 to 1 because it is so hot there.[21]

Even Marlin compared itself to Mineral Wells, as well as to Carlsbad. After visiting Mineral Wells in 1905, one Marlin citizen enjoined his city to pitch its virtues:

> W. W. Allen, who has been visiting in Mineral Wells is at home [in Marlin]. He says that there are something like 1000 visitors now there. The virtues of the water in Mineral Wells do not begin to compare with our water; we have a beautiful and healthy location and [nature] has blessed us with most favorable surroundings in every way, and yet we have nothing like 1000 visitors here now.[22]

After visiting several resorts, some healthseekers compared experiences but credited recovery to a certain locality, often Mineral Wells. Competition for such testimonials reached a fever pitch as resorts jostled for attention. J. H. Blackburn, M.D., of Brenham, who suffered from rheumatism, diabetes (which had caused his blindness), and gout for eighteen years, visited Hot Springs, Arkansas; Monterrey, Mexico; Wootan Wells and Burdette Wells, Texas; and Buffalo Lithia Springs, Virginia. But after his stay in Mineral Wells, he testified that his eyesight and his health improved. Other healthseekers, however, thought less of Mineral Wells' health claims. One lady swore that twelve or fourteen years of drinking Mineral Wells' water did not relieve her rheumatism and stomach troubles, but after thirty months, Putnam's water restored her health. A superintendent of the Texas Central Railroad noted, "I am thoroughly convinced that the Mangum water is better than the Mineral Wells water and this being the case, with depot accommodations, it will soon make a good town."[23]

Nevertheless, Mineral Wells continued to attract the largest number of healthseekers as well as much unsolicited publicity from other spas. Yet some people believed the town needed even more promotion. Former governor T. M. Campbell wrote:

Texas does not realize what she has in that town, and it is not advertised half enough. Every time I go there, I come away with a greater belief in its possibilities. It is Nature's resting place, and health resort for Texas and all the world. It is destined to be one of the greatest watering places in America.[24]

Part of the reason for Mineral Wells' success lies in the aggressive policy of the town's Commercial Club, which did its best to promote the spa. Under the leadership of secretary J. W. Register, the club printed and distributed small three-by-five-inch booklets, titled "Health and Pleasure at Mineral Wells," " 'The Better Way': Mineral Wells Water (Route) to Health," "Read What Physicians Say," plus hotel guides, a quarterly magazine, testimonials, and articles.

In a 1905 letter reprinted in the *Texas and Pacific Quarterly*, the author compared Mineral Wells to other resorts in the country:

Of course, it is not in any regard to be compared with the elegancies and luxuries of Northern and Western resorts to which the financial princes of America resort for pleasures and to spend their money, but for suffering humanity, who are seeking relief from their afflictions, it offers all the comforts necessary, and that, too, for a price that the poorest can afford, and is, to my mind, of the highest consideration.[25]

This simple statement articulated the philosophy and strength of all Texas spas, emphasizing facilities for sick, indigent, and poor people. Most resorts accepted this assertion as reality and utilized it to their advantage.

Railroads continued to play important roles in facilitating access to these watering places in the early 1900s. The Texas Central Railroad, for example, offered to build a depot in Mangum, provided the town deed alternate lots to the company. Its superintendent believed that the spa's water was better than that of Mineral Wells. Like Mangum, many resorts served as dining places along a railroad's route: two trains stopped daily at Mangum to allow passengers to visit the community and sample its water and local cuisine. In addition, "immigrant cars" offered cheap rates for people to explore possible homesites or to move household belongings to new settlements. These rates also lured potential investors to resort communities.[26]

Decline: 1920–1949   Just as railroads facilitated the promotion of new spas with well-tested mineral waters, the automobile began to play a dual role in resort life: it both helped and hurt business. Smaller resorts began to decline after it became possible to drive to larger, more famous spas. After 1915, when several fires destroyed much of Wootan Wells, nearby Marlin benefited from the town's demise. It was easier, it seemed, to drive to Marlin than to wait for the owners to rebuild Wootan Wells. On the other hand, the automobile facilitated access to more-distant watering sites, such as springs on the Rio Grande. In 1929, at the relatively hard-to-reach spa at [Langford] Hot Springs in Brewster County, owner J. O. Langford counted more than six hundred cars carrying healthseekers to his resort.

Aided by improved transportation, both resorts and sanitariums grew up around mineral waters in West Texas. In contrast to resorts, sanitariums drew upon a pool of more critically ill patients who undertook long, sometimes difficult, journeys for a cure. The privately owned Grogan Wells Sanitorium in Sweetwater utilized steam baths and mineral water treatments, shipped out bottled water, and built a hotel and pavilion. On the South Concho River south of San Angelo, the Christoval Mineral Wells bathhouse (later called Percifull Chiropractic Sanitarium) offered sulphur water from about 1920 until the 1980s. The town of Carlsbad sported a mineral well, a pleasure pavilion, a public bathhouse, and the state sanitorium, which probably used mineral waters in its therapy after its construction in 1912.[27]

Several resorts, particularly in West Texas, grew up independently of nearby towns. With the ease of the automobile and improved highways, travel to remote places became easier, especially if the waters were regarded as special. These resorts, the last to become established, survived into recent times. Jewel Babb, a white healer or *curandera,* operated Indian Hot Springs on the Rio Grande River until World War II, when gas rationing hurt operations. In 1967, H. L. Hunt restored the hotel and built a bathhouse. Indian Hot Springs remained accessible to visitors until 1974, when Hunt died. West Texas' Kingston Hot Springs, also called Ruidosa Springs, blossomed late as well. It closed in May 1990, and local folks considered this action "the end of an era."[28] Toward the close of the decade, it would reopen under different ownership as Chinati Hot Springs.

Mineral water spas once accommodated healthseekers and pleasureseekers alike across the state in an east-to-west trajectory. While many spas clustered together, their success depended to a great extent on the accessibility of their locations, and their locations, in turn, relied upon the presence of healing waters.

CHAPTER 4

Places Lived:
Recapturing Past Landscapes

How WONDERFUL ARE THESE health-giving wells, scattered throughout
Texas, affording natures grand panacea for the thousand and one ailings
which afflict humanity!
— Texas Prairie Flower, *October 1883*

A
s I soaked my exhausted body in hot water after having driven
to Truth or Consequences, New Mexico, I surveyed my unusual
surroundings—an enclosed room with a large twelve-by-twelve-by-five-foot
natural-bottom pool in a small 1950s-era tourist court. Many similar such
baths exist in this town, once christened "Hot Springs, New Mexico." These
old motels were certainly rather dowdy, unappealing structures for a health
industry centered around baths, health food stores, and massage parlors. Yet
the waters obviously attracted older people who could not afford more expensive and luxurious lodgings. This small town's environment cannot be
too different from that of many small watering places in Texas' heyday.

How important is the milieu to this particular practice? And what un-
derlies our fervent search for that elusive fountain of youth and immortality? How far-fetched can it be to believe that water might possess a power
as healing as any medicinal plant found in some rain forest? I imagine that
if we ever find a panacea for our bodily ills, it will be something simple,
ever-present, and obvious—like water. After all, our bodies are about three
fourths water.

The viability of a spa depended upon both the strength of its waters and
visitors' perceptions of its site and situation. The predominance of certain
dissolved minerals in some waters often determined the attractiveness of the
spa. Thus, Marlin's hot sulphur water attracted a large number of arthritic
and dermatological patients, and the iron waters of Harrison and Cherokee

Counties were touted for alleviation of anemia and blood diseases. Yet because the outdoors was itself considered a sanitarium to the nineteenth-century healthseeker, a spa's natural surroundings were an important factor in the decision to go there. This was especially true for people in search of pleasure as well as a cure.

With its wealth of both natural springs and mineral wells, Texas offered a wide selection of possible sites for watering places. Where people chose to go depended on what they searched for. People endowed natural features of the terrain with the power to affect them physically, emotionally, and spiritually. Descriptions and visual images of the physical setting of watering places conjured up mythic landscapes that were well suited for health and relaxation.

Mythic Landscapes

Symbolically, the waters represented life. Healthseekers believed that the Creator gave them as a gift to mankind, to be used judiciously and wisely. As the sacred waters allowed the healthseeker to turn back the clock and become young again, they also represented an earlier time when others, too, instinctively recognized the waters' sacredness. Myths and legends grew up around these places and further reinforced the waters' symbolic appeal.

In today's world a myth often describes something that happened in the distant or imagined past, but it can also be a psychological tool, with intuitive and spiritual dimensions. Even though these were not mythical waters, the emergence of a myth underscores the importance of the waters in people's minds. Myths may arise from attempts to explain natural phenomena or landscape features, especially if they are unusual or strange. The claim that mineral waters could heal denoted an extraordinary natural phenomenon that needed further corroboration. Myths and legends explained how these natural resources came about and how our ancestors used them. They thereby enhanced people's expectations of the power of the waters.

References to Spanish rule over Texas also added a romantic allure. Illusory qualities about a myth do not diminish its importance as a tool for understanding perceptions about sacred places. Many myths and legends, in fact, contain factual material.

A nineteenth-century myth about Lampasas' springs explained their origin, their value for human needs, and how they changed through human actions, thereby enhancing their sacredness.[1] In 1735, St. Juan, a priest, and his retinue set out from San Antonio to inspect missions throughout the Southwest. Near Lampasas, however, the company found its water supplies nearly exhausted; it had been a year of devastating drought, and though the group spread out to find water, they found none. One by one, they began to die off. The confused priest did not understand the suffering. As he watched his men and his faithful burro die, he stomped on the ground and pronounced a curse on the country. The devil, seeing a unique opportunity to lure the priest to his domain, started to approach the holy man, who then regretted his outburst, grabbed his crucifix, and began praying for his company. At each spot where a member of his party lay, a spring emerged, carrying with it the sulphur left from the devil's retreat. The waters carried as well a gift of healing to the beleaguered group.

The priest and his retinue in the myth defied death and the nether regions. Several mythic elements occur here: First, both the factual and the mythical come into play in the selection of a saint to preside over the historical reality of missionaries' visits to scattered missions. Although the San Saba mission was not built until 1757, priests did travel between the missions of San Antonio and new ones established elsewhere in Texas. Second, specific geographic references also fixed actions at familiar locations. The citing of local place markers seemed to substantiate the story. The myth accounted for the specific location of the springs, although it incorrectly placed them closer to the Colorado River. Third, creation of the waters explained their power, now more valuable to later settlers and visitors. The priest and his company survived because of the waters, as others would thereafter. This myth invested the springs with power to heal. A saint, not just a priest, empowered and sanctified the waters and made them holy.

Mythic stories also reveal universal symbols. Springs, as openings to the underworld, represent an *axis mundi,* or center, that connects earth, sky, and underworld. The demon's emergence in response to St. Juan's curse explained the sulphurous nature of the waters, suggesting brimstone from the infernal regions. The triumph of righteousness over the devil endowed the waters with extraordinary powers.

Myths revolving around Spanish settlement of Texas gave the waters a patina of age and hence a historical continuity to their value. Although less colorful and explanatory than the Lampasas myth, another myth, concerning Santa Monica Springs near Austin, simply suggested a plausible cause for the basins where people bathed for medicinal effects. Some mission fathers, who had accompanied early Spanish settlers in Texas up the Colorado River in search of the source of particles of gold, stopped at these springs for rest. They considered the waters extraordinary and carved a basin, seventeen feet by four and a half feet deep, in the shape of a Mexican gourd. Several known elements of Spanish involvement in the New World exist in this brief capsule—a search for precious metals, a search for souls, and their resultant landscape artifacts. The 1890 Chamber of Commerce brochure *Something of Interest Concerning Austin,* which described this story, sought to draw interest in the place through the appeal of myth and legend.

Stories about the origins of springs often involve Indian tales of discovery. Occasionally they reflect the romantic notion of the noble savage who through a primitive unity with the forces of nature discovered the waters' powers. Native American lore and legend clouded the veracity of many accounts. Springs often became sacred sites where enemies met in peace. For example, Karankawas, Tonkawas, and Caddos supposedly put aside their animosities to bathe at Sour Lake.

Legends also elicited curiosity about local sites. One about Lovers' Retreat, a popular picnic place near Mineral Wells, told of a Comanche maiden about to marry the chief's son although she loved a different brave. When her wedding neared, she fled to the top of a cliff and jumped. In another legend, a Spaniard, taking $10 million in gold bars, reportedly buried the treasure on Mineral Wells' East Mountain when he fled from Santa Anna. Although these two tales did not address local waters, they created an interest in place—such an interest, in fact, that the treasure legend resulted in much destruction of the top of East Mountain.[2]

Some spa names reportedly are derived from Indian words. In one account "Tioga" means "fair and beautiful" and in another "swift current." Conversely, one local Tioga resident claims that an Indian woman once assured her that "Tioga" meant "healing waters." Likewise, the word "wizard" in Wizard Wells supposedly represented a Kiowa medicine man.[3]

Myths and legends often laid the groundwork for the choice of a spa. The establishment of a successful resort, however, required other amenities. Visitors' perceptions often depended upon a place's images as health-promoting, picturesque, romantic, or Eden-like. Some of these images derived from promotional literature, which can indeed manufacture an interest in a certain place. However, they reflect contemporary archetypes and sentiments as well. As important as the reality of place is the perception of place, for these mental impressions can propel people to undertake safe or perilous journeys.

Perceived Landscapes

Besides the waters, other elements that attracted people to these places and contributed to a sense of well-being were picturesque, Eden-like landscapes and an air of mystery and enchantment. Foremost, however, was the image of Mother Earth as nurturing: the spring or well created, in a sense, a natural sanitarium. It often could also accomplish the miraculous—stop the processes of aging.

NATURAL SANITARIUMS AND FOUNTAINS OF YOUTH

Taking advantage of the healthseekers' scorn for human-made prophylactics, resort owners coined the phrase "nature's sanitarium." Nature, in other words, healed humanity's ills. According to promotional pamphlets, Sour Lake was "nature's sanitarium," while Mineral Wells represented "nature's great sanitarium." The Missouri Pacific Railway Company characterized San Antonio and Southwest Texas as "nature's own sanitarium," a "health belt" with "no marshes, no bayous, no swamps, no sluggish streams" to give febrile afflictions. San Antonio's Hot Wells brochure expressed this sentiment also, as well as the image of earth as Mother, caretaker of man's afflictions:

> Nature has disclosed her secret long hidden from man, and has yielded up
> a fountain of youth, beauty, and health, the gift of "Old Mother Earth"
> to afflicted humanity. It is the only natural hot water resort located in a
> climate that constitutes in itself a sanitarium. . . . a prescription prepared
> and put up in the vaults of nature's own laboratory—a God-made remedy.[4]

The waters from Tioga were drawn "from the bosom of the earth sparkling and free from deleterious elements," and they consequently created "nature's powerful restorative, the Tioga Mineral Water." Rosborough called itself "nature's laboratory." When J. W. Torbett, M.D., built his 1908 clinic in Marlin, he played on this image, calling his institution a "sanatorium" rather than "sanitarium" because "it used climate and the forces of nature, like heat, light and mineral water." [5]

The natural "sanatorium" must also possess certain climatological factors crucial for the restoration of health. In the 1880s, a West Texas physician, W. M. Yandell, enumerated the preferred attributes: dryness, coolness, rarefaction (less than sea level pressure), sunshine, temperature variability, mountainous topography, moderate winds, radiation and absorption of heat by rocks and sandy loams rather than damp clay soils. Most physicians eschewed unhealthy air from the lowlands: "The elevation here [Lampasas] is a continuation of the high ridge running north and south in the vicinity of San Antonio. There are no swamps or marshes which so frequently accompany mineral springs." [6]

Scattered communities pushed the health benefits of their "ozone-rich" atmosphere. Putnam advertised its location as ideal for health: "In this rich, ethereal clime disease and poverty are dethroned while health and prosperity reign supreme. The average altitude is 1700 feet and every breath of this pure, ozone-laden atmosphere gives a new lease of life." [7]

Farther east, in the Palo Pinto Mountains, Mineral Wells was at an "elevation of 1,450 feet, ensuring pure air, heavily laden with the life-giving element, ozone, to inspire new life and vitality in the afflicted, who come much depressed from the influences of the lower altitudes." On hills overlooking Marshall, Hynson Springs claimed to be in the "Ozone Strata," with the temperature entirely uniform throughout all seasons of the year. Hynson Springs also warned that communities lower down experienced more yellow fever. [8]

Promotional brochures, testimonials, and newspaper accounts repeatedly referred to these places as "fountains of youth." References were enthusiastic endorsements of a simple magic elixir. That they recurred frequently suggests that they were not completely the fabrication of imaginative, sales-hungry promoters.

Mineral Wells' Carlsbad Well depicted Ponce de León in stained-glass windows. The motto of Hot Springs (Brewster County)—"the fountain of youth that Ponce de Leon failed to find"—mimicked a Hot Sulphur Wells brochure that read: "If the lamp of life has not burned too low, ten chances to one you will have found Ponce de Leon's mystical 'fountain of youth.'" [9]

Such excessive use of the image may have somewhat diminished its effectiveness. One Marlinite chided resorts in general for this practice:

> Most of the mineral springs in the country claim to have been discovered by Ponce de Leon in the course of his unsatisfied quest for the Fountain of Youth which makes unique the fact that our well was not discovered by the worthy Senor,—at least not during his life. At the time of his wanderings, and for a few centuries more, its rejuvenating waters were locked tight in their stony cavern where the gnomes of the nether world kept a-boil their cauldron and prepared their concoction which today brings back health to thousands.[10]

Nevertheless, people still believed in this "fountain" of spring and well waters. Some testified about miraculous cures. A seventy-year-old man who wrote a letter to the Sutherland Springs newspaper in 1910 recounted that he suffered from sciatica and had not been able to dress himself, but after bathing in Sutherland Springs' black sulphur springs, he declared, he experienced no pain. He professed that "the springs have been to me the fountain of youth so diligently sought by Ponce de Leon." An 1888 pamphlet proclaimed that one woman who had wasted away to 62 pounds immediately improved after arriving in Lampasas and bathing in the springs. When she left the resort, she weighed 112 pounds.[11]

Journalist Frank Tolbert attributed Indian Hot Springs' reputation as "the Apaches' Fountains of Youth" to the oral tradition spread by the Mexicans who lived in the area. In several columns, Tolbert described one spring, the Chief or Geronimo Spring, that was supposed to rejuvenate and to "[revive] the interest in life of older men"—an earlier version of the modern-day "wonder" drug Viagra. He also suggested that there were 1,967 men who would testify to the spring's medicinal effects. In particular, he mentioned three men whose ailments either cleared up completely or were relieved.[12]

Newspapers added significantly to the lore. One account boldly declared that early pioneers often recounted how Ponce de León came over an "Old Spanish Trail" near Sour Lake to find the Fountain of Youth because he had heard in Florida about such waters. The Myrtle Springs newspaper asserted that "to these gurgling Fountains of Youth do the ailing denizens of the vicinity go, instead of to the apothecary shop, for relief; and they are never disappointed, for beneficent nature assures healing with every draught, without money and without price."[13] One local Tiogan wrote a similar tribute to his town:

I am an oasis in the busy world where the cosmopolite may find a fellow
from whatsoever clime or country. . . . I am the builder of flesh and bone.
All but make the dead stand up and shout, "Oh thou fountain of youth." [14]

Less obvious but still important to the image of a desirable place for
recuperation were a resort's physical qualities, which appealed to the emo-
tions or to aesthetic sensibilities. Viewpoints and vistas were among the attributes that could make a resort pleasing and uplifting and thus a most
"picturesque" destination.

PICTURESQUE LANDSCAPES

For many people the century's search for the picturesque was to be
fulfilled in watering places. People sought out sites with high elevations,
rugged scenery, sweeping vistas, and meandering features. One nineteenth-
century chronicler suggested that Hynson Springs embodied the essence of
this appeal:

> These springs [Iron Mountain Springs, later known as Hynson] form
> quite a romantic feature in the picturesque scenery surrounding Marshall.
> They are situated at the apex of a high bluff, the road leading up to them
> forming a long spiral sweep around the spur of the eminence, the top of
> which commands lovely views on all sides. [15]

Hikers at Mineral Wells climbed Inspiration Point to view the far hori-
zon (see fig. 7). The distant view and the curve of the winding Brazos River
made this spot a popular place to pass the hours between baths.

In 1883, one journalist described the setting of her hotel in Mineral
Wells:

> [We] found our hotel (the Piedmont), was at the foot of a mountain
> which rises to a height of from one hundred and fifty to two hundred
> feet—some say three hundred feet but I think the latter an exaggeration.
> Across the town, half a mile distant, is another lofty peak, and on all sides
> are these rocky declivities until they lose themselves in the distance ren-
> dering the valley exceedingly picturesque and lovely. [16]

The author also mentioned that she had seen "so little of the sublime in
Texas," but found it at Mineral Wells as she glimpsed the sun strike the
mountain scenery. At Devil's Canyon and Lovers' Retreat, popular spots for
visitors to early-day Mineral Wells, giant boulders and a quiet, serpentine
creek provided the backdrop for countryside fun and frolic (see figs. 8 and

7. Inspiration Point, near Mineral Wells, Texas, 1924. Author's postcard collection.

9). Women in long dresses and men in suits and coats seem stuffy and formal to contemporary eyes, but they embraced the outdoors in appropriate social attire. Social outings became part of the "cure."

MYSTERY AND ENCHANTMENT

Another commonly quoted landscape attribute had to do with "mystery" and "enchantment." As recently as the 1960s, journalist Frank Tolbert called Indian Hot Springs an "enchanted place." He attributed this "mystery" to the area's remoteness and to the reputed effects of the gushing springs (see fig. 10). He was not, however, the only one to recognize the mysterious qualities of the place. Around the same time, a geologist also described his impression of the springs:

> The country around Indisprings [*sic*] has a strange effect on me; its vastness, ruggedness, stark contrasts and brilliant colors are mixed with some mystery that always touches me deeply, reviving something that life in modern society has smothered. I returned to the business world from Indisprings feeling once again a child of the universe and in harmony with God and man. Even more inexplicable are the waters of Indisprings.

8. Devil's Canyon, near Mineral Wells, Texas, 1907. Author's postcard collection.

9. Suspension bridge at Lovers' Retreat, near Mineral Wells, Texas, 1920s or 1930s. Author's postcard collection.

10. Indian Hot Springs, Texas, 1992. Author photo.

11. A Sunday jaunt around New Sutherland Springs, Texas. Source: *Health Resort*, 1911.

I wonder of their origin and the beneficial effects have not been satisfacto-
rily explained to me or by me in my Master's thesis of the area, but I am
in a position as a geologist that felt his lifeless fingers regain movement
and sense of touch, to say that the waters cure what medical science cannot. I write you now using the hand that was crippled.[17]

Other types of landscapes sparked the same sensations. The ruggedness,
stark contrasts, and brilliant colors of West Texas contrasted strikingly with
the soft, shadowy milieu of places in the south central part of the state. One
visitor to New Sutherland Springs near San Antonio (see fig. 11) experienced "a feeling of awe, reverence, or a sensation of being in the land of
enchantment."

According to an 1877 letter in the *Western Chronicle,* Sutherland Springs
possessed an otherworldly appearance, with shadows, ethereal and gossamer spirits, a mysterious silence, and illusion pervading the atmosphere surrounding the springs:

The woods to me have a peculiar and weird appearance, the trees with
their straight and slender trunks being densely massed together, and the

foliage so light and quivering, flecked with occasional gleams of sunshine or vanishing away in the deep shadows of the evening, while the mysterious silence which reigns in their midst, give the impression that they are only habitable by ethereal and gossamer spirits, though the illusion is frequently dispelled by real live specimens of humanity which we often meet with in our drive.[18]

Only an enchanted land could deliver the elusive key to immortality, as one letter to the editor of the *Glen Rose Citizen* described the town in 1885: "[There] one feels like he were in an enchanted land, where were fountains of perennial youth."

Visitors also perceived individual landscape features in several different ways. One in particular, Spanish moss, exemplified several qualities most noted about these watering places—romantic, picturesque, and healthful or deleterious. Unique to the southeastern part of the state, the moss often hangs profusely from trees, sways with the breeze, and often hides a clear view of any structures behind it. Descriptions of Sutherland Springs frequently noted Spanish moss on surrounding trees (see fig. 12). Images of Sour Lake with its "cluster of oak trees" and the trees "fantastically draped with Spanish moss" conjured up mystery:

Within a few yards of the lake is a giant cluster of oak trees, just close enough together for beauty and just far enough apart to allow the cool gulf breeze to pass through on its benevolent mission. Here, on the long verandas, sit the seekers after health, eagerly drinking in the pure air wafted in through the trees, as well as the beauty of the rich foliage, the quaint forms taken by the giant oaks, and the long branches, fantastically draped with Spanish moss, that wave back and forth their soft grey drapery as the winds direct. Day after day a perfect picture in softest tones is spread before them, with the blue sky beyond and the fleecy clouds floating over, giving the added beauty of light and shadow.[19]

Also called Spanish Beard, the moss gave to Sour Lake's "fantastically draped" trees an unreal, imaginary quality.

An 1876 railway guidebook to Texas also noted the moss's "most grotesque and wierd-like [*sic*] appearance." This mystery in form and shape corresponded to a confusion about the moss's effect on the salubrity or healthfulness of a locality. People were ambivalent about damp places because of the "idea prevailing in the low lands of Louisiana that no place can be healthy in which moss grows. That this moss does grow in places which are un-

12. Sutherland Springs Hotel, New Sutherland Springs, Texas, ca. 1910. Author's postcard collection.

healthy is very certain, but it also grows in localities of remarkable salubrity." [20] Another chronicler echoed this widespread confusion:

> I was led to believe, by any information I could receive from others, or any observation of my own, that where moss grew on the trees, it was sickly; and that according to the luxurious growth of that singular production, so did the inhabitants of its vicinity, upon an equal vein, suffer by bilious attacks, and intermittent fevers. I was the more confirmed in this opinion, by seeing such vast quantities of moss, alias Spanish beard, in the lower parts of Texas, and the people so sickly looking.
>
> But how was I astonished, when I found many a solitary tree particularly live-oak, and many a lonely grove, especially post-oak, miles upon miles apart, far upon the highest of the highlands, dressed out with equal profusion in their long flowing robes of sober gray, waving in a clear atmosphere, over the driest of situations; where the inhabitants, by their good looks and athletic frames, shook *my former theory to the very center!* (chronicler's emphasis) [21]

The author also refers to the prevailing belief in the unhealthy nature of "bad" air, or miasma.[22] People sought fresh air and flowing water, indicative of movement, energy, and life.

Although the nineteenth-century suspicion of swampy waters and low, wet places would seem to have forestalled frequenting mineral springs, water proved alluring in its fresh and free-flowing form. Historian David Edward expressed this seeming paradox:

> In examining the water of a draw-well, which was sunk by mishap, through rotten lime-stone, I found it as unpalatable in taste, as it was unbearable in smell and unhealthy in nature; but I found the lime-stone water which was exposed to the air in a running stream, not only the most pellucid to the eye of any other, but pleasant to the taste, and as healthy as any that ever dropped from the clouds, and was purified in a cistern![23]

Moving water meant water alive with vital energy. Not surprisingly, this additional image of the fountain as dynamic force was prominent in nineteenth-century newspaper articles touting Texas springs. "Living fountains of medicated waters" graced the state, according to the *San Antonio Daily Herald* in 1866, while both Glen Rose and Rogers' Springs (Caldwell County) were proclaimed as fountains of health.

Images of Paradise

The literature promoting some resorts even evoked images of the promised land, an Eden-like environment. The following excerpt resembles the first chapter of *Genesis*, in which the Creator purposely placed certain features on earth:

> Nature has been kind to Lampasas. The Creator endowed it with many of his choicest gifts. When he made this goodly land of Texas and the great southwest, he must have looked about him and said: "Right here in the center of the choicest land which I have made for My people will I cause springs of life-giving waters to come forth from the earth that they may heal the people against their sickness and their infirmities, and will cause great trees to spring up, nut bearing trees, and trees of oak and of maple that their branches may overspread the people and make it joyous to rest between their shades; and I will cause rivers of sparkling waters, yea of health-giving waters, to flow through the land that My people may come and bathe in them and be well; and close by will I establish hills and mountains with their trees and shrubs of green and of brown and the many tints of the rainbow that they may tempt the people from the cities

that they may climb them in search of their beauties and thus be made well." [24]

In this passage the author specifically refers to three salubrious components—life-giving springs, health-giving rivers, and the healing beauty of hills and trees. Water, it seems, was a major healing power of nature. Rocks, trees with Spanish moss, and flowing water were components of an idyllic, health-restoring landscape.

In 1909, the editor of the *Hot Springs Daily News* described the illusion created by the location of Mineral Wells between two mountains: "The little city of 8,000 population, like Mount Zion of Holy Writ, is beautiful for situation, nestling in a fan-shaped valley between green-verdured hill ranges, and expanding in a level plain below." [25] Healthseekers could view Mineral Wells as the promised land, offering redemption from bodily burdens.

In a 1918 description of Glen Rose, the author saw the handiwork of God in the surrounding landscape:

> This touch and throb of nature is real health to both body and soul. Here we breathe the real ozone of life, and hold converse with God's creation and list to nature's teaching, and "think God's thoughts after him;" for nature, as it presents itself about Glen Rose, is poem full, beauty-full, and sermon-full and God full. As the old Hebrew prophets, poets and seers would say, "The Lord is in this place." [26]

Biblical references also reinforced the idea of water as living and holy. In 1979, when the Texas Historical Commission dedicated a historical marker at Midyett Springs, the Reverend Jack Midyett, the principal speaker, compared the spring to the well where Jesus told the Samaritan woman about God's "living" water (John 4:10). He continued: "There are several parallels here that I could mention. The comparisons were of the many thirsty people who had found refreshment, and the memories that had filled the thirsty places of lives touched by the Spring." [27] In the early 1900s, a preacher even suggested that Glen Rose's waters could change a person's life: "And go to quiet Glen Rose, stroll into the fields or the forests, climb the hills, drink of its life-giving waters. . . . God who put beauty into the surrounding hills has put virtue into these healing waters." [28]

Other biblical references endowed the waters with sacred powers. One brochure from Wizard Wells used Old Testament language in its copy: "Ho! Every one that thirsteth, Come Ye to the Waters." [29] A Sour Lake spring was like the "troubled" waters of Bethesda's pool in Jerusalem where the sick and blind waited for the angel to move the water (John 5:2–7): "The lake—the larger one—bubbles like a cauldron. It has mineral constituents that give it an acrid taste, and is charged with natural gases, by force of which its restorative elements are commingled like stirred-up Bethesda's of old."[30] Marlin's J. W. Torbett capitalized upon this image when he named his bathhouse the Bethesda. Although this structure was later torn down, citizens of Marlin must have liked the name because when another bathhouse was built in the 1960s, it was named Bethesda. Some early bathers missed the point of the word, however. A local newspaperwoman commented on "Bathhouse Row" in Marlin:

> The bathing public seems to prefer an easy name for a bathhouse. . . . And as for the Bethesda, it hardly knows its own name. It has been called the "Besda," the "Bethesby," the "Thesda," and one lady remarked that she never could get any nearer to it than Mthuselah. A number of people spell it with an "a" making it "bathesda," which merely shows that they consider the purpose of the place more than the origin of the name.[31]

Another biblical reference comes from the story of a blind man whom Jesus told to wash his eyes in the pool of Siloam to regain his sight (John 9: 7–11). In 1906, Captain Jeff of the Texas Rangers described Indian Springs in Hudspeth County as follows:

> They mounted and turned their course for the once famous Hot Springs, on the east side of the river. The old signs and trails leading in to the springs indicated that the Indians held the virtues of these springs as the people of old Biblical times held the Pool of Siloam.[32]

One observer described Sour Lake with the same metaphor:

> My last [letter] brought us past the various springs between the hotel and the Lake, and left us standing upon the margin of this pool of Siloam— or rather upon the edge of the little water that is now to be seen upon the vast expanse of mud, dignified by the title of Lake. The weary invalid standing on this spot need not pray for an angel to come down and stir the waters of the pool, as it is constantly agitated by the bubbling up of the gases contained therein, and this is all the stiring [sic] it will bear in its present condition.[33]

For some people, then, many waters offered contact with the Divine. In 1910, an Illinois Baptist pastor called Mineral Wells' water "God's remedy and not man's." That sentiment was by no means limited to the late nine-teenth or early twentieth century. A Tioga woman who still believes in the healing powers of the local waters calls them a "God given gift."[34]

If God gave the waters to man to heal himself, then he could also wor-ship there. Springs provided the ideal venue for outdoor reverie. Worship at these sites further reinforced the image of sacred waters, emblematic of a holy place.

Sulphur is symbolic of fire and brimstone. In alchemy, sulphur was the nonburning fire and represented the masculine, fiery principle. Water, on the other hand, was the wet, feminine principle. Together they symbolized a union, or the making whole of an ill body. Appropriately, sulphur springs provided the setting for many revival meetings. It is assumed that baptism took place in most of these springs. One letter to the editor of the *Lampasas Daily Times* verified baptism in at least one of the town's sulphur springs:

> When the spirits the other night cast Mr. Sweet, the leader of spiritualism here, into the sulphur spring horizontally with his back downward, he struck the water kur-splash, kur-chunk, chow-row; and this is the voice of spiritualism that is heard in our town. Brethren, this proves beyond a rea-sonable doubt that the correct mode of baptism into the faith of spiritual-ism is by immersion in sulphur water. And the smell of brimstone is still on our clothes.[35]

Revivalists often traveled to revered watering holes. Organized revival meetings, common in the 1800s in open arbor settings, enhanced the percep-tions of water as a vehicle for a new beginning. During the Second Great Awakening, a time of religious fervor from 1800 to 1830, revivals stimulated individual conversion experience, largely in camp meetings, a significant re-ligious practice of the frontier years.

Open-air revival meetings began in the eastern United States in the early 1800s and grew popular in Texas after the Civil War. Families from as far as fifty miles away gathered for several days of preaching, singing, and talking. Camp meetings became major social events for isolated farmers and ranchers to meet their neighbors and also provided opportunities for family vacations in a spiritually regenerative setting. Bodily self-renewal harmonized well with such spiritual concerns.

Although many camp meetings sprang up around seaside resorts during the 1860s and 1870s, about the only physical requirements for a site in Texas included water, a large flat, open area, and a tree or brush arbor. Camp meeting organizers favored areas with springs. Contemporary observers noticed a parallel between the ever-flowing waters and everlasting life. In fact, because most mineral springs originated deep below the earth's surface, they continued to flow during droughts. These meetings held at mineral springs sacralized the waters, and when those waters were used for baptism, consecrated these places.

The watering holes at Sutherland Springs particularly seemed to attract religious zeal. Each year, a union camp meeting took place at Sutherland Springs' Sour Spring, under the auspices of the Methodist and Presbyterian churches. An 1877 edition of the *Western Chronicle* recorded one such happening: "There has been quite an interesting religious meeting going on this week at the spring near Mr. Coopers. We understand that there was [*sic*] eleven converts to the Presbyterian and Methodist churches." More than thirty years later, in 1909, the springs were continuing to draw such patronage. The *Wilson County Journal* reported a two-week camp meeting, and that same year the Southwest Texas Baptists Workers' Conference chose Sutherland Springs for its annual encampment. The Baptists owned twenty-five acres on the Cibolo River (as it was called then), and in 1910, 2,500 persons attended a revival there.

Other camp meeting sites included Midyett Springs and Welch Springs. In 1872 Dr. John H. McLean, a Methodist minister, held a revival under a brush arbor at Hughes Springs. In 1879, and again in 1885, Major William Penn, a nineteenth-century circuit preacher, held camp meetings in an arbor at one of Lampasas' springs. He described this uplifting yet tragic experience there:

> At Lampasas we had a large brush arbor which seated several hundred people—perhaps a thousand. It was full at every meeting, and many were in the seats for prayer at each meeting. . . . One night when we were singing the first song a lady came to the rostrum and stood by Bro. Smith and looked on the book with him to sing. We had a very solemn meeting, and when we arose to sing the last song some one struck one of the large tin lamps hanging on a post near the organ. The lid came off and about a quart of oil poured out. The lady who was looking on the book with Bro. Smith, ran, struck another lamp, and was almost covered with the oil, which was soon in a blaze. She ran out some distance from the arbor and fell on her knees with the flames away above her head. . . . There were over three hundred conversions in eleven days, and nearly all of them

joined the church in Lampasas, were baptized, and some took letters and joined at their country churches.[36]

Other sects also enjoyed Lampasas' springs. An 1889 edition of the *Lampasas Leader* noted how the Christadelphians camped at Cooper Spring and held large gatherings in their tent. With or without organized camp meetings, religion played an integral role in the everyday life of the tenters at the early springs, especially the sulphur waters of Lampasas and Sutherland Springs.

The ideal salubrious landscape would thus be mythical, healthful, picturesque, mysterious, enchanted, and approved by the Creator. These attitudes showed respect for Nature and a belief in its healing power. Attraction to these resorts was contingent not only upon the waters' capabilities but also on the spirit of place, offering beauty, hope, and allure. All that remained was for visitors to transform these idyllic settings into landscapes of human activity.

CHAPTER 5

Daily Spa Life

THE REASON FOR DOMINOES in Texas is strongly fundamentalist Baptist.
If a Baptist preacher walked into the living room, and there was a deck
of playing cards, it would be like there was a naked woman there. It was
the worst thing in the world to be caught with a deck of playing cards. So
what did they do? They played dominoes.

—*Dr. Neil Buie Jr., 1990*

We drove to Indiana's French Lick Springs Resort, home of
the famous Pluto Spring and noted historic watering place.
The water still flows from a small springhouse behind the hotel, but French
Lick is more of a recreational resort now, with golf and tennis packages, than
a destination for health-conscious travelers. The Pluto water is rarely beck-
oned from its infernal domain.

In front of the hotel, an electric trolley car built in 1930 carries passengers
a mile away to West Baden, a resort once as popular as French Lick. Built in
1902, the round hotel was an architectural wonder, crowned by a 200-foot
glass and steel dome more than 135 feet high and so grand that even circus
shows entertained guests underneath it. Accommodations for a thousand
guests included a convention hall, a bath department floor with sulphur and
hot mud baths, and a complete medical and surgical clinic. A garden with a
scattering of Greek Revivalist springhouses surrounded a covered bicycle racing track. Even by today's standards this place was fit for royalty. It had been
closed as a spa for many years, although new owners were planning to renovate it. How strange that this magnificent place lies derelict while only a mile
away another grand hotel flourishes!

We study events, or people, or places, but less often do we study how
people inhabited places—what they did there, what they thought about

those places, and how they connected with others in those places. The resort experience required mingling with friends, family, and strangers in a community setting. In fact, the healing regimen depended to a great degree on the sharing of stories and recoveries.

In the early days, resort life centered around the presence of mineral waters, with scattered activities for pleasure and exercise. Water dictated certain rituals and recreational patterns. At first, healthseekers lodged in crudely built accommodations and sat in bubbling springs. Visitors moved from lodgings—tents, cottages, or boardinghouses—to bathing or drinking facilities. Often they also visited a doctor. Recreation near the watering hole involved outdoor picnics, camp meetings, or promenades. Each site around a spring specialized in its own activity, and visitors moved from site to site to satisfy their needs.

After railroads and automobiles ushered in greater flexibility in travel, the choice of available resorts depended less on access and more upon the amenities. Activities became more generalized as drinking and recreational pavilions combined recreation with health-seeking. Simple bathhouses—no more than one-room shacks with several tubs—gave way to large buildings with vaulted ceilings and separate swimming pools and segregated tubs for men and women. Physicians sometimes relocated their offices to bathhouses for easier access. Some offices grew into clinics and sanitariums with facilities for medical consultations, baths, cooling rooms, and massages.

Although outdoor recreation still occurred, indoor activities grew more important. As a resort evolved, its facilities expanded to meet all the traveler's needs. Although boardinghouses survived, elaborate hotels with varied food menus catered to most patrons' whims. They were *grand* hotels, and they offered a range of bathing, recreational, and transportation services. In fact, the visitor did not need to stray far to participate in desired activities. The Baker Hotel in Mineral Wells, for example, offered golf, tennis, medical clinics, shopping, a beauty salon, a drinking pavilion, a nightclub, and a bathing department. Indoor activities thus displaced outdoor ones. Recreation halls or city pool houses replaced the sparkling, clear-flowing waters that once provided the backdrop for most gatherings—camp meetings, Sunday school get-togethers, and picnics. Fancy accommodations and assorted social pursuits attracted sophisticated, fashionable pleasure-seekers. Activities became divorced from the locale and concentrated more and more on secular entertainments.

Lampasas, Mineral Wells, Marlin, and San Antonio (Hot Wells) exemplify towns where different resort activities and facilities developed to accommodate people through the years. Each place manifested the spa experience in its own unique way. Lampasas as a watering hole particularly thrived during its tenting and camping days, when the few accommodations housed healthseekers. After entrepreneurs developed the springs in a grand resort style, its days as a resort were numbered. On the other hand, Mineral Wells quickly surpassed its rough-accommodations period, as many facilities sprang up to serve its visitors. Assorted pavilions and outdoor recreational activities encouraged social gatherings around the wells and their immediate surroundings. Later on, emphasis on life in grand hotels eroded some of the qualities that had been the town's strength, and many of these gathering places disappeared. Marlin produced only a few resort facilities, where physicians and the community catered to invalids for years. However, many local citizens opened their homes to the flood of visitors. The medical services and the boardinghouse experience drew a loyal contingent of healthseekers. Finally, San Antonio's Hot Wells illustrates the rapid demise of a spa when visitors came to be more interested in recreation than in recuperation.

Lampasas

In his 1872 diary entries, James Billingsley described everyday life in camps around the Lampasas springs. Despite the apparent dangers of the area, they nevertheless seemed to be crowded with healthseekers involved in activities centered around the sulphur-rich waters:

> July 13: We arrived at the springs about 3 o'clock and after much hunting around for a suitable place finally pitched our tent on Sulphur Creek on the outskirts of the many campers sad [sic] to be about 600. July 18: Grand ball at night well attended by lots of pretty women. July 19: Thornington sick last night and is quite sick today. He has bathed too much and taken cold. . . . Many campers coming in from all directions. Report in camps is that four white men came across six Indians. Had a skirmish. White killed one and wounded one Indian but after close examination, he was found to be a white man. July 23: Campers still continue to come. July 28: Riddell and Billy and Thornington have been very regular attendants at night meetings during our stay at Lampasas.[1]

13. Hanna Springs, Lampasas, Texas, 1909. Author's postcard collection.

The Lampasas newspapers often reported on tent life at the several springs in the area (see fig. 13). The *Dispatch* of April 25, 1878, noted: "Some 10 or 12 camps are pitched at the Gooch Springs, while as many have stopped at the Hancock Spring, besides the great numbers seeking quarters in town."

Campers also made special arrangements in these early years:

> Campers are coming into our springs, and many invalids may be seen in our town and vicinity. Mr. Hanna is enclosing the Cooper Spring and the adjoining grounds and campers who desire to be free from the annoyance of hogs and other stock, can make arrangements by which they can have elegant shades convenient to the springs and have their stock secure and their camps unmolested.[2]

Most resorts preferred to draw wealthier clientele, but their unembellished, simpler physical structures deterred such an exclusive entourage. In 1877, visitors to Lampasas constituted "generally the substantial farmers, business and professional men of the country from which they come."

Townspeople also participated in activities around the increasingly popular waters. They did not simply sell their services or wares to visitors, but made the springs a part of their lives. Columns in local newspapers noted the presence of prominent people at the springs, particularly on Sundays:

> More than 1500 people drank at the Hancock springs on last Sunday, and nearly as many at the other springs about Lampasas. . . . The Upper Springs are the great center of attention on Sunday afternoons. In addition to the visitors and campers from a distance, the whole population of the town and surrounding country seemed to be on the ground last Sunday. The different streets and roads leading from town to the springs were filled with wagons, hacks, carriages and buggies going and returning from the springs with their loads of living freight. Everybody seemed to be in good humor and enjoying themselves.[3]

Social events planned around the springs allowed residents to mingle with visitors, an uncommon practice at more developed resorts. Serenades by local singers took place in 1878, according to the *Lampasas Daily Times,* while the *Dispatch* reported the popularity of informal markets set up by townspeople at the springs. Informal markets also contributed to the economic life of the town, and anything from buckets to soap to tents were hot items there. The *Dispatch* even warned readers that "a good deal of humbugging will be done during the summer."

Whether to a local citizen or a recently arrived outsider, the springs proved inviting on a warm summer evening:

> Groups of children sally forth for their evening walk to the springs, accompanied by numerous dogs of every size and breed. They romp and play, chase and pelt each other with pebbles, until overcome with fatigue. An old man soon makes his appearance in the midst of these childish sports, bent with rheumatism or afflicted with some other disease, who winds his way to the springs with his cup or bottle. He has come to quaff of the healing waters, with a faint hope that he may be relieved. Old, middle-aged and young come from every direction and congregate at this, their favorite resort.[4]

Moonlight walks to Hanna Springs were popular with young couples, as were the dances that filled spa nights with music and song. Although usually an indoor activity, dances in the early days often took place outdoors, as a July 1878 edition of the *Daily Times* announced: "Preparations are being made for a grand barn dance at the Hancock Springs tomorrow night." Evidently dances were in demand, for a decade earlier the *Lampasas Dispatch* complained: "We have six dances a week and still many of our young folks are not happy."

Although diversions included walks, picnics, and dances, tenters often found it necessary to create other forms of amusement:

> They've got a new game at the Hancock spring. It's a board with a number of nails driven far enough into it to hold, fastened to a tree; the player stands a few feet off and tosses four iron rings at it. If he lodges all four of them, he gets another play free; if he doesn't, he sets 'em up for the crowd.[5]

Despite the social whirl, conditions could be unpleasant and boredom could set in. The *Lampasas Daily Times,* for example, reported in August 1878 that a visitor to Hancock Springs was "prejudiced against ants, and amused herself last Sunday by catching the industrious pests and putting them in doodle [bug] holes, to see the doodles nab 'em." These particular springs, once a stop along a branch of the Chisholm cattle trail, on occasion attracted a rowdy crowd, ripe for practical jokes and rough-and-ready amusements like riding bucking mules.

No wonder spa-goers appeared ripe for proselytizing. The *Daily Times* reported that "Reverend Mr. Weaver preached under the trees at the Hancock." Four days later a similar event took place across town: "There is a minister camped north of the Hanna Spring who preaches to his tenting neighbors occasionally."

Educational pursuits also accompanied the quest for bodily health and recreation. Self-improvement became a moral duty, and many watering places promoted the institution of "Chautauqua." The *Lampasas Leader* in 1888 described Chautauqua as a discourse where "speakers of renown, political, literary, non-sectarian and scientific were engaged, some even from England, to address the people to be gathered. Imagine then the Chautauqua as a school for the masses." It was in fact a traveling college.

Because the Central Texas Chautauqua, operating out of San Marcos, was searching for a permanent home, officials paid particular attention to Lampasas, a place renowned as a resort and perfect for the Chautauqua's prerequisites: "a healthy section, high and dry, with plenty of water and shade right or as near as possible to the railroad." Evangelists also promoted similar sites for camp meetings, although in the early years they demanded brush arbors to shelter the crowd from the elements.

In the early 1880s, the Lampasas spa experience began to change. Its

14. Hancock Bathhouse, Lampasas, Texas, ca. 1900. Author's postcard collection.

metamorphosis began in 1883 when a syndicate of wealthy railroad men from Galveston built the Park Hotel on two hundred acres of land overlooking Hancock Springs (see fig. 14). Patterned after Galveston's Beach Hotel, this two-story structure had a front that extended more than three hundred feet in width, with banistered porches along both floors of the building. With more than two hundred electrically lighted and carpeted rooms, a reading and writing room, a music room, a dining room with seating capacity for 150, three parlors, and a billiard room with four tables, the hotel was the epitome of grace and elegance rarely seen in small frontier towns. Reminiscent of eighteenth-century southern resorts, two rows of cottages—one for families and one for bachelors—stood behind the hotel. A boardwalk led from the hotel to the extension bridge over the creek near the bathhouse. The owners also built a large circular dancing pavilion in front of the hotel. In the summer season of 1888 in Lampasas, bands gave concerts three times a day.[6]

The resort's owners had succeeded in transforming the rough, primitive campground of a decade earlier into a fashionable watering place. The scenery around the hotel presented an almost idyllic retreat:

The park at Hancock contains miles of drives and walks lined with superb forest trees, their foliage throwing o'er the passer by [*sic*] their pleasant, protecting shade; in places they approach and run close to the limpid Lampasas river, its beautiful banks clad with water plants and shrubs, and taller trees whose limbs graceful, bending, now rising, now falling, their tips seeming to dally with its crystalline waves. . . . At night the paths seem specially designed for lovers' walks and cupid illumes them with fire fly lamps whose intermittent scintillations of light lend special beauty and charm to the scene.[7]

Although tenting continued at Hancock Springs and to a greater extent at Hanna Springs, the social focus shifted. Many years later, an early-day resident recalled that in the afternoons ladies would ride out in buggies and sit in the parlors or on the hotel's porches to chat with friends or eat in the "fashionable" dining room served by "expert" black waiters. A nearby racetrack also helped pass the hours between baths; even ladies could witness the proceedings, as the track was within plain view of the hotel's gallery.

Shooting tournaments took place inside the racetrack. In July 1883, for example, the media reported: "This evening closed the greatest shooting match ever held in Texas." Such events attracted people from all around, and newspapers proclaimed that the area featured "delightful social events nightly." Because of such publicity, a company called the Lampasas Street Railway and Transportation Company provided a streetcar service from the depot past Hanna Springs to Hancock Springs. Mules pulled the cars. After reaching the destination, drivers hitched the mules to the opposite end and retraced the route. Folks knew when the cars were coming because of the "constant jingling of the sleigh bells on the mules."[8]

Lampasas also attracted conventions and get-togethers. The National Guard held its state encampments there in 1885 and again in 1886. In 1889, the county's ex-Confederates held a reunion at Hancock Springs. Three years later, 150 members of the Veteran Sons of Texas celebrated their annual reunion at Hanna Hall, where they dined, drilled, and danced. That same month 600 Mabry Guards also drilled there. Other noteworthy events at Hanna Springs included the State Democratic Convention for presidential electors, in which they nominated Grover Cleveland for president.[9]

Increased tourist business tempted local entrepreneurs. Even in 1879, preacher Homer Thrall estimated that more than two thousand persons a year visited Lampasas' sulphur springs. At that time Lampasas' springs attracted people from throughout Central Texas, but primarily from the northeastern and southeastern parts of the state, including Galveston. A few years after the Park Hotel opened, the *Lampasas Leader* reported:

> The income from this source alone is enough to support a large town.
> The past summer, there was a floating population of 2500. Each one will
> average a daily expenditure of at least $2.00. One season lasts about 135
> days. Figure this and you have the immense amount of $675,000.[10]

More than six thousand baths were recorded during the following summer at the smaller Hanna facility. By then, many lodgers were coming from out of state by railroad.

Some chroniclers have suggested that the lure of watering places further west stole Lampasas' glory. After the railroad extended its track west in the 1880s, they say, the town began to lose vacationers.[11] However, it took several years before growth slowed appreciably. By the early 1890s, the Park Hotel could not lease all its rooms and eventually closed. Hancock Springs' bath-house remained open a few more years, but then that also shut down. On the other side of town, Hanna Springs continued to attract campers and healthseekers to its simple, relatively undeveloped pool and bathhouse until after 1900.

Lampasas' days as a health resort passed quickly, and despite a trickle of healthseekers, facilities deteriorated. In a 1905 article in the *Lampasas News,* a concerned citizen lamented the loss of the watering tradition:

> Its resources are in many respects unlimited, but as in many like cases its
> own people do not appear to appreciate them; they are indifferent; they
> forget. They treat God's gifts as though they hold them in utter con-
> tempt. Hanna Springs, once the pride of many people, wears a neglected
> look. The fences have gone to decay, rank weeds grow everywhere mixing
> their poisonous breaths with the life laden odors from the springs, the
> once beautiful bath house and auditorium has long since lost its paint,
> the shutters are down, the floors are rotting, and all about the place is
> evidence of that decay which is the inevitable result of neglect. Once hun-
> dreds came to drink there where now only an occasional person is seen;
> once there was constant life, gayety, happiness; now—but why say more?
> Lampasas does not care, for Lampasas is surely dying.[12]

In 1904, however, the *Lampasas Leader* reported "visitors coming from all points of the compass, and it is nothing rare to see a crowd of people at

15. Abney Well, Lampasas, Texas, 1909. Author's postcard collection.

the Hanna spring from 6 to 8:00 A.M. and from 8 to 11:00 P.M." These visitations occurred after the pool was reported to have lost its appeal. Indeed, the 1904 *Texas Almanac* noted Lampasas as a "health and pleasure resort" with "the largest sulphur springs in the world." What accounted for these claims of rejuvenation? Or was it essentially a last gasp?

In a final effort to revive spa life, Lampasas' boosters sought to promote water from an exploratory well drilled for oil in 1903; instead of oil, the well furnished water said to contain 1.25 percent lithium. The new Abney Well (see fig. 15) featured a small, open-air, Victorian pavilion with benches around the perimeter. It displayed an almost sanctuarylike quality, to which an individual could retreat and meditate in a quiet, parklike atmosphere.[13]

As recently as 1936, local people lauded the medicinal qualities of the waters from Hanna Springs and the Abney Well. Throughout the 1930s visitors continued to come in small numbers to sample the waters, and in 1948 another local citizen tried to resurrect the town's image as a resort by building a motel close to the waters, but to no avail.[14] Spring life gradually faded in Lampasas, leaving only memories of tented camps, moonlit walks, grand amusements, and healing waters.

Mineral Wells

As in Lampasas, tents surrounded the newly discovered waters of the future site of Mineral Wells, but they proved more temporary and were quickly replaced by hotels. The unique social life found around Lampasas' camps never had a chance to develop in Mineral Wells. In addition, Lampasas' resort activities centered primarily around the two natural springs, located adjacent to but outside the immediate downtown area. In Mineral Wells, by way of contrast, the newly drilled, cold-water wells became the focus of town building and eventually were scattered throughout the downtown.

In 1881, the year J. A. Lynch first described the therapeutic effects of the water from his well, three thousand people at one time camped on his property. Shortly thereafter, a building boom began that eclipsed Lampasas' endeavors to build a resort. J. H. Baker wrote of the excitement of discovery:

> July 21, 1881: Sent the wife and children to the medical well today. There is considerable excitement in the country below the mountains, beyond the river concerning a well that has been dug, the waters of which seem to be benefitting those who drink it. August 16: Left Ed in the office and went to the mineral well to see my wife. There are several hundred people there for the benefit of their health. There is but one well and it does not offer enough water to supply those who are there. . . . Two other wells are being dug.[15]

H. M. Berry, Mineral Wells' first schoolteacher, arrived a month after the town was laid out, in the fall of 1881. As an eyewitness to the frenzy of early town building, he reported on the importance of mineral waters as the raison d'être of the town's formation:

> Many wells were drilled soon after this. A boom was now starting. By the first of October it looked like a small army was camped here. Tents were everywhere. In laying out the original town they made the Lynch well the starting point and put it in the center of the block. This block was reserved by Judge Lynch as a public square. . . . The original town was then laid out covering the 80 acres, then 3 rows of blocks were laid out running east and west on the south part of the Wiggins addition. . . . Mr. Pritchett came here about October 1 and opened a hotel in a large tent. . . . By November 1st the sound of the hammer was heard in all directions. Carpenters had come by the dozens. The road was lined with wagons hauling lumber from Weatherford and Millsap. . . . Several wells

were drilled so near the same time I don't think anyone remembers which was drilled first. The DeBellet well, the Starr well, the Gibson well and what was known as the white sulphur well were all mineral wells.[16]

Berry noted that eight to twelve hacks (taxis) met arriving trains of the Texas and Pacific Railway in Millsap and would continue to do so for the following nine years. Many enterprising persons arrived in town as invalids, saw its business prospects, and began to cater to others who were in similar unfortunate circumstances:

> Mr. J. M. Allen, an old pioneer came here an invalid, drank the water about a month. It made him sick. He swore he would not stay one hour longer than he could help in Mineral Wells. He got on the Millsap hack early in the morning and spent the day in Millsap. While there the reaction came and he felt so much better he paid his dollar, and came back to the wells. He soon got sound and well. He then built a hotel where the east wing of the Crazy now stands. He found a wife somewhere, and they ran the hotel for about ten years.[17]

The water was in such demand that twenty-five years later, Mr. Lynch remembered that he had to adopt stringent measures when the limited daily supply of one hundred gallons proved inadequate. He required each applicant to sign a declaration that he or she was indeed sick and needed the water. Two years after the water's discovery, 125 wells doled out the healing liquid, and one man had begun to manufacture soap, an eye salve, and crystals made from the water that flowed from his well.[18]

From early on, bathhouses, pavilions, and hotels dominated the built landscape. Although the town contained the largest number of such structures of any Texas resort, the average bathhouse remained open only a short time. Fires took their toll, and names changed as frequently as the owners did. The *1909 Hotel Guide* listed four bathhouses—the Bimini, Lamar, Bethesda, and Anna Bell; seven wells and pavilions—the Crazy, Gibson, Texas Carlsbad, Lamar, New Beach, Star, and French Iron; two sanitoriums—the Mineral Wells Sanitorium and the Rountree Sanitarium; forty-six hotels and boardinghouses; and nineteen rooming houses. Owners of these wells, pavilions, and bathhouses often chose familiar names, such as the Vichy Well and the Carlsbad Well, after famous European resorts. One man based the design of his Lamar Bathhouse on one in his hometown of Hot Springs, Arkansas.[19]

There was a well-established social routine at Mineral Wells. Mornings were set aside for bathing and "calling," afternoons for drives or donkey rides, and evenings for balls and band performances. Early-morning routines began with bathing and imbibing mineral water. Socializing often took the form of playing games in pavilions or boardinghouse lobbies. Aficionados spent countless hours on verandas or in drawing rooms playing dominoes. One 1905 report estimated that "there are 3,000 visitors here and 2,800 are domino mad." Even in 1952 dominoes were popular; as one writer described the scene in the Crazy Hotel lobby: "You hear the 'bones'—the dominoes—clicking on the tables. West Texas stockmen and Kansas wheat farmers, and their wives, love to play dominoes. Some of the visitors play all the time except when eating, sleeping or taking the treatment." [20]

On Sunday, however, a reporter noted, "The lid goes on the dominoes. Then the visitors climb the mountains, visit the lake and drink water." Other Mineral Wells visitors climbed the "sick thermometer" or the flight of steps up the nearby hill.

In the afternoon, outdoor retreats were especially popular, if the pavilions' activities did not seem particularly inviting. In its early days, the town advertised walks to Inspiration Point, with its impressive view of the Brazos River. Other outings took sightseers to Lovers' Retreat, Devil's Hollow, Lake Mineral Wells, Witches' Rock, Hanging Rock, Revelation Point, the Pinnacle, and Jackson Park. Visitors could in fact select from a greater variety of outdoor recreational opportunities at this resort than at any other spa in Texas. Horseback rides carried them to the brakes of the Brazos River, while in the resort's early years, burros—called Texas Nightingales because of their ability to "sing"—carried parties up East Mountain (see fig. 16). One observer noted that it was worth the $10 fee to "catch a glimpse of a 250 pound woman astride of a 90 pound burro coming down the mountainside." [21]

If these outdoor recreation options did not seem enough, enterprising men endeavored to create their own. In 1904, Edward Dismuke and Cicero Smith decided to build a lake for visitors and later organized the Mineral Wells Lakewood Motor Car Scenic Railway to run from Mineral Wells to Lake Pinto. The motor cars, nicknamed the Scenic Railway, ran every fifteen minutes from Gibson Wells Park to Lakewood Park; they included two "Dinky Cars," small gasoline-powered cars on tracks. [22]

Streetcars also took visitors to Elmhurst Park, south of the city, to "skate, boat and see 'high-class vaudeville.'" Elmhurst, situated on a hundred acres, included a lake, a bandstand, dancing pavilions, cafes, a merry-go-round,

16. Burro riding, Mineral Wells, Texas, 1918. Author's postcard collection.

and a casino capable of seating 1,500 persons. With the 1907 inauguration of the electric system and the opening of Elmhurst, Mineral Wells classed itself with the "larger cities of Texas." Indeed, with its bathhouses, pavilions, and amusement park, the town claimed activities and structures that larger cities did not possess.[23]

Drinking pavilions, elaborate descendants of the eastern sheds called springhouses, offered many recreational activities, particularly in Mineral Wells. In 1911, the Standard Pavilion in Mineral Wells covered almost an entire city block and housed various activities, including movies, a playground, a swimming pool, a flower garden, and a dancing pavilion. An earlier picture of the Standard (when it was called the Beach) shows small pools of water dotting the sandy soil (see fig. 17). It resembled a bathing pavilion commonly seen around Galveston. A 1906 postcard of Sangcura Sprudel Wells with its adjoining bowling alley in Mineral Wells also reveals a similar openness to the elements with its surrounding verandas (see fig. 18).

Most pavilions provided space for reading and games. Some also boasted bowling alleys and billiard rooms. The French Well, Mineral Wells' first

17. Beach pavilion, Mineral Wells, Texas. Note the small pools in the sandy fenced area behind the open pavilion. Author's postcard collection.

18. Sangcura Sprudel, Mineral Wells, Texas. Note the openness of the pavilion and the bowling alley in the rear. Author's postcard collection.

drinking pavilion, sported a dancing room and skating rink. Clearly, competition to outshine nearby pavilions was intense. The Mineral Wells Commercial Club offered a detailed view of a typical structure:

> One of the drinking pavilions completed in 1909 is a two-story and basement building, 100 x 200 feet, constructed of white pressed brick, concrete and steel, equipped with steam heat, electric fans, a handsome drinking fountain, ladies' and gentlemen's separate rest and writing rooms, sanitary toilets and wash rooms, telegraph and cable office, post-office box, news stand, hundreds of rockers and chairs, manicure parlors, etc., and cost approximately $100,000. . . . There are three or four other drinking pavilions where the various waters are served (cold or hot) to guests from 6 A.M. to 10 P.M. every day in the year. Guests can be [as] comfortable on the inside of these pavilions as in a modern hotel, and three of them have beautiful "park grounds" adjoining where guests can enjoy the open air and sunshine.[24]

In addition to morning visits, people particularly liked to congregate at the pavilions in the evenings to dance the night away:

> [When] "night lets her curtain down and pins it with a star," then the merriment begins! Electric "Stars" gleam, entrancing strains of music from various instruments are wafted on the summer breeze, and now the favorite waltz, the exhilarating two-step, or the old-time dance of our ancestors, the stately and dignified minuet, can be witnessed at any and all of these popular resorts.[25]

The facilities provided venues for "spooning," a popular romantic pastime encouraged by a mayor who "invites all persons, young or old, afflicted with spoonitis, to come to Mineral Wells, drink the water and play at the great national game."[26] To encourage it, there was a public dance every night at Hawthorne Hall.

Vacationers registered at a pavilion and for one dollar could drink all the water they wanted for a week. As a result, they tended to frequent the same pavilion for the entire seven days. At the first Crazy Well pavilion a small orchestra played mornings, afternoons, and nights during the summer. In the later, more elaborate structure two to four persons dispensed free water from 9 A.M. to 12 P.M. and 3 P.M. to 5 P.M.:

> Hundreds of people gather, and even more in the evening. A splendid band furnishes music, while the visitors amuse themselves by playing dominoes, or pass the hours in several ways, ever and anon quaffing

glasses of water at intervals of every half hour. The extent to which the Crazy Well is patronized may be imagined when it is stated that from two to four persons are kept busy from morning until 10 o'clock at night behind the water counter filling glasses from freely-flowing faucets and passing them over to the "drinkers" always lined up, sometimes four deep.[27]

Other activities occupied townspeople and resort-goers alike. As in Lampasas, the Chautauqua attracted prominent speakers during the resort's early days. In 1905, Mineral Wells erected a Chautauqua Assembly Hall where the Texas Chautauqua held an eight-day meeting, with two programs daily. One local historian recalls some sessions:

> The first chautauqua sessions were under the direction of Homer T. Wilson, minister of the Disciples of Christ, from San Antonio. They were held during the summer, and there were three sessions daily. In the mornings were bible lectures; the afternoon and night meetings were diversified programs. An orchestra played for all the meetings. William Jennings Bryan delivered one lecture. He had just returned from a world tour. . . . General Pickett's widow lectured on the Battle of Gettysburg, where her husband led the famed Pickett's men in that decisive battle.[28]

Seven years later, the town demolished the building—a preview of changes to come.

In the 1930s, the social focus in Mineral Wells shifted to large hotels, with all the facilities on-site. The Baker Hotel in Mineral Wells emulated Hot Springs' Arlington Hotel (see fig. 19). It provided all amenities. In the spirit of modern-day resorts, it offered a barbershop and a beauty shop, coffee shop, laundry, dress shop, drugstore, stockbroker, bowling alley, bus terminal, garage, rooftop ballroom, swimming pool, gymnasium, and facilities for horseback riding, golf, and tennis. For the healthseeker there were a drinking pavilion, mineral baths, and a medical floor that housed three physicians, a dentist, and an optometrist. The 200-room Crazy Water Hotel tried to compete with the 450-room Baker, with facilities that included a dining room, coffee shop, barbershop and beauty shop, dress shop, drugstore, shoeshine parlor, newsstand, bus station, telegraph and long-distance phone station, doctors' office, curio shop, florist, bookstore, valet service, recreation department, drinking pavilion, and bathhouse.[29]

The Baker Hotel, looming above the skyline, dwarfed the Crazy Water

19. Baker Hotel, Mineral Wells, Texas. Author's collection.

Hotel: "No other city in the country the size of Mineral Wells, with a population of 10,000, has a hotel as big or as comfortably ornate as the Baker,
which is a profitable one."[30] From its lofty position, the building made it
clear to all observers that it alone embodied the "real" resort. Folks, proud
of its fame, forgave such pretentiousness. When it first opened in 1929, the
Baker epitomized luxury befitting any first-class European resort. One local
citizen recalled:

> It was quite elegant; that era will never come back. The Baker was a hang-
> out for oil and cattle men. I remember vividly the automobiles most of
> all—the Packards, Rolls Royces, chauffeur-driven limousines, and black
> Cadillacs. There were ice carvings from the kitchen, a smorgasbord on
> Sunday, and hors d'oeuvres and cocktails at 5 P.M. each day. Sunday lunch
> at the Fairmont [in Dallas] is what the Baker used to be. I don't know
> where you get that kind of luxury today.[31]

Large hotels employed many "big bands" and drew many celebrities.
Lawrence Welk played in both Mineral Wells and Marlin. Guy Lombardo
crooned in the Baker's rooftop club. Other performers included Mary Mar-
tin, Dorothy Lamour, Sophie Tucker, and Pat Boone. The baths attracted
Will Rogers, Judy Garland, Marlene Dietrich, Tom Mix, and General John J.
Pershing.[32]

When the resort business died in Mineral Wells, so did the Baker. A case
could also be made that when the Baker died, so did the resort business there,
as the hotel overwhelmed the industry in that town. It now sits vacant, a
fitting symbol of a bygone era. People enjoyed playing there as much as bathing and drinking the water. While early Lampasas developed into a ranching
and market center, the economy of Mineral Wells depended upon resort-
goers until World War II. Thereafter, the city courted industrial firms to
diversify its economy. Mineral Wells thus remains vibrant, though its name
alone bears witness to the story behind its settlement.

Marlin

The reputation of Mineral Wells' cold waters equaled that of Marlin's
renowned hot-water therapies. Although Mineral Wells offered a variety of
medical services in complement to its social activities, Marlin's medical practitioners entirely controlled the city's spa phenomenon. Marlin's attempt to

match Mineral Wells' success and transform itself into a playground for the rich and famous, however, was short-lived.

In the early 1890s, ten years after the discovery of Mineral Wells' underground treasure, Marlin drilled for a city water supply. Disappointed to find heavily mineralized artesian water, the townspeople let the hot water flow undisturbed. According to a writer for the *Marlin Democrat,* a sick and despairing man entered the newspaper's office and "enlisted the sympathy of this writer and others." For five weeks he bathed in a barrel of water provided by the Marlin townspeople. When he finished, his "loathsome disease" appeared to be healed. The water had "cleansed" him, and the barrel demonstrated "the wonderful and unexcelled healing power of the Marlin water."[33]

The writer must have referred to some venereal disease—possibly syphilis, a disease considered "unclean" and incurable at the time. Almost overnight, people flocked to sample this amazing discovery, and they continued to do so for many years. Marlin obviously held an appeal for a certain audience.

Medical practitioners also considered the water beneficial for other ailments. Two doctors founded an institution for chronic diseases, focusing on mineral water treatments. One of them, J. W. Torbett, credited the water with aiding his recovery from malaria. After discovering the water's medicinal effects, the local medical profession celebrated Marlin's waters as curative and widely promoted them.

Soon other aspects of resort life appeared. Train depots attracted bands and boosters who met arriving resort-goers. In the 1880s, in Lampasas, for example, hack drivers met the trains and shouted the names of their respective hotels. This tradition continued in other places but blossomed in Marlin, where hustlers also hawked the names of doctors' offices and bathhouses, endeavoring to capture the business of arriving healthseekers. They guided them to hotels, boardinghouses, bathhouses, or medical people. Enterprising boys and men often accosted persons as they climbed off the train, creating such a nuisance that the city was forced to restrict such activities.

In 1904, the Marlin City Council passed an ordinance regulating this boosting of hotels and bathhouses. It prohibited the soliciting of anyone arriving by train except within certain prescribed limits. Entrepreneurs had to stand behind a white line painted fifteen feet from the train tracks and wait for twenty minutes after the passenger crossed this line at the depot before soliciting his patronage. Clarita Buie, a local resident, described this lively but somewhat hazardous experience:

> The boosters tried to outshout one another from behind the "booster line," a white line painted on the sidewalk 15 feet from the train tracks. Before Mayor Kennedy and his council passed a city ordinance establishing the line, visitors had occasionally been knocked down by overzealous boosters. More than one had been forced to accompany a captor to regain possession of his luggage. *Marlin Democrat* publisher, Mayor Kennedy, was in attendance at train times to scout for news, as well as to collect the $16 fine if the line were violated.[34]

Frank Oltorf, a Marlin historian and rancher, even recalled a local "booster" prank played by a young Marlin man:

> There was a local man named Tom whose father was a district judge, a distinguished old man, and his mother had a Cadillac or one of those big cars. Tom was just as wild as he could be, so to amuse himself he would get his mother's car and go meet the train and say [for example], "This way to the Ben Jefferson House." They [the train's passengers] would see that fine looking car and get in. He'd take them up to the front [of what they thought was a boardinghouse] and let them out. They'd thank him profusely, and when they got in [the building], it was a black cat house.[35]

A booster earned room and board plus a dollar for every customer. Ruby Harris, owner of a boardinghouse in Marlin from 1939 to 1972, remembered her husband's days as a booster:

> My husband was one [a booster]. He worked for his brother. They would meet the trains. At that time we had trains and buses both. Mostly they met the trains. They'd go down to the depot, and they would say, "Harris House, Harris House, Harris House. Come stay with us. Room and board so much a week." Every one of them would have one or two boosters. They would just fight over anyone that got off that train. In fact, people did get hurt. He [Mrs. Harris' husband] met the buses and trains for fifteen years. That's when [when people drove their cars there], boosters didn't work anymore.[36]

Many local citizens continually complained about the insolence and unscrupulousness of these men. In a 1909 letter to the editor of the *Marlin Democrat*, for example, one person wrote of a young woman's experience with a booster who was employed by a certain physician in the resort town. Upon her arrival on the midnight train, the fatigued healthseeker turned to a booster for assistance in finding the hotel and physician to which she had been referred. Neither was available, according to the booster, but he was delighted to take her to another hotel and doctor—his employers, of course (the doctor paid him a 40 percent commission). In closing, the letter pronounced: "The boosters' business is in reality trafficking in flesh and blood, for many a case of lifelong invalidism,—many a death even,—may be laid at their doors."[37]

Although not all professionals adopted the practice of employing boosters, enough did to spark disapproving comments from both local and visiting physicians. One Marlin physician, for example, warned about these industrious men by verse:

> Now boarding houses dot the place and feed you very well,
> But one thing more they often do, of which I wish to tell;
> They work for faking doctors here as their commission men,
> And try to be your friend at once, that they might "boost" you in.
> So, warn your friends before they leave, to know what they're about,
> Or the "boosters" will catch them if they don't watch out.[38]

Although state legislators tried to outlaw the practice, it continued into the 1930s, when travel by automobiles became more frequent. Even then, the booster spirit did not die out completely; Mrs. Harris continued to pay taxi drivers if they brought guests to her boardinghouse.

Boarding- and rooming houses proliferated at Marlin. In these establishments visitors with fewer financial resources paid lower rates, received their meals, and still took baths in nearby bathhouses. At one time Mrs. Harris estimated that Marlin had thirty-two boardinghouses catering to bathers. At her Harris House, she rented thirty-eight rooms and attracted all age groups (see fig. 20). Leon Hale, journalist for the *Houston Post,* called it typical of "the old boarding-house look—white frame, two story, a porch with swings, and men sitting out front waiting for the dinner bell." Mrs. Harris further described the boardinghouse experience:

> We served three meals a day. Breakfast from 7 to 9:00 A.M., dinner at
> 12:00, and supper at 6:00 P.M. We had six tables set up—four long
> tables with twelve chairs and two tables with six chairs. We could serve
> 60 people at one time. We rang a bell at 12:00 and everybody had their
> regular seats in the dining room. They came here on the basis of weekly
> baths. The course of the baths, when we first started, was three weeks.
> One a day. They came from everywhere to take the baths. When we first
> bought the place in 1939, there wasn't anyone come unless they were pre-

20. Harris Boarding House, Marlin, Texas, ca. 1950. Author's postcard collection.

pared to stay the entire three weeks. At that time room and board with three meals a day was $8.00 per week.[39]

Social life drew people to Marlin's boardinghouses. Mrs. Harris recalls lifelong friendships and romances that were formed at her establishment. Adding to the ambience at Harris House were card tables and a big domino table, where enthusiasts played continuously from 8:00 A.M. to 10:00 P.M. Other activities included sitting in the nearby open-air pavilion, telling stories, and meeting people. In later years, visitors took advantage of country club privileges to swim and play golf. Before the club built a pool, they swam in the country club lake or fished in the Brazos River, where the most popular outing took place at the Falls. A bus picked up passengers at hotels and boardinghouses and conveyed them to the Falls of the Brazos, where they waded across on a concrete crossway. The twelve-foot concrete crossover also permitted less mobile folks to drive across from one bank of the river to the other. On the banks, some townspeople set up temporary stands to clean and fry catfish.

Marlin's patrons also drank mineral water at pavilions (see fig. 21). The pavilion held benches, a fountain of continuously flowing hot water, and, in

21. Marlin's Hot Well, Marlin, Texas, 1924. Author's collection.

the early days, a stand that provided mineral water and soda. In 1909 the town began to charge patrons to drink the water. But since the water flowed incessantly, the practice must have been difficult to institute. (Even in the 1990s, people could freely drink from the fountain.) The Ladies Social Club added a second fountain in 1912, and another wooden pavilion later covered this one. These pavilions were simple affairs compared to those of Mineral Wells. Nevertheless, they served as a focus for informal gatherings among strangers and townsfolk alike. Frequenting the pavilion was a social event, so people dressed up. In 1908, one reporter described the social bustle that the pavilion encouraged:

> The pavilion is a simple structure whose primary object was to shelter from the ardent rays of the Texas sun those health-seeking pilgrims who wished to loaf around between drinks. A progressive drug store contributed some benches by way of advertisement. These have been added to until the place now resembles an audience hall. An electric piano has been installed and discourses sweetly at 5 cents a tune. These aids to sociability and musical entertainment enhance the value of the spot as a place for congregating; and still the water flows and still the pilgrims drink. They assemble here, a motley crowd, and as "one touch of rheumatiz makes the

whole world kin," they need no introduction to their neighbors, but are on friendly terms immediately. . . . When summer comes and an orchestra is secured and the pavilion suddenly blossoms into a social center, a concert is given here every other night. It furnishes an occasion for paying respects to the melodious muse and at the same time meeting one's friends and disseminating the latest hearsay. During the intermissions, the big folks chat, the small folks romp, and the young folks flirt; all ages and sizes being represented. And the popcorn man does a thriving business.[40]

In addition to these activities, a rather unusual pastime came about at Marlin's pavilion. It seemed that clear glassware turned amber after about six hours of sitting under the ever-flowing, sulphur-rich water. It seemed "to afford [the ladies] great pleasure as they [sat] on the long bench [to] watch the clear glass turn into a golden tint." One enterprising ticket clerk for the International and Great Northern Railway treated glass paperweights in the water "until they present[ed] all the tints of the rainbow" and sent them as advertisement to prominent railway men. He even sent one to President Theodore Roosevelt as a birthday gift; the president appreciatively acknowledged it with a note. Even into the 1960s, two bathhouses displayed shelves of the amber glassware, from costume jewelry (rhinestones, especially) to vases. Because of the demand for golden trinkets, one man remained in business for more than twenty-five years coloring glass for clients.[41]

Marlin provided other amusements also—there were two large lakes for fishing, an opera house, and dancing arenas. During the first few decades of the twentieth century, the *Marlin Democrat* often announced orchestra recitals on hotel lawns, at the park, and at the hot-well pavilion. In 1911, for example, the Marlin Juvenile Band played at the pavilion on Tuesday and Friday nights. The Ladies Social Club and the Marlin Commercial Club promoted Marlin as a health resort and a desirable place to live. They held dances in the Arlington Hotel or, later, on the top floor of the Hilton Hotel. The clubs also sponsored events for teenagers at the pavilion in Bartlett Park.[42]

In contrast to the early days of Lampasas, local townspeople in Marlin never participated to a great extent in visitors' activities. Oltorf attributes this separation of residents and visitors to the town's social structure: "Marlin was a very old town. And it was a rather snobbish town. These old families around here had intermarried. Like when the Giants trained here, the daughters were never allowed to go with one of the Giants."[43]

Professional baseball teams often moved their spring training to Texas resorts because of the climate and the healthful waters. From 1908 to 1919 the New York Giants trained in Marlin. The Giants, in fact, owned a baseball park and grandstand there until the 1970s. Other teams that came to Marlin included the Chicago White Sox, the Philadelphia Phillies, the Cincinnati Reds, the St. Louis Cardinals, and the St. Louis Browns. The Giants, in particular, chose Marlin because of the mineral water; they considered bathing in it and drinking it essential for physical conditioning. In 1908, Sam Crane, a sportswriter who traveled with the group to Marlin, described its importance to the team:

> The players will have the benefit, and it is a great one, too, of the bath house run with the hotel. It is a pretty and commodious brick building next to the impressive looking big brick hotel, and has all the conveniences that can be found in any up-to-date turkish bath in New York. This will be a big advantage to the players, and, in fact, is half the training.[44]

The sanctioning of balneology by the medical establishment reached its fullest expression in Marlin (see fig. 22). In 1940, for example, Dr. J. W. Torbett incorporated his sanatorium as the Torbett Clinic and Hospital. The American Medical Association's Committee on Health Resorts approved the Buie Health Clinic, located in the Marlin Sanitarium and Bath House, for listing by the Council on Physical Medicine and Rehabilitation. Marlin (as well as Warm Springs in Ottine, near Gonzales) also featured a crippled children's hospital, where polio patients in particular received hot mineral water baths.[45]

Many other aspiring spas in the state did not become as well known because they lacked a charismatic person like Dr. Neil Buie to back their resort enterprise. Part of Marlin's success as a medically oriented spa indeed derived from the magnetism and political acumen of Dr. Buie, former Senator Tom Connally's brother-in-law. According to Frank Oltorf, Buie customarily greeted his patients warmly: "'I'm so glad to see you, old friend, and we're not going to let you suffer. You come in here and talk to me.'" He then spent nearly an hour with each person, Oltorf recalls, "and for the rest of his life, if you asked him [the patient] who his ten best friends were, Buie would have been among the ten." Oltorf, however, used to tease Buie's son, Neil Junior, about the clinic's secret for success:

22. Bethesda Bathhouse, water fountain, and lemonade stand, Marlin, Texas, 1907. The sign reads HOT LEMONADE—A HEALTH DRINK. Author's postcard collection.

You know your father's secret weapon? It was a girl. Her father was a doctor there [at Buie's clinic]. She was red-headed and cross-eyed and with a figure every bit as good as Marilyn Monroe's. She was also a nymphomaniac. So no matter what you came to Marlin for, you ended up being treated for the clap.[46]

Dr. Buie also never lost track of his patients; he even sent them Christmas cards. But the doctor could not tolerate every annoyance. Oltorf recalled the one time that Buie appeared upset with a patient, an occasion when he used the mineral water to its maximum potential:

There was this one lady came from Wichita Falls, and she was just as mean and cantankerous as she could be. She went to the clinic, saw every doctor, all the X-rays, the blood tests and she got ready to leave. They gave her a bill for $130. She said, "Oh no, $21 is all I owe." So Dr. Buie's secretary said, "You don't understand. That's just for the baths. All the clinic work and the X-rays were extra." "That's not the way it was told to me," the old lady said. The secretary went in to tell Dr. Buie. He said, "Let me talk to her." He came in and she pulled this same thing on Dr. Buie. The secretary said that she had never seen Dr. Buie angry, but she could see that his face was flushed. So when she got ready to leave, you know the Marlin mineral waters are powerful laxative. Dr. Buie said, "Have you tried any mineral water?" She said, "No." He said, "Now that's the best thing we have. Now when is your bus leaving?" She said, "In about 20 minutes." "Well, you have time to go over there and get some. It's free." She said, "Free?" He said, "Yes." She said, "Well, I think I'll go over and have a glass." He said, "Oh, one glass won't help you. Take around three." So when she left, Dr. Buie grabbed the secretary and they rushed down to peep out and watch the old lady drinking out of the fountain. So when she downed the third glass, Dr. Buie said, "Do you realize the first stop for this bus is 30 miles away?" [47]

In 1930, Hilton's eighth hotel in the state opened in Marlin. The hotel garden contained a miniature golf course, and there was a sunroom large enough for dances and banquets, but it was a modest enterprise compared to Mineral Wells' Baker or Crazy. When the Depression brought fewer guests to the hotel, the National Hotel Company took it over. A retired rancher bought and remodeled it in the 1960s, and it finally closed in 1984. The Falls Health Spa in the old Marlin Sanitarium also shut down at the same time.[48]

Although Marlinites had hoped that the Hilton would transform the town into a vacation destination, spa-goers primarily sought Marlin's health therapies rather than its social pastimes. In later years the local hospital displaced the sanitarium's medical functions, employing the sulphurous waters in physical therapies. Eventually, however, even the hospital stopped pumping the water for health, though it continued to use the hot water to cut down on heating bills.[49] The healing waters of Marlin, though still utilized by some physicians, were thus transformed in value.

San Antonio's Hot Wells

While Marlin excelled as a *health* spa and Mineral Wells and Lampasas thrived as *health and pleasure* resorts, San Antonio for a few years claimed the status of a first-class *pleasure* haven.

In 1900, on the east bank overlooking the San Antonio River and within

23. Hot Wells Bathhouse, San Antonio, Texas, ca. 1900s. Author's postcard collection.

sight of the old Mission San Jose in the distance, two thousand people attended the opening of the Hot Sulphur Wells Bathhouse. In 1900, the *San Antonio Daily Express* reported that "the very best people in San Antonio attended the affair, some of the younger society yet preferring to [dance?] in their shirt waists and dresses in the ball room of the Sanitarium to having avoirdupois in the bubbling waters of the pool." Although Hot Wells appealed to the rich and famous, it also welcomed the less affluent, who often stayed in the nearby boardinghouses and private homes while they bathed in the famous wells (see fig. 23). Nevertheless, the *International Blue Book* determined that Hot Wells made San Antonio a "modern, high-class resort center."[50]

The opulence of the Hot Wells Hotel with its fountain, palm trees, and covered walkway to the bathhouse seemed to justify such claims. Situated next to the new bathhouse, the three-story, eighty-room hotel featured modern conveniences, such as steam heat, electric and gas light, individual telephones to the office, and hot and cold water. A local reporter captured a sense of its luxury:

> The parlors are fitted like those of a palace, the dining room is like that of
> a millionaire, furnished in fine carved woods of home manufacture, the

bed rooms are as easy as my lady's bouduoir, the kitchen is as clean as any housewife's in San Antonio and the other departments are likewise up to the same standard. Everything is furnished elaborately and the silver service was made especially for exhibition at the Buffalo Exposition. The table ware is all Haviland China, which is in itself a rarity for a hotel.[51]

In 1906, the management turned away approximately two thousand visitors because there was only the single hotel and bathhouse. The Southern Pacific Railroad had touted San Antonio for its curative Hot Wells, Harlandale Hot Sulphur Well, and Terrell Wells. Although Terrell Wells boasted a sanitarium, it and Harlandale Hot Sulphur Well never achieved the fame of Hot Wells.[52]

Hot Wells drew visitors primarily because of the gambling and social displays—bowling, racing, and visits to the resort's zoo and alligator and ostrich farms. The manager of the first natatorium had acquired a menagerie, including a black bear and a mountain lion, from Langtry's Judge Roy Bean. The zoo grew. In 1902, an ostrich farm relocated to the Wells from San Pedro Springs and remained there until about 1920. (The feathers were harvested to decorate ladies' garments.) Gambling took place in the Hot Wells bathhouse, where a Jockey Club bookie placed bets, often on Sunday ostrich races held north of the hotel. One man who worked at the resort reported cockfights held north of the ostrich farm in 1917–18.[53]

By 1920, however, the spa's heyday had ended. By that time the waters had become only a minor attraction, a development that usually portended the demise of spa life.

Places Lived and Loved

The stories of these four resorts recount life around springs and wells. All the towns prospered because of their underground elixirs, but only Mineral Wells and Marlin blossomed as resorts and flourished for more than a few years. Tent life in Lampasas probably enhanced the experience for both townsfolk and visitors. Lampasas' days as a health spa peaked during those twenty-five years. Resort-goers embraced the springs and established a sense of community around them. They relished the outdoor life, and even local citizens caught their enthusiasm. After only a few years of grand hotel living, however, people sought the waters less and less frequently. The earlier social whirl around the springs quieted, and the waters became places of solitude and retreat for people who still believed in their healing powers.

Mineral Wells developed differently. It thrived because its early pavilions fostered a sense of fellowship, while its mountainous setting provided a wide range of outdoor leisure activities. With its grand hotels extending the life of the resort for about twenty more years, activity patterns changed. Visitors did not climb the mountains anymore or hike to Inspiration Point, or sit in an outdoorlike pavilion to read or hear music. As indoor activities became increasingly popular, visitors placed less value on the physical setting, which was previously considered important in the healing process. They lost contact with the land—the very thing that made Mineral Wells and Lampasas appealing.

Marlin's healing waters took center stage throughout the spa's existence, though the town later tried to become more of a pleasure resort with the building of the Hilton Hotel. Spa life in Marlin thus lasted longer than at the other resorts because it kept its attention centered on water and health. The medical profession ensured its continued success for many years.

Hot Wells closed its doors after only thirty years of operation. Although as famous as Mineral Wells and Marlin, with waters as sulphurous and hot as those at Marlin, it did not establish the pavilions, the tent life, the outdoor activities, or the substantial medical support that characterized the other watering places. Instead it spent its brief heyday primarily as a pleasure resort.

Regardless of a resort's focus, rhythms of daily life at these and other Texas spas promoted a familiarity and sense of belonging. Some people settled at these places. Others just played there, and taking the waters became synonymous with socializing at the waters. Attracted to the lifestyle that the spas offered, visitors embraced these places and returned to them again and again.

CHAPTER 6

Marketing the Waters

THERE ARE, IT IS SAID, within a radius of two miles of the village [of
Sutherland Springs], not less than 100 mineral springs, varying in size,
and in the medicated character of their waters. It is these springs, which
give to the place its special importance, and which must in the near future
of this progressive era in the history of Western Texas, give the locality
a fame co-equal with that of the great health resorts and watering places
of America.

—San Antonio Daily Express, *June 5, 1877,*
as quoted in the Western Chronicle, *June 15, 1877*

While Marlin and Mineral Wells displayed long-term successful attempts to capitalize on the hopes of healthseekers and
pleasure-seekers alike, other prospective towns tried to emulate their success
but achieved less satisfaction. Nevertheless, their stories tell of the importance of this natural resource for the state's settlement. Even their short-lived
fame served to bring settlers or railroads into the area.

In the late nineteenth and early twentieth centuries, development companies were formed to initiate settlement by proclaiming the waters as their
key to prosperity. In some cases the only remaining evidence of such endeavors is an old prospectus in which hyperbole ran rampant, emphasizing peculiar or fantastic features. Sutherland Springs (Wilson County), Hynson
Springs (Harrison County), and Putnam (Callahan County) mentioned the
Native Americans' fascination with the area, but Putnam outdid them in its
exaggeration. Putnam's boosters boldly suggested that Putnam was once an
Aztec capital and offered so-called proof: "On the sealed door of a recently
discovered cave near Putnam the emblems of MASONRY [boosters' empha-
sis] were found as inscribed by some Aztec Sculptor ages ago." Although New
Sutherland Springs boasted that their waters were the "red man's" cure, they

also flaunted their assertion that they possessed the South's largest concrete swimming pool. Sour Lake suggested that

> the invigorating character of Spring No. 3 for both men and women has long been known, and dates from the days of Ponce de Leon, who being directed to the port of Sabine Pass by the aborigines, missed the location and searched unsuccessfully in Florida for the Fountain of Youth.[1]

The more incredible the story, it seemed, the more attractive the resort. New resorts often lasted twenty to forty years and then failed. Hynson Springs, Caldwell County's springs, New Sutherland Springs, and Wootan Wells provide examples of how promoters marketed these places and how some early town-building schemes folded after initial success. Although each site was located in significantly different landscapes from Mineral Wells, the first three resorts compared their chances for success to Mineral Wells' prosperity. East Texas' Hynson Springs overlooked Marshall from the top of a nearby pinnacle. Caldwell County's springs emerged from the flat coastal prairie south of San Antonio. New Sutherland Springs sprang up in a riverine environment on the coastal plain, also close to San Antonio. On the blackland prairie, however, Wootan Wells faced stiff competition from nearby Marlin.

Hynson Springs: The "Hill of Health"

Hynson Springs typified a rustic retreat. It was located

> on the summit of a mountain overlooking a vast valley embracing thousands and thousands of acres of towering pine trees. The view of the surrounding country is indeed a rare spectacle with the sun flashing on the noble heights. . . . There is a Lover's Lane with the limbs of fragrant cedar trees interlocking above a grassy promenade scented with the perfume of wild flowers . . . more than a hundred of them [springs], and the summer houses and pavillions with their rustic benches.[2]

Since more than one hundred springs flowed from the top and sides of the hill, the place earned the Indian name translated as "Hill of Health."

In 1851 the *Texas Republican* called what was then Marshall Springs a "modern Eden," meant for "habitation of the muses." Few would-be poets could reside there, however, as the proprietor had built only ten cabins for public accommodations. Hynson Springs derived its name from its next owner, Colonel Hynson. By the 1870s he had built a house and fitted a stage-coach for daily trips to the springs. After he sold the resort in 1890, the new owner built the luxurious Randall Hotel. The hotel, the "best ventilated one in the South," offered 128 rooms, all facing the outside, and more than a mile of verandas and corridors. In 1905, a real estate company speculated that the property would become more valuable if developed further. The Inter-State Investment Company cited a familiar precedent, claiming that purchasers of its Lawn Terrace enterprise in Mineral Wells realized more than 200 percent on their investment in a mere twelve months. At Hynson Springs the company proposed to sell one thousand lots, claiming already to have sold half as many summer home sites. Since 1892, they surprisingly bragged, 100,000 guests (plus 30,000 children) had visited, with only four deaths since the resort's opening.

The company's unusual promotion stressed the hill as a "paradise for children," where "countless ill children had recovered." It boasted that at one time in 1903 sixty-seven children had resided at the springs and that "children in all stages of illness have been brought to the place, some on cots, or pillows, the last resort of their respective physicians, and there has never been a child lost." Their postcards even featured children playing on the hill (see fig. 24). One year later the resort closed for unspecified reasons. Shortly thereafter, the hotel burned down.[3]

The story of Hynson Springs depicted one of the state's earliest marketed springs, one blessed with unique waters and a picturesque location. Yet suddenly the resort completely shut down, and the site has lain derelict for years. A similar fate awaited another early spa.

Caldwell County's Spas: Davy Crockett's Retreat?

As at Hynson Springs, many new owners conceived elaborate development schemes after a resort proved itself marketable over a number of years. Sour waters underlay the oil fields between Lockhart and Luling. J. K. Crook, a physician who wrote to owners of the country's mineral spas and later compiled their responses into a book, extolled each area's claim to fame. Caldwell (also spelled "Cardwell" in some sources) Springs' proprietor must have bragged of their famous visitor, for Crook noted that "tradition has it that the aborigines employed the waters for medicinal purposes, and that Colonel

24. Hynson Springs, Marshall, Texas, ca. 1900. Author's postcard collection.

Davy Crockett bathed his wounds in their cool and limpid flow after his famous single-handed fight with the Mexican lions in this vicinity."[4]

In 1877, the *Galveston Daily News* reported that fifty people lodged at Burditt's Well (also spelled "Burdett's" or "Burdette's") while nearby, the recently opened Cardwell Springs had thirty boarders in its hotel and as many campers. A week later, a follow-up letter indignantly complained of the report's unjust treatment of Cardwell Springs:

> He [the writer about Burditt's Well] forgets to mention the interesting
> facts that the water of "Burdett's Well" is muddy and nearly tasteless,
> and not so "strongly impregnated with alum—the other minerals being
> scarcely perceptible;" but proceeds with the clever statement that "the
> springs are in a crude state, but it is proposed to continue improvements
> until the grounds and accommodations are both attractive and commodi-
> ous," from which the reader should by no means infer that "Burdett's
> Well" is *less* crude, or furnished with *more* "attractive and commodious"
> accommodations.[5]

Claiming impartiality, the writer observed that the springs offered a "picturesque" view of the area, "clear and sparkling" waters, "courteous and attentive hosts," and "satisfactory" accommodations. Although such competition between small adjacent resorts might imply that both could not survive, these two operated well past the turn of the twentieth century. Cardwell's became Rogers' Springs, known for its crystals, and Burditt's Well continued to attract a few patrons:

> This wonderful health resort has had its many "ups and downs" like all
> other health resorts, but for the past few years it has been gradually forg-
> ing to the front and is now in some splendid hands. Mrs. Farris, the excel-
> lent lady who now has charge of the property, is doing well with business
> and is rapidly gaining favor with campers and boarders from almost all
> points, some of whom come a long distance.[6]

Investors realized that development was needed to capitalize on its fame, so they formed the Burdette Mineral Wells and Hotel Company "to create a health resort similar to the one at Mineral Wells, Texas, and already a $5,000 modern bottling plant, a $5,000 amusement pavilion and a twenty-room hotel and cottages are now installed." In the plan they projected a new $40,000 hotel and bathhouse, cement sidewalks, and a cotton gin. They platted one thousand business and residential lots; one half of them sold. Again a budding resort envied Mineral Wells' success:

Some idea of the profits that may be derived from an investment in a resort of this character may be obtained by comparison with Mineral Wells, Texas, where, twelve years ago, lots were on the market for $250 each. It was then a town of about two thousand inhabitants, with two hotels and twelve boarding houses. It is now a city of twelve thousand people, has twenty two hotels and over one hundred boarding houses and lots are now selling at five to six thousand dollars each, and the resort and mineral water business there brought about these results. Last summer there were over six thousand visitors there drinking water at the various wells (10 in number) paying $1.00 per week each for the privilege, an income of over $25,000 per month from these wells.[7]

The land company also published a list of ninety-three businessmen, including bankers, merchants, and physicians, who had purchased lots. One San Antonio businessman was "surprised that such a fine location for a town in such a thickly settled and fine agricultural country as this is should have been so long neglected. Your mineral water alone should build a small city." Potential investors stayed in the hotel and toured the grounds. Visitors and nearby residents frequented the amusement pavilion and drank the waters, particularly on Sundays. Little more was accomplished, however, and the wells gradually stopped attracting patrons by the 1920s.

Developers of both Hynson Springs and Caldwell County's springs already possessed successful resorts, proven in their ability to attract patrons, but they longed for prosperous new towns. Sutherland Springs was both a well-respected resort and a small community when developers of New Sutherland Springs dreamed of nothing less than a completely new community across the river. Fate smiled on their hubris and briefly cooperated—but ultimately had other plans in store.

Sutherland Springs: The Town that Moved Twice

In 1840 George Bonnell called these "celebrated white sulphur springs . . . the most beautiful springs in the world." Located east of Cibolo Creek, they were unimproved, consisting of "a large basin, similar to a bowl of twenty feet in diameter, dug out of a solid rock. The water boils up from the bottom and runs off with a bold stream." Other early explorers and observers of Texas' natural resources such as Orceneth Fisher, Francis Moore Jr., and Viktor Bracht likewise noted these springs "held in high estimation by the aborigines for their medicinal qualities."[8]

The original developer of Sutherland Springs, Dr. John Sutherland, had been at the Alamo during the famous siege of 1836, but escaped the others' fate when early in the battle, William Travis sent him to Goliad to carry a message. After the war, Sutherland briefly left the state and then returned and built his plantation on the bluff west of the creek in 1848. Six years later he commissioned a teacher to lay out the town nearby at a major intersection of the "Chihuahua Road" and the "Goliad Road."

Although Sutherland utilized the springs in his medical practice, especially during cholera epidemics, the springs remained in their natural state until hopes for further development arose in the late 1800s. By 1877, local citizens hoped to improve the viability of the community, which had declined after the Civil War. With the arrival of the Galveston, Harrisburg, and San Antonio Railway to San Antonio and the opening of a newspaper that same year, hopes were rekindled for a growing tourist market at the springs. J. B. Polley wrote:

> Conspicuous among [the springs] which are Black and White Sulphur, Magnesia, Seltzer, Alum and Chalybeate waters, and many other varieties not yet identified, two large Sulphur springs, the one white, the other black sulphur are much resorted to for bathing, and are said to be unsurpassed in their invigorating effect on the human system. The other waters are used for drinking. The Sour Spring notably is most resorted to on account of the coolness and refreshing acidity of its water. The owner of the land on which these springs are situated has as yet made no improvement on it, the springs being kept in order by the citizens of the town, who have also prepared to accommodate all visitors. A commodious line of hacks runs between San Antonio and Sutherland Springs and soon there will be a line of coaches from Seguin.[9]

The springs prompted social gatherings—picnics, target shooting, hunting and fishing, and religious meetings:

> Driving over to the sour springs one evening this week, we were somewhat astounded to find the beautiful pecan grove there, filled with visitors who are spending the summer at our different hotels, all engaged in different amusements. Whilst some were having a lively game of croquet, others, ladies included, were practicing target shooting.[10]

Frequent notices in the new daily, the *Western Chronicle*, advised readers of the cultural activities taking place at the local hotel: "Concert at the Messinger House on Friday the 15th. Vocal and instrumental music and four act plays of Cinderella will be presented with a full caste of amateur actors," or "Anniversary ball at Messinger House—fortnightly parties are to be given at the House throughout the summer months." The paper thanked Dr. Messinger for the "substantial improvements" he put up at the white sulphur bathing springs. That same year, the annual Union Camp meeting was held at the sour springs, although it seemed "little religious interest" was generated.

In 1877, the owner of the spring wished to sell six hundred acres to a Galveston group to improve bathing facilities and to provide accommodations so that the "little village would become a point of importance; neat residences would spring up on the green hills and in the arbored glens about." He failed, but thirty years later a company formed and platted the waterfront property across Cibolo Creek from the original townsite and near the depot of the San Antonio and Gulf Shore Railway Company, built in the late 1890s. The Sutherland Springs Development Company's location seemed ideal—a thousand acres, including frontage on the creek and twenty springs.

In 1909, after the first year, the company proclaimed that twenty thousand persons had visited the new town. In 1910, they sold twenty-eight lots in one week alone and by December, eight hundred persons had bought property at New Sutherland Springs (see fig. 25).

The initiative seemed earmarked for success. The railroad was especially interested in revamping the depot:

> W. G. Van Vleck, manager of the Galveston Harrisburg & San Antonio Railway, accompanied by all the superintendents of the entire Atlantic system of the Southern Pacific railway, visited here yesterday for the purpose of a general inspection of the wonderful mineral waters, and the developments recently made at this place. The object of this inspection was to decide upon the size and location of the new depot already in contemplation. They seemed very much enthused over the prospects at New Sutherland Springs and were especially pleased with the new hotel, now almost completed.[11]

By 1910, officials of the Sunset Route had spent $14,000 on improvements. The *Health Resort* reported that town boosters applauded the railroad:

> The purchasers of this property are such men as Colonel Ike Pryor, Judge M. H. Townsend and J. L. Kerr, and the purchase price was nearly a quarter million dollars. The Southern Pacific Railroad Company have [*sic*]

25. Sutherland Springs pool and bathhouse, New Sutherland Springs, Texas, 1910. Author's postcard collection.

spent and is spending a great sum in a new station, additional trackage facilities, etc. and have put on special rates every point on their lines in the states. When these men and this company show such faith in the future of a proposition of this kind, you must know that it is sound, substantial and extraordinary.

Excursion trains carried immigrants, vacationers, and investors for the winter seasons. A 1914 commercial brochure noted that "tourists one season frequently become homebuilders the next." Many stayed. The Southern Pacific "Sunset Route" offered a discount rate from East Texas to Sutherland Springs when a passenger bought a tourist ticket to Houston or to San Antonio. On December 6, 1910, the newspaper *Health Resort* mentioned a "Homeseekers' excursion" train to arrive on December 8 and that "a large number [of homeseekers] will winter here." Many excursioners came for their health. The December 20, 1910, edition mentioned a Hoosier who was a town promoter and not interested in buying land but who came because of his wife's health and ended up buying four lots.

As at Hynson Springs and Burditt's Wells, Mineral Wells provided the model by which the company measured success. The town's newspaper declared: "You seekers of Health have made Hot Springs, you have enhanced the value of property at Mineral Wells over 1000%; you have made a splendid little city of Excelsior Springs; you are building Sulphur, Oklahoma." The development company considered New Sutherland Springs to have better prospects than the other locations because of its site, climate, and the "greater variety and more efficient mineral waters." [12]

In anticipation of continued growth, the company platted two hundred acres into town lots and streets. By June of 1911, the town consisted of four hotels and boardinghouses, two restaurants, three real estate companies, four physicians, two bakeries, one grocery, one general store, one poolroom, one bank, two drugstores, one dry goods store, two meat markets, one ice house, two lumberyards, one cotton gin, two blacksmiths, two barbers, and one stable. One doctor reported that in twenty-one years of practicing medicine in Sutherland Springs, he had seen at least "10,000 people from the south, north and west." The resort also attracted local and regional groups. According to one witness, it was not unusual to see three or four thousand people there at week's end. San Antonians particularly frequented the park on weekends:

> Saturday the Methodists invaded Sutherland Springs in force, and spent the day in the park in their annual Sunday school picnic festivities. Tickets to the number of 427 were sold out of San Antonio for the special excursion train, which means that counting children and all, there were at least 500 visitors from the Alamo City on that day. [13]

In 1910, the first Baptist encampment on Cibolo Creek attracted 2,500 persons to the Chautauqua meeting. The railroad recognized that the resort also "was ideally located for suburban homes for the hustling and growing city of San Antonio."

The pool and the bathhouse sat next to the creek, while the springs gushed from the bank or creekbed. Floods frequently filled the springs with mud, which the owner continually had to dredge. A disastrous flood in October 1913 destroyed the bathhouse and bankrupted the company. Shortly thereafter, T. J. Williams, a lumberman from East Texas, bought the property and soon erected a bathhouse, a sanitarium, and a dancing pavilion on stilts. To facilitate access, he ran a trolley line from the railroad to his park. After the quality of the clientele declined and his wife died in the early 1920s, Williams closed the resort, although the pool remained open for recreational purposes. Newspaperman T. C. Richardson noted that the pool and hotel

26. Sutherland Springs pool as it looked in 1992. Author's photo.

still drew customers, but said that the new owner "lacked the vision to capitalize his assets." By the late 1920s the hotel had closed, and the community was virtually a ghost town. As a new highway connected the old townsite to the coast, businesses and homes moved back across to the west bank of Cibolo Creek, where Dr. John Sutherland had originally established his plantation in the 1840s.

Little remains today of the planned community except the exterior of the old bank, with its exposed but unopened vault and a plant-choked pool on a peninsula jutting out into the creek (see fig. 26). Although the old town died, the community of Sutherland Springs still exists, primarily because of its location on prime transportation routes. Another planned town, however, lacked such assets.

Wootan Wells: A Planned Community

On this blackland prairie three miles from Bremond, F. M. Wootan dug for water for his farm in 1878. He sent samples to be analyzed and found

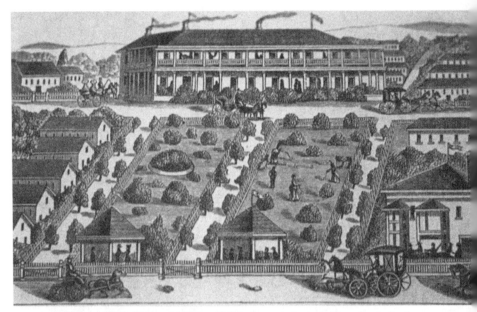

27. Wootan Wells, Texas, and Union Hall in Saratoga Springs. Note the similar layout of the resorts. Sources: *1884 Texas State Gazetteer,* courtesy of Center for American History, University of Texas at Austin, and *Frank Leslie's Illustrated Newspaper, 1865,* as pictured in Henry W. Lawrence, "Southern Spas: Source of the American Resort Tradition," *Landscape* 27, no. 2 (1983).

that it contained minerals purported to have medicinal properties. In 1880 Wootan formed a partnership with T. W. Wade to bottle the water and build a resort. This "Old Wootan Wells Company" dug four wells, built four hotels, and laid a mile and a half of railroad track so a mule train could carry passengers and bottled water to and from the Houston and Texas Central Railway. A later partnership, the Wootan Wells Company, added further improvements to the resort.

Specifically planned as a resort town, Wootan Wells exemplified a modest but comprehensive spa. Its small hotels, pavilions, cottages, and bottling works revolved around the waters. Although most watering places displayed buildings randomly placed around a spring or well, Wootan Wells' highly structured morphology appeared similar to that of the plan of Union Hall in Saratoga Springs, developed in the 1860s in the new national style. This national style included "long verandas, rambling site plans, loosely connected wings, an increased concern for openness and freedom of movement, and a

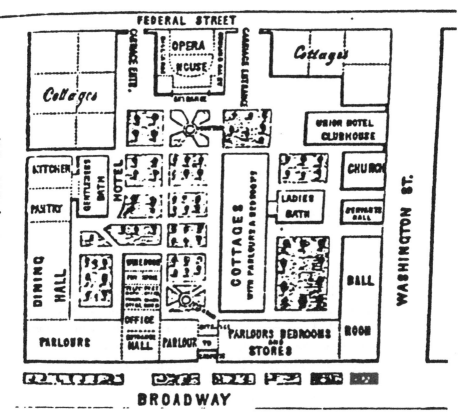

greater integration of buildings and grounds . . . an increased emphasis on courtyards, connecting walkways, and the grouping of buildings to suit the topography." [14]

Wootan Wells displayed a central plaza or park area with pavilions at one end, similar to Union Hall's central park, with fountains at each end (see fig. 27). In both plans cottages lined the park. While the opera house overlooked Union Hall's park, a large hotel with long verandas dominated Wootan Wells' landscape, with the opera house tucked away on the periphery of the settlement. Further similarities included connecting walkways and the placement of individual trees equidistant around the green space. The congruities between the two places suggest that in the 1880s developers recognized a resort style used elsewhere in the country. In 1883, the editor of *Texas Prairie Flower* recounted the neat array of buildings:

Beyond the park, immediately opposite the hotel, are the wells, covered with neat, tastily-built sheds, and floored, where the water is dispensed by men who remain at their post day and night. These wells are in a row, about twenty feet apart, and each possessing different medicinal properties. It is the fashion to drink from number one first, then from number three, and stroll over to the only store of the place (Wade Bros.) and weigh. Numbers four and five are used almost exclusively for bathing purposes. . . .

To the left of the hotel is a circular building used as a skating rink, dancing hall, and for preaching on Sunday. There is also a billiard hall but no saloon, making it one of the most orderly places to be found anywhere.[15]

The military-like, ordered spacing of the facilities contrasted with the haphazard placement of structures at most resorts.

Interest in the resort waned after the discovery of Marlin's hot water. A bankruptcy and several fires in the 1920s doomed the town. The bottling works was the last building to survive; it burned in 1926.

Although some planned towns failed, those towns that survived or were already established near springs sought ways to market their waters. Promoters displayed a wealth of knowledge about the attributes of famous resorts, and they were not averse to some inventive comparisons.

Other Marketing Strategies

Many Texas resorts tried to convey the impression that their waters equaled or surpassed those of famous resorts in the United States or Europe. For example, both Lampasas and Sutherland Springs pictured themselves as the "Saratoga of the South," while Sour Lake was the "winter Saratoga," destined to draw visitors from the colder North. In the 1800s, a Southeast Texas town named itself Saratoga after the New York spa in hopes of capitalizing on natural springs. Other budding communities blessed with medicinal waters similarly called themselves Bath, White Sulphur Springs, and Carlsbad. One of Lampasas' springs, the Hancock, was supposed to "surpass in medicinal virtues the waters of the famous Blue Lick Springs of Kentucky, and [was] nearly equal to the ancient Harrowgate [sic] Springs of England."[16]

Many waters reportedly resembled those of Carlsbad, a famous resort in Bohemia, which was once part of Czechoslovakia. Referring to Mineral Wells, the *Texas and Pacific Quarterly* noted, "Palo Pinto [County] claims the only genuine Carlsbad on the continent of North America." Some of its early wells, with names like Sprudel, Hygeia, Bernhardt, Newbrunnen, and Schlossbrunnen, reinforced that impression. Mineral Wells compared itself to Carlsbad so often that a story spread about a Texas man (in some versions a woman) whose health prompted him to go abroad to Carlsbad, where specialists, after examining him completely, unknowingly advised him to go to Mineral Wells to be healed.

Comparisons to Carlsbad also became commonplace among other Texas spas. Putnam, "New Carlsbad of America," competed with Hot Sulphur Wells (near San Antonio), also the "Carlsbad of America." In 1890, a University of Texas chemist portrayed the water of Santa Monica Springs, near the city of Austin, as "the celebrated Carlsbad water." Another chemist, who analyzed Gonzales' water, argued that it surpassed Carlsbad's with its "large quantities of sulphate of magnesia and sulphate of soda which [more accurately] resembles Hunyadi-Janos of Hungary." [17]

Other springs in the country drew comparisons as well. The evaporated mineral salts of Rogers' Springs (near Luling) resembled those of the "celebrated Crab Orchard Spring in Kentucky." One spring near Marshall reportedly equaled "the famous Lythia Springs of Virginia." A chemist compared Mangum's waters to the magnetic waters of New York and the Sheboygan waters of Wisconsin. Promoters of Hot Sulphur Wells commented: "It [the spa] has a better summer and winter climate than Hot Springs, and presents a marked contrast to that of Central Texas resorts, where the conditions are decidedly malarial." Fans and promoters of certain resorts even penned extravagant odes to their places of choice. One North Central Texas spa, for example, boasted: "Welcome is the stranger within my gates who finds me with more beauty and health-giving properties than Venice, more culture than Athens. I am to have more history than Rome. Fate gave to the world but one of a kind. I am Tioga." [18]

If the waters displayed such wonders, maybe healthseekers did not even need to journey to the spa to experience them. They could use them in their own homes.

DRINKING TO HEALTH

Bottled waters, crystals, and salves made from mineral water supplemented other business activities and became increasingly important to Texas and the nation. According to the USGS, sales of mineral water between 1889

SALES OF TEXAS' BOTTLED WATER

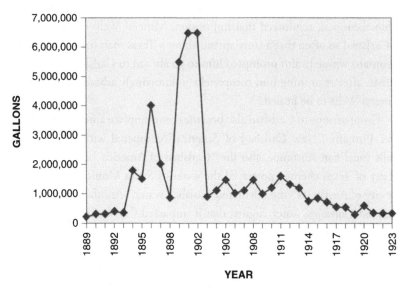

28. Sales of Texas' bottled water. The number of springs reporting each year varied from 10 in 1891 to 21 in 1902, and 40 in 1911, decreasing to 38 in 1913, 18 in 1919, and 9 in 1923. Compiled from USGS.

and 1923 fluctuated from a low of 213,700 gallons to a high of 6,651,750 gallons (see fig. 28). The high figure was achieved shortly after the state's peak resort years. Texas' percentage of national commercial sales fluctuated from a high of 16 percent in 1896 to less than one percent in 1923. The haphazard number of springs reporting sales varied from a low of ten in 1892 to a high of forty in 1911. However, the 1929 *Texas Almanac* reported that "commercial usage of these waters is largely through the establishment of resorts which attract healthseekers, but there is also an appreciable distribution of bottled water." The resort business thus earned significant income from bottled water sales.[19]

Medicinal demand accounted for most Texas sales (see fig. 29). In 1907, three classes of medicinal waters included purgative, lithia, and sulphureted—the last rarely sold in bottles but drunk in large quantities at the resorts. When the USGS began to differentiate between medicinal waters and table waters in 1905, medicinal waters accounted for most of Texas' sales. These sales averaged more than 90 percent yearly except for 1910 and 1911, when 77 and 79 percent of the respective sales were for the healing waters.

TEXAS' SHARE OF SALES OF US MEDICINAL WATERS

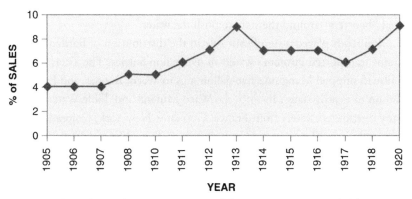

29. Texas' share of sales of all medicinal waters of the United States. Compiled from USGS.

Texas' share—except for 1909 and 1919, when figures are unavailable—
was from 4 percent to 10 percent of the nation's sale of medicinal waters. In
1912 Texas was fourth in sales. The role of Texas' resorts in providing an
ongoing supply of mineral water increased significantly.

In 1877, W. H. Lillie sent ten different varieties of Sutherland Springs'
medicinal waters to San Antonio. A San Antonio newspaper advertised sealed
bottles of the water: Sour Water and White and Black Sulphur Water at
fifteen cents per bottle, plus Dr. Burditt's Sour Water from Burditt's Well
at five cents a glass. Later, Sutherland Springs systematically marketed the
water:

> Last week the Sutherland Springs Hygeia Water Co. was incorporated
> under state laws, at a capitalization of $30,000. W. E. and H. P. Nelson
> and Judson Hume are the incorporators, but a number of other local
> people are stockholders in the new enterprise. Plans are in the making for
> the construction of a bottling plant. This is the first company in the field
> to undertake the systematic marketing of our waters, and we predict for it
> a high measure of success.[20]

By 1911, an investor could buy into the newly organized Hume Sour
Water Company for $10 and receive one share and forty-eight half gallons
of water.

In 1879, proprietors of Burditt's Well shipped twelve thousand gallons
of water reportedly all over the United States in five- and ten-gallon contain-
ers. By 1911, a $5,000 bottling plant had been built, and bottles were shipped

on a railroad spur to points within a 250-mile radius. The company's plans were ambitious, though, for it planned to employ six hundred to eight hundred "boosters" around the state to push the water.

Railroads played a significant role in the distribution of bottled waters. Trains transported Putnam's waters in five-gallon bottles. The Texas Central Railroad shipped Mangum's five-gallon jugs to Waco, Ranger, and Eastland, and on to nearby states. In 1910, the Waco Mineral and Table Waters Company distributed waters from France, Germany, New York, Colorado, Indiana, and Texas. Texas' waters included those from Mineral Wells (Gibson and Sangcura No. 2 and 3), Mangum (Pete and Maurice Mangum), Wootan Wells, Marlin, Hubbard City, Arlington, and Tioga. In 1913, the owners of the Crystal Bathhouse asked the railroad to change the name of the town Vineyard to Wizard Wells and send mineral water by railroad. Other bottled waters came from New Birmingham (near Rusk) and Tyler.

Mineral Wells bragged about being the "largest mineral water shipping point in the South," as shipments (for 1910) were said to exceed three million bottles. Water companies shipped to Chicago, St. Louis, Memphis, Kansas City, Joplin, Oklahoma City, and other places in the North. By 1913, twenty-one mineral water companies operated out of the town. The town's newspaper also printed extravagant and sometimes humorous medical advertisements about the water. Texas Carlsbad Mineral Water from Mineral Wells claimed that its water "makes a man love his wife, makes a wife love her husband, robs the divorce court of its business, takes the temper out of red-headed people, puts ginger into ginks and pepper into plodders." [21]

CRYSTALS AND SUCH

Crystals also supplemented business. If nothing else, the sale of these mineral salts ensured name recognition of the springs or wells. For instance, Crazy Water Crystals, a well-known Mineral Wells product, sometimes hailed from less "zany" locations. In the 1930s Marlin built a crystal factory that operated for about ten years. Several local residents remembered that Mineral Wells often marketed Marlin's crystals as its own. [22]

Enterprising persons made mineral water crystals from as early as the 1880s. Supposedly a man at Mineral Wells' Piedmont Hotel discovered crystal making in 1882 by taking water from rooms to bathe his sore feet. Evaporation formed crystals from the heavy concentration of dissolved salts. Crystal making then spread. In 1884, Mineral Wells' Gibson Company marketed crystals, condensed water, oil, salve, and soap. These articles grew to be in such demand that by 1893 twelve wells in town provided sources for crystals, oils, and other medicines. The Star Well Water Company also made and shipped crystals, oils, and condensed waters.

Crystal making was so popular that even the smallest places manufactured products. The *Myrtle Springs Herald* claimed that the spa had "an expert as to the therapy of mineral waters, [who] purposes soon reducing water from the Castleberry well to crystals; and perhaps may extend the investigation to other wells and springs at Myrtle." [23]

The waters provided not only crystals but a versatile array of other products. A Confederate pharmaceutical laboratory located at Headache Springs near Tyler during the Civil War manufactured medicine from the water; it was said to have a rather acid taste similar to that of aspirin. Others countered that the spring's name derived from the "bust-head" whiskey made there. Sour Lake's businesses shipped water, mineral mud, and tar, plus ginger champagne, sassafras, and beer made from the waters. Mineral mud reputedly cured "Eczema, Putrid Sores, Rheumatism, Syphilis" and "all blood disorders without the use of mercury." Sour Lake Tar sold at $6 to $8 per gallon and was used for "Catarrh, Pneumonia, Lung Troubles and Piles." The brochure claimed that their "Sour Lake Tar Ointment" was used by Drs. Stuart and Boyles in their Houston infirmary. [24]

Healers also used another unusual product for therapy. A San Antonio doctor claimed that after exposure to air, the most valuable properties of Terrell Hot Wells' water precipitated into a form called "sulphuria." He then collected it, compressed it into tablets touted to relieve Bright's disease or diabetes, and made a salve by grinding the sulphuria to powder and adding oils. The salve, he maintained, was especially beneficial for skin eruptions. Mineral Wells also boasted a healing salve. In 1930, Mineral Wells' Crazy Hotel advertised baths using Crazy Crystals with an after-bath massage using the Crazy Residuum. The residuum was touted as Crazy Water in its most highly concentrated form, left over in the evaporation vat after the condensation of crystals.

Mineral Wells' Crazy Crystals, perhaps the most famous crystals in Texas, was not the town's only product. Water from the Famous Mineral Wells evaporated in an open-kettle process into a product called Dismuke's

Pronto-Lax. A dosage before breakfast equaled the drinking of four or five glasses of natural mineral water, the marketers contended.

Tioga offered Tioga Mineral Salve, Atlas Water, condensed mineral water (fifty times its natural strength), and Radium Mineral Water. Local historian Ross Estes described the process of condensation:

> They had outfits built out of bricks about so high and a pan set on it. Cook that water like cookin' syrup. Boil it down. It takes 40 gallons of water to make a gallon condensed. They was makin' it a few years ago. I don't know whether they make any now or not; don't think so. It wasn't very syrupy, but it changed the color of it to a yellowish-brown color. . . . That condensed water, you could drink a teacup of that and you couldn't hardly get to the barn.[25]

In summary, Texas played a significant role in the nation's mineral water business, from its sales of bottled waters and other products to its share of resort-goers. Promoters marketed waters from resorts primarily by comparing their superiority to that of waters from more famous resorts. Towns founded upon the bubbling brew, however, often foundered, and even the most vigorous promotional schemes could not resurrect them. Those towns that remained had to be satisfied with whatever mineral water business they could muster. They often drew a small, dedicated contingent of resort-goers who quietly drank and bathed in the water as needed over the course of the years. Something more elemental attracted the diehards to these places.

CHAPTER 7

The Experience of Bathing

To ENTER AND COME to inhabit a place fully means to redraw the limits of our bodily existence to include that place—to come to incorporate it and to live it henceforth as ground of revelation rather than as panorama.

—*Bernd Jager,* Dwelling, Place, and Environment

I TOOK A BATH THE NIGHT we arrived and one the next morning. I have had five surgical operations in connection with my arthritis and have visited many spas. The water from the Chief Geronimo Springs is the finest water that I have ever felt.

—*Gene Tunney, former heavyweight champion,*
commenting on Indian Hot Springs

As I drove past a crude, faded sign pointing the way to Stovall Hot Wells, I hoped to see crowds of people patronizing the last bathhouse operating in Texas. A wistful hope—the possibility was remote, at best. As I slowly pulled into the long driveway on this Brazos River floodplain, which was bare of trees and other vegetation, the air was calm and quiet. Nearing the distant gray buildings, I began to feel almost suspended in time. This sensation heightened as I approached the main building. I didn't know that living anachronisms still existed—places forgotten in time, neglected but not abandoned, patronized but not really alive. I reached for the old 1930s postcard I had bought at a paper show (see fig. 30). With the exception of the automobiles parked in front of the bathhouse, the resort before me looked identical to the image on the postcard. The same messages beckoning passersby to take the miraculous waters lured me into a reverie of sorts—as if I were driving a Model T, with my grandmother sitting next to me, looking as if she were sixteen again and on the way to an illicit rendezvous at the wells. The handwritten, foot-high signs on the corrugated tin

30. Stovall Hot Wells, Texas, ca. 1930. Author's postcard collection.

walls alerted patrons to the waters: BATHE YOUR WAY TO HEALTH, BOIL OUT
THE POISON, and HOME OF THE FAMOUS HOT MINERAL WATERBATH. The
black, bold-faced words looked newly painted against the silver-gray background. They weren't faded and disappearing like the old Mail Pouch tobacco signs I had seen back home on Indiana barns.

As I entered the main building, the lobby also seemed to have changed
little from its earlier days when it was the focus of weekly community sings
or square dances. The sulphur smell was as strong as it had been in the hall
outside my high school chemistry lab. An old sign touting a long list of
diseases that the water cured hung next to the window where the owner
greeted guests. Sixty years had brought few renovations, as attested by the
deteriorating interior and the sparse number of bathers. This place used to
attract people in droves, as much for the many amusements available then as
for the mineral water; the amenities had included tennis courts, croquet, a
cafe and barbershop, a lighted ballpark, and skeet shooting grounds. In 1938
the *Graham Leader* boasted that "the skeet grounds have become a famous
place in this part of Texas, for here some of the outstanding skeet artists of
the nation have shot and regular shoots are held there each week."

I was curious to see how the water fared. Only two large communal tubs accommodated female bathers. As I stepped into the hot, black, oily water, I looked at the older, naked ladies already soaking in the brew. I hadn't relinquished my modesty yet, so I climbed into the tub in my bathing suit. That was a mistake, according to my companions, because I wouldn't get the full effect. I smiled self-consciously and changed the subject to their enjoyment of the waters. Both women lived in the area and took the baths religiously. One had moved back specifically to take the waters for a stubborn skin condition, which had not cleared up until she started a bath regimen. The more we talked, the more streams of perspiration coursed down my face, but I thought I could tough it out at least as long as these elderly ladies could. I looked around the room, bare but for a clock and a sign on the wall warning the bather to stay in the water only a few minutes the first time. I sipped my bottled water, but by then I was dying. Finally I couldn't stand it anymore and crawled out of the water. Looking as if they had just stepped in, the ladies remained in the tub and smiled knowingly. It must have been easy to separate the avid dippers from the newly dipped. Shamefaced at my unsophisticated lack of endurance, I wrapped a towel around my dripping suit and walked to the changing room. I could take only so much in the name of research.

A place becomes real if we experience it fully with our senses. Although all the senses—sight, touch, taste, smell, and hearing—contributed to the bathing experience, few people actually described their baths, perhaps because it was such a private activity, especially during the 1800s. A few bathers experienced enough differences from bathing in their own homes to record their impressions. Some noted a distinctive physical sensation after stepping into the waters or described the feel of their skin afterward. To others, the unusual smell or taste of the waters warranted a whimsical explanation. Some springs even looked pure or medicinal to the bathers, depending upon whether they displayed particular colors.

Stimulation of all the senses may occur simultaneously, although one response may predominate. Bathing is often a taken-for-granted activity, and the temperature of the water is the one thing we notice.

The most obvious, fundamental sense involved in bathing, and the most difficult to describe, involves the sense of touch. Except for hot, lukewarm, or cold temperature designations, language falters in descriptions of the sensation of water touching the body. The words "wet," "fluid," or "moist" convey only inadequately how water feels.

Physical immersion in a body of water involves complete contact with an element of nature. Water enwraps, surrounds, lifts, and supports the body. Pleasure from bathing in a natural setting such as a lake or spring is more acute than from bathing in built structures with piped-in water. Lovie Whitaker, daughter of J. O. Langford, who constructed a bathhouse at Hot Springs in Brewster County, described her experience in one hot spring:

> The lower spring for a long time had nothing more than a bathtub dugout in sand where the water welled up, and it was a rather pleasant sensation to get in that and feel the hot water surging up gently and along with it the grains of river silt and sand brushing your skin. It was quite a pleasant sensation.[1]

Similarly, a visitor from the state of Colorado wrote to Sutherland Springs' local newspaper:

> The white and black sulphur are the principal springs and burst from the ground with such force and strength as to render the water perfectly buoyant, and we have fully realized the fact of which we had been told, that it is impossible to sink in it . . . once you are in the spring which is so buoyant, exhilarating and refreshing that one is tempted to remain in longer than might be beneficial. . . . The sulphur water leaves a glow after bathing, similar to a mustard bath, and is so penetrating that it seems impossible for rheumatic or neuralgic sufferers not to be benefited.[2]

The inside bathtub, however, did not necessarily detract from this sensory experience, as Pat Ellis Taylor suggested when she recorded her impressions of the Chief Spring at Indian Hot Springs:

> I stretched out in the trough, listening to the hum of the water pump, studying the cobwebs in the corners of the ceiling, the water so full of minerals that my body floated, and when the tub filled up, I could simply lay my head back on the water like a pillow and let my body bob up and down like a worm an anemone long arms of seaweed dead woman's body.[3]

While a water's buoyancy enhanced the bathing experience, both Whitaker and Taylor enjoyed the feel of their skin after bathing. Whether it was the minerals in the water or the heat of the waters that was responsible, many people recalled how soft their skin felt after a bath. In 1892, George Walton,

a physician who studied mineral bathing, ascribed a smooth, sometimes unc-
tuous texture to many mineral waters. Indeed, many of Sour Lake's springs
exuded an oily film. Oiliness may also result from silicates or organic matter,
such as algae.[4]

Some sensations, however, were unwelcome. According to the *Galveston
Daily News,* some bathers had trouble with the local wildlife:

> The sensations of the bath are as pleasant as could be desired, bating [*sic*]
> an occasional attack from a big black hog which skims over the water like
> a seagull and dives at the nearest—and sometimes the most sensitive—
> point of the human corporation, inflicting an incision or a circumcision,
> and carying [*sic*] off a sweet morsel under his tongue. This, however, only
> gives zest to the exercise which ought always to be continued during the
> bath, and adds an additional glow to the flush of a brisk and steady fric-
> tion of hands and towels.[5]

While touch was infrequently characterized—and then mainly by
women—odors emanating from the water merited comments from many
bathers. Some waters smelled horrible. According to one early-twentieth-
century doctor, the soils through which water flowed, the gases that charged
it, and its mineral content all contributed distinctive odors. Smell, however,
is usually indicative of the release of hydrogen sulphide gas.[6] Many Texas
waters exhibited sulphurous qualities, commonly perceived as being beneficial because of their odiferousness.

Local newspapers offered rather humorous explanations. One familiar
boast of Lampasas' Hancock Springs was that the "fumes of these waters can
be smelled fifty yards or more, and are so strong as to tarnish gold coins, to
the color of copper, in fifteen minutes, if exposed to the open air near the
springs."[7] The editor of the *Lampasas Daily Times* facetiously described
nearby Hanna Springs:

> Our devil says the next time he visits his dominion, he will go via the
> Hanna Spring and investigate the source of its delightful odor. Passage by
> that route, he thinks will be easy and direct. Anyone desiring to accom-
> pany him can do so, free gratis and for nothing by applying early.[8]

A Sutherland Springs writer echoed these sentiments, noting that at the
black sulphur spring "the water discharges gases which forcibly reminds [*sic*]
one of all the defunct embryo chicks in the infernal regions."[9]

Potent odors rarely prevented people from consuming the waters or bathing in them. On the contrary, because physicians considered sulphur beneficial for the skin, many women, in particular, sought out these waters. In 1857 an observer at Sour Lake noticed a "curiosity of nature":

> A few steps farther brings us to a small and bare depression of the soil, which we might regard as a nearly dried up mud hole, unworthy of notice, were not our olfactory nerves saluted with a peculiar and rather disagreeable odor, revealing the proximity of something which any smelling committee would feel bound to investigate. There is a long pole, sharpened at one end, lying near, and with this we pry up a fragment of the moist soil, and pass it to the vicinity of anybody's nose. Anybody draws back, with certain involuntary facial distortions, and pronounces an unfavorable judgment upon the quality and decency of the article. It *is* rather "hard to take"—yet it is said the ladies *do* take this *Mineral Soap* and use it freely for the improvement of their complexions. It is also said to be a certain enemy and destroyer of freckles, tan and sunburn, and to give an unusual brilliance and transparency to the human cuticle.[10]

In addition to a spring's odor, its color was frequently remarked upon. Besides the flow and motion of water—either smoothly flowing, erupting as a fountain, or still and stagnant—the only other visual qualities that waters occasionally possessed were turbidity and color. Flowing mineral waters are usually clear, suggesting freshness, but few chroniclers mentioned a water's clarity.

Color often suggested the nature or the strength of the principal elements in spring water. In the late nineteenth century, Dr. George Walton explained the frequency of colors according to a water's chemical constituents. He ascribed a whitish color to the precipitation of sulphur and a pure white to the precipitation of lime carbonate. Blue resulted from the suspension of slate or clay, and red was from the precipitation of iron oxide. A change in sulphur molecules gave a yellow cast to the water. While this explanation may seem simplistic today, the presence of certain constituents signaled possible medicinal benefits. For example, most nineteenth-century observers assumed that red water must contain iron and consequently would help anemic conditions.[11]

Red water, commonly called chalybeate, usually did contain iron. Journalist Frank Tolbert attributed "chalybeate" (sometimes pronounced "claybeat") to a Choctaw Indian word meaning "water with iron." Others have traced the word to the French *chalbs,* meaning "steel." The Chalybes, reportedly from Pontus in Asia Minor, were famous for their iron and steel work. Therefore, "chalybeate" suggests a taste resulting from the presence of iron. Any reddish hue seemed to justify describing springs as chalybeate, even though they may not have contained iron:

> The spring called Chalybeate, which is about one hundred yards above the Boiling Spring [Hancock Springs], contains no iron, or, if any, but a trace. The red deposit which may be seen is probably a calcareous earth and oxide of iron; but there is not sufficient carbonic acid in the water to hold any appreciable amount of it in solution.[12]

At Red Mineral Springs in Mount Pleasant, there emerged red, blue, and clear springs. One of the first promotors of these waters called them the "Iridescent Springs," for they exhibited rainbow colors as if reflecting energy from the sun.[13]

Sulphur water manifested several colors. White sulphur seemed a particularly valuable attribute. In 1925 Glen Rose had two hundred flowing white sulphur wells, although the town advertised its white and black sulphur and chalybeate waters. One letter to the editor of the *Dallas Herald* stated: "This water, clear as crystal, cold and pleasant to the taste, is sufficiently impregnated with pure white sulphur to have excellent curative effects on those ailments reached by such means." Many chroniclers believed that sulphur could impart any color to the water. J. De Cordova, in describing the sulphur spring that emerged from the banks of the Colorado River, noted that "the bed of this stream, which is about three yards wide, is thickly lined with a snow-white sediment. . . . The water is as clear as crystal, and the escaping gas gives it a most beautiful, sparkling, silvery appearance."[14]

Reminiscing about Sutherland Springs' sulphur waters, one local woman wrote:

> Two bathing pools, one for the men and one for the women, were located in the bends of the river screened by trees and shrubs. The white sulphur water was used by the women, and the black sulphur water by the men. There was no mixed bathing then as there is today. The other springs were for drinking. It was here that people would come to camp in the summer, particularly when there was a revival meeting going on under a brush arbor. . . . The many young people rode horseback; the women, with long, flowing, black riding skirts and tight basques, the skirts almost trailing the ground, rode on steeds prancing in the deep sand to the springs.[15]

Other places with black water included Oran, near Mineral Wells, and Dalby Springs, whose waters "were about the color of weak coffee." Frank Tolbert further recorded a local man's reminiscences: "Those springs have a wonderful mineral content, and yet the waters aren't heavy. And, it's a funny thing, I don't remember the Black Spring ever freezing even in coldest weather." Others, however, countered that Dalby's waters exhibited various shades of red. Tuscaloosa Springs, or Wyser's (near Huntsville), also appeared to be red, black, and white.[16]

Green water, a color not necessarily perceived as healthful, occurred at only one locale. Sour Lake's waters exhibited a "greenish tinge, and the exhalation of the gases keeps it constantly bubbling." Perhaps for that reason, former governor James Hogg did not find the waters appealing.[17]

A rather unusual but attractive color was blue. Piedmont Springs had three sulphur springs—two reportedly rather mild white and one with very strong sulphur water, which was called the "black spring." One of Piedmont's three springs, however, still emerges from the ground with a distinct bluish cast, leaving a white deposition. Myrtle Springs' blue sulphur water supposedly "never fail[ed] to give prompt relief in all kidney afflictions."[18]

In addition to variations in color, resorts offered waters with different tastes. Healthseekers practiced crounotherapy, or the "drinking cure," as actively as balneotherapy, the bathing cure. Taste was related to effect. Generally, people believed that the worse the waters tasted, the more beneficial they were. One doctor, writing in 1913, attributed that singular quality to their popularity:

> It was too nasty to drink; it was too cold to lie down and soak in. There was only one thing it could be good for, and that was medicine. This is precisely the method by which many of our most famous remedies, particularly the bitter tonic class, have been raised to the level of the medicine shelf. Anything which has a bitter or other vile taste and is poisonous in large doses, is sure to be "good for you," in small ones.[19]

Many tastes resulted from particular salts. Sulphur gave water a bitter or salty taste; carbonic acid gas gave it a pungent and agreeable taste; and ferruginous waters left an astringent taste. People prized the occasional sour wells and springs. In 1875 a geologist described Sour Lake's water as "quite sour," with "a disagreeable fetid odor from the presence of petroleum or mineral oil, which rises . . . in the form of globules and floats upon the surface of the water."[20]

Other waters received mixed reviews. During the Giants' spring training in Marlin, Sam Crane experienced Marlin's water for the first time:

> So I walked about half a block to the pagoda, which is open to the public, and drank a tincupful of steaming water, at about 150 degrees. It was about as hot as a cup of tea at tasteful heat, but the water needed disinfecting, according to my ideas, and it showed it plainly when I screwed up my face.[21]

Although the fountain's water left a potent aftertaste, people still drank it.

No matter what the taste, people trustingly consumed the waters. Some elderly people from Longview, who were forced as children to drink a cup of water from Capp's Wells every day, described its taste as "horrible," "bitter," or "just awful." A local resident thought that Mineral Wells' water "tastes a bit like Perrier mixed with Alka-Seltzer." Mineral Wells probably attracted many people specifically because the mineral water was "odorless, clear, and palatable." Judge Lynch, the town's founder, claimed that the water's best feature was its palatability compared to other waters "that the hogs won't drink."[22]

The sound of water trickling out of the ground or flowing over rocks and tree roots enhanced the relaxation aspect of outside bathing. After bathhouses and inside pools became the norm, bathers listened to water dripping from faucets or an occasional pounding of someone's muscles in a vigorous massage, all of which seemed to break the stillness and echo from the tiles, reminding participants that health-seeking was a communal affair.

If the physical sensations of taking the waters contributed to their popularity, bathers also indulged themselves for several other reasons. Besides the social benefits of sharing the waters in a pool, bathers realized that water possessed several attributes that could aid them in their quest for health. In short, water could cleanse them both externally and internally.

Cleansing and Purification

A concern for hygiene surfaced in the late 1800s. Cities installed public baths as well as hospitals and water treatment plants. Bathing, however, was not a common practice. An improvement in personal hygiene must have added to the perception of the efficacy of the waters. In the first decade of the 1900s, Waco's two natatoriums offered many hydropathic practices, but one physician complained that the city "hardly appreciated the importance to itself and suffering humanity of the healing waters which exist in such abundance that all the sick and suffering of the world might 'wash and be clean' and yet not exhaust the unlimited supply [of artesian waters]."[23]

Symbolically, water—a universal solvent—also connotes internal cleansing, a purging of the gross and unhealthy. Mineral waters contained salts that produced a purgative and laxative effect on the body. The manager of the Marlin Sanitarium and Bath House observed this "boiling out" process:

> I have seen people, for example, who are heavy smokers and wrap them in a sheet. After they sweat 20 or 30 minutes in that steam room, after they come out, after they've been in the tub and sauna and steam room, I've seen a white sheet just as brown. That's nicotine coming out of the pores of your skin. It would come out through the pores. I've seen that happen.[24]

Ruby Harris remembered that certain months brought many visitors to Marlin. In February and October some came with the purpose of getting acclimated physically for the following spring or winter. A local historian echoed similar sentiments for the sulphur springs of Tyler County. It was advantageous to camp in springtime, she said, after the harsh winter and a banal diet.[25]

The Bath Encounter

To accomplish the necessary purging of bodily tissues, most resorts advocated similar bath routines, emphasizing both external treatments and internal consumption of the waters. The bathhouse, as we will see, provided an important venue for these activities. First, however, the spas had to attract visitors to their facilities, a task aided by Texas' location and climate.

SEASONAL VISITS

Visitors preferred summering at most resorts, but healthseekers arrived throughout the year and usually stayed one or more months. In its early years, Lampasas' season extended from May to August: "At least 20 counties are represented by visitors now at Lampasas in attendance upon the virtues of these celebrated waters. From this time on to the first of September many thousands will be here, and the life-giving effects of our springs will be tested by many an invalid." [26] By August 29, observed the *Lampasas Daily Times:*

> Only a very few remain, and the life and bustle of a few weeks back is no longer to be seen at the Springs. A goodly number are still at the hotels, but the watering season may now be said to be over, so far as the number in attendance is concerned; and not until the warm season of next year will there be a return of the gay and festive scenes of this summer. [27]

Ten years later, with the springs further developed, the locals expected resort activities to last about 135 days of the year.

Promoters often justified development attempts by alluding to the duration of warm weather. In nearby San Saba County, an early would-be spa on the Colorado River celebrated its most important asset—its climate. It aimed to lure visitors by promising a longer watering season:

> The salubrious and health-restoring atmosphere which is enjoyed at this point will ever commend it to the valetudinarian and the seeker of plea-sure . . . and we doubt not that ere long this choice spot will become the GREAT WATERING-PLACE of the South, with a reputation fully equal to that of Saratoga or Baden-Baden. . . . It must be kept in mind that one cause of the Northern watering-places not realizing to their owners the immense fortunes, they would otherwise is the extreme shortness of "the season," which does not last longer than two months, while in our climate "the season" would commence by the 1st of April, and would not close before the 15th of October,—six months and a half. [28]

Farther south, at Sutherland Springs, visitors also remained later. According to the local newspaper: "Our hotel accommodations are crowded just now to their fullest capacity by summer visitors to our mineral springs. We are glad to hear our visitors are fully satisfied with the merits of the waters. The season we understand will not close until about the first of October." [29] On the other hand, at Hot Springs in Brewster County, visitation lasted year-round, although slightly more people registered in the winter.

With comfortable and adequate accommodations, as at Marlin or Mineral Wells, the time of year mattered less than the length of stay. Ruby Harris noted that during the 1930s and 1940s more people came for the full three-week course of treatment; as years progressed, however, fewer stayed as long. Folk would stay two weeks at a time, then one week, then stop coming altogether.

The older, more elaborate resorts in the eastern United States encouraged cyclical visits, but Texas' retreats did not. Without a "Grand Tour," some persons spent an entire *season* at a resort. Mineral Wells attracted persons from the North and East. One young girl visited, fell in love there, and wrote about her social debut years later:

> I knew, from what Father had said, that in winter, when northern latitudes are wrapped in an ice-fringed mantle of snow, the greater portion of the visiting population came from the extreme East, the far North and the breezy West. And that when warm weather began to creep over the states south of Mason and Dixon's line, the flood-gates of travel were truly opened and thousands of people went to this "City of Healing Waters."[30]

The *1909 Quarterly Guide* boasted:

> Mineral Wells has long been looked upon as a summer health and pleasure resort only, but of late years the improvements made in the best hotels and bathing houses by steam heat, etc., have been the means of bringing many Northern and Eastern people here to spend the winter.[31]

Mineral Wells indeed did bill itself as "a winter resort for Northerners" and a "summer resort for Southerners" (see fig. 31). Since social touring seemed less important in Texas, the time of year mattered less when adequate accommodations offered greater convenience and comfort.

No matter which was the season of choice, visitors made the selection of destination partly based on the bathing experience that they expected. Comfortable accommodations depended upon the services a bathhouse could offer—and still can, as I learned during a 1990 visit to one of the few that remained operative in the United States.

THE BATHHOUSE

The most outstanding symbol of Stovall Hot Wells, described at the beginning of this chapter, or any spa, for that matter, was the bathing spot, whether it be a small spring camouflaged by shrubbery or a massive complex of offices and rooms catering to the pleasure and enjoyment of the guests. Bathhouses varied so greatly that there was no standard model. Yet there were always identifying features—communal pools, individual tubs, cooling tables, massage tables, sometimes doctors' offices, sometimes machines and exercise equipment. Stovall Hot Wells' bathhouse represented a simpler version, but one bathhouse on the Rio Grande offered only the bare necessities:

31. Mineral Wells advertisement, *Texas and Pacific Quarterly*, July 1905. Courtesy of Center for American History, University of Texas at Austin.

walls, tubs, and some shelters of vegetation constructed at the request of J. O. Langford.

What desperation fueled the malarial, weakened Langford to take a ten-day covered-wagon trip from Alpine to his new home at Hot Springs (now in Big Bend National Park), where there was no nearby hospital and no physician in residence? Perhaps Lovie Whitaker provided a clue to her father's hopes for this place when she discussed the relief that quicksilver (mercury) miners from Terlingua received from the waters at Hot Springs:

> These people came to get relief from mechanical injuries they had suffered at the mines, crippling effects aside from the regular ailments that other people anywhere and everywhere seemed to get—arthritis, rheumatism, and what not. Also among these people from the mines were those that were injured by heavy metals—lead and mercury and these were the saddest cases of all. Basically because of extreme poverty a family or two families would get together when they could scrape up enough money and enough foodstuff and they would make their way down the harsh narrow track of a winding road from the Terlingua area downstream to the Hot Springs.[32]

In 1910, Langford hired a German stonemason to built a small bathhouse on the Rio Grande. The twenty-by-twenty-foot stone bathhouse with stone and cement-plastered tubs spaced along the walls had a three-foot-thick wall facing the head of the river to withstand floods (see fig. 32). A pump on the top of the second story issued water to each tub. In addition, a small enclosure with a concrete tub on a bluff overlooking the springs accommodated those bathers who had "social diseases" (Lovie Whitaker's terminology). Langford also provided cane and brush shelters for privacy at a small downstream spring.

The Langfords left because of unrest in the area during the Mexican Revolution, then returned in 1927 to find the bathhouse in disarray. Langford rebuilt it on a smaller scale. He then circulated in the area a small brochure touting "the Fountain of Youth that Ponce de Leon Failed to Find," in which he advertised fifteen- and twenty-five-cent baths (fifty cents for social diseases). A 1938 flood later washed away most of the bathhouse. Today, curiosity seekers can still bathe in the ruins of the tubs where the warm spring flows, protected from the river water.

Most bathhouses were simple affairs, though usually more elaborate than Langford's. Some included drinking pavilions, physicians' offices, danc-

32. Langford's Hot Springs Bathhouse, ca. 1940s. Author's postcard collection.

ing rooms, and occasionally sanitariums. Mineral Wells' Lamar Bathhouse typified the average bathhouse of the time. It contained a consulting room, a reception room, cooling rooms, sweat rooms, and the baths. The Palo Pinto Bath House offered plain, Turkish, Salt Glow, Russian Massage, and Vapor baths. Several sanitariums—the Rountree Sanitarium, the Milling Sanitarium, the Mineral Wells Sanatorium, and the O'Neal Sanitarium—never replaced the bathhouses but operated in conjunction with them and with separate physicians' facilities.[33]

Marlin's bathhouses displayed all the accoutrements necessary for successful physicians' practices. After the discovery of the mineral water in the 1890s, Marlin attracted many doctors. J. W. Cook operated his Imperial Bath House and Sanitarium with its "X Ray Apparatus, Static and Electric Machines" at the same time that J. W. Torbett advertised his Sanatorium and Bethesda Bathhouse.[34]

Started by Dr. Neil Buie, the Marlin Sanitarium and Bath House in conjunction with the Buie Clinic contained doctors' offices, baths, cooling and massage rooms, and a tunnel linking the facility to the Hilton Hotel, later called the Falls Hotel, across the street (see fig. 33). Appropriately attired bathers could conveniently reach the sanitarium and bathhouse through the

33. Marlin Sanitarium and Bath House and Buie Clinic, Marlin, Texas, 1928. Author's postcard collection.

tunnel. When Conrad Hilton built his hotel in Marlin in 1929, the townspeople had to contribute $40,000 to help pay for the structure. Buie worked closely with Hilton to arrange all the details, and the hotel was constructed across the street from his clinic. Dr. Torbett (one of the first doctors to recognize the medicinal benefits of the water) and a local businessman, owner of another bathhouse in Marlin, worried that they would receive little benefit from Hilton's hotel. Frank Oltorf remembers how Buie managed to secure the remainder of the amount needed for the hotel:

> One of the doctors with Dr. Torbett told me this. Howard Smith, Dr. Torbett and Mr. Cheeves went up to meet Conrad Hilton in Dallas. Mr. Cheeves spoke his objection that it [Hilton's planned hotel] was too closely associated with Dr. Buie's bathhouse. . . . He [Hilton] said, "Oh no, we're going to treat you exactly the same. You'll get as many as stay in our hotel as Dr. Buie will. We can guarantee you that. I'll be glad to put it into writing." Dr. Torbett, the old fiddle-playing doctor, said, "Oh, Mr. Hilton, that's unnecessary. Your word is your mark as far as we're concerned." They were halfway back to Marlin and Cheeves hadn't said a word. Finally, he said, "Torbett, you have made a terrible mistake by not letting him commit that to writing." Dr. Torbett said, "Oh, I don't

believe so." When they got back and had the checks [made out], that
night Dr. Buie called a special meeting of the city council. His bathhouse
manager was a member of the council. They passed a resolution for the
city to build a tunnel connecting Dr. Buie's bathhouse to the Falls Hotel
[the Hilton hotel]. They started construction on it at night. So then, who
got all the business? [35]

Few resort accounts mentioned facilities for the African-American population, but among Marlin's medical practices was that of a black physician. A
Marlin Chamber of Commerce brochure featured a picture of the available
accommodations for blacks: a small building called the Hunter Clinic, Sanitarium, Hospital, and Bathhouse. The clinic, built in 1921, featured six tubs,
and the operators tallied around forty baths given daily (see fig. 34). It and
the oriental bathhouse, with eight tubs, also served the black employees who
worked in the white establishments but could not take baths there until the
1960s. Blacks also imbibed the sulphurous water at a separate fountain near
the railroad tracks.[36]

34. Hunter Clinic, Sanitarium, Hospital, and Bathhouse, Marlin, Texas, ca. 1900.
Source: "Health Begins in Marlin," pamphlet, Marlin Vertical File, Center for American
History, University of Texas at Austin.

35. Hot Wells Bathhouse, ca. 1910. Author's postcard collection.

If Marlin's and Mineral Wells' bathhouses offered visitors a greater array of services, San Antonio's Hot Wells Bathhouse put all the others to shame. It featured all the amenities desired by the elite visitor (see fig. 35). Famed railroad magnate E. H. Harriman, father of diplomat Averell Harriman, built a spur from the San Antonio and Aransas Pass tracks to the Hot Wells Hotel so that he could bathe there when he was ill. In 1909 he had seven tents erected behind the hotel to house himself and his entourage. In each tent he set up wooden floors, electric lights and heaters, rocking chairs, a reading table, and iron bedsteads.[37]

The Hot Wells indeed catered to those of prominence and renown. In 1911, the Star Film Company, which filmed *The Fall of the Alamo*, headquartered at the bathhouse. Visiting the hotel at the time were Sarah Bernhardt, Cecil B. DeMille, and Jack Hoxie, a western film star.

The most imposing feature of the bathhouse at Hot Wells in San Antonio was the natatorium. Three swimming pools, each sixty-four by ninety feet and lined by white-enameled brick, contained separate pools for ladies, for men, and for families. The pools, with water ranging in temperature from 80° to 95° F, were emptied and cleaned every forty-eight hours. The ambience of the three pools juxtaposed with the bicolored support beams suggested a Spanish-Moorish element. The bathhouse replaced an earlier, shorter-lived natatorium, which had burned in 1894. The bathhouse itself contained forty-five private bathing areas with tile floors, marble partitions, and porcelain tubs. There were separate compartments for Vapor, Turkish, Russian, Roman, Needle, and Shower baths, as well as massage and cooling rooms. There were also two hundred individual dressing rooms and sixteen bedrooms for bathers who needed to retire after the bath or stay close to their treatments. Men and women had their own wings.

Besides preparation areas set aside for bathing, the bathhouse provided other amenities such as an ice cream and soda water parlor, a buffet, a billiard room, a ballroom, large parlors, and the aforementioned notorious Jockey Club. Bathers were warned to remain indoors until their bodies could cool down to their normal temperatures. If they chose to return to their hotel, however, they could use the enclosed and heated second-story walkway to the hotel next door. Finally, there was an operating room and sanitarium in the bathhouse. Rates ranged from $5 to $15 per course of twenty-one baths, depending upon the amount of service.

While the more complex structures often evolved from their simpler forerunners, Lampasas' Hanna Springs Bathhouse took the opposite route. In 1889, Hanna Springs' 60-by-120-foot pavilion offered two large swimming pools, each 28 by 30 feet, with the ladies' pool one foot deeper than the gentlemen's five-foot depth. The office and the ladies' reception room also were on the lower floor. The bathhouse offered fourteen tub baths of hot water and two shower baths. Outside bubbled the nonbathing pool of sulphur water, 60 feet across and from 10 to 16 feet deep. Sulphur water flowed continuously from four hydrants near the pavilion.

In 1910, Hanna Springs' owner advertised a remodeled bathhouse:

> The Hanna Springs Bathhouse is equal to or superior to any other bath house in Texas, as to the number of baths, the quality of our far-famed Sulphur water, sanitation, attendants, electric baths, steam and hot dry air baths, shower and vapor baths, the famous Epsom salts baths, medicated baths, salt rubs, Turkish baths, massage, hot medicated packs. Also two of the finest swimming pools in the world, filled with pure, fresh Sulphur water. Rheumatic patients are taken on the "no help; no charge" plan. Testimonials furnished on application. Bath houses open the year round.[38]

The owner must have shortly thereafter torn down the bathhouse, since by 1912 a simpler affair graced the grounds. Not many years later, only the round pool would remain; from the bottom of it the sulphur water trickled into a nearby ditch. Even in 1990 the water slowly flowed, giving drink to thirsty cattle grazing nearby.

Why have no bathhouses in Texas been restored or remembered, or saved from destruction? Is it that we don't want to be reminded of our frailties or that we denigrate this now forgotten therapy? Are the structures simply unimportant because they did not display the elaborate architecture of Hot Springs' Bathhouse Row in Arkansas or because presidents did not typically visit them, such as the bathhouse at Warm Springs, Virginia? Yet as a society we reenact scenes from famous gunfights and bank robberies. We memorialize war, epidemics, disasters, but we do not commemorate places where hundreds testified their lives were saved, where people flocked to start a new town, where people gathered year after year in pursuit of health, pleasure, or immortality. Perhaps we have completely convinced ourselves that these practices did not work, that we had lapsed into a brief moment of insanity—or worse, that we had only catered to a fad.

Perhaps the answer lies in the essential nature of a bathhouse. Although not a haven for illicit activity, as are the gay bathhouses of recent origin, a bathhouse exposed a person's vulnerability while providing a haven for broken bodies. In many cases, the bathhouse was the closest institution to a hospital in an area. We rarely honor that which reminds us of our weaknesses, our limitations. Yet people exited these buildings feeling better than they did when they entered.

As many buildings at the resorts progressively decayed, so did our memories. Texas has not renovated or reestablished mineral water spas. In fact, few watering sites are commemorated with historical markers. Even memory may lose its connection with place. There is no marker, for example, beside Hanna Springs in Lampasas; the marker is on the courthouse grounds, approximately a mile away. Even though San Antonio's Hot Wells lies within the Mission Historic District, its dilapidated condition has deterred many investors.

Although these scattered and disparate buildings have disappeared, the rituals inside the bathhouse proved similar and consistent throughout the hundred-plus years of observance of the bathing tradition in this state.

THE BODY ROUTINE

Bathhouse procedures must have seemed strange to some visitors:

A stranger coming to take his first bath is easily spotted. Sometimes he is
one whose proximity to godliness has been kept up by the use of the tin
wash basin at home, and a porcelain bathtub is a novelty to him. He is
rather timid in his new surroundings, and no wonder, for the first thing
he knows the manager places a box in front of him and bids him yield up
his valuables, which surely looks like a hold-up. When he has been convinced of the fairness of this procedure he is ushered into the sanctum
sanctorium and begins to ask questions, a sample of which is: Do I have
to take off my clothes?[39]

Marlin offered a widely accepted form of treatment. When clients visited the Buie Clinic, located in the bathhouse, Dr. Neil Buie Jr. filled out a
spa prescription (see fig. 36). The regimen included the amount of mineral
water the patient must consume and the required number of baths, also possible prescribed hot packs, vapor cabinet treatments, salt rubs, or rubdowns.

Bodily indulgence in the waters, not completely a private affair, warranted bath attendants who poured out waters and adjusted their temperature. They gave out mineral water drinks during the bath and placed ice bags
on the patron's head to keep down the body's temperature. Assistants also
wrapped clients in towels and hot packs, and masseuses and masseurs usually
ended treatments with their particular form of body work. Velva White of
Mineral Wells managed the Baker Bath Department for twelve years. She
described the typical routine:

You would first take as hot as you can tub bath—about fifteen minutes.
Then if you had arthritis, you were put on a cot and wrapped in blankets
with hot packs wherever your pain was. Or if you were just trying to get
rid of impurities in your body or losing weight, you were put in the steam
cabinets or the steam room where you lay on a slab. The room was so
completely full of steam, you couldn't see your hands in front of you.
Then you would lay down on a cot in the middle of the big hall of the
bath department until you cooled off. You then took a needle shower
and then the best part—you got your wonderful massage.[40]

This carefully orchestrated ritual would be repeated each day that the
patron stayed at the spa. One reporter eloquently described the camaraderie
engendered by the ritual:

SPA PRESCRIPTION
Marlin Rehabilitation Center
BUIE CLINIC AND HOSPITAL — MARLIN BATH HOUSE
MARLIN, TEXAS

Date _____

Patient _____

Address _____

_____

R̸   **CLINIC EXAMINATIONS:**

    Complete Examination: _____

Special Studies: _____

_____

MEDICATIONS: _____

_____

Mineral Water Drinking (laxative): _____

Diet: _____

Coffee _____ Tea _____ Alcoholic beverages _____ Tobacco _____

PHYSICAL MEDICINE:

☐ Mineral water baths   ☐ Vapor cabinet   ☐ Hot room
☐ Hot packs   ☐ Rub down   ☐ Salt rub

    Exercise Therapy (Registered Physical Therapist Supervised)

☐ Special corrective: _____

    General Muscle Building

☐ Walking: distance _____; frequency _____
☐ Golf   ☐ Stationary bicycle   ☐ Shoulder wheel
☐ Swimming   ☐ Walking bars   ☐ _____

    Other Physical Agents

☐ Infra red   ☐ Diathermy   ☐ Ultrasound   ☐ Special massage
☐ Whirlpool bath   ☐ Paraffin bath   ☐ Ultraviolet   ☐ Baker
☐ Cervical traction   ☐ Galvanic   ☐ _____   ☐ _____

RECREATION: Active _____ ; Semi-Active _____ ; Passive _____ ;

REST: Sleep at night _____ ; Afternoon nap _____

_____ M. D.

36. Spa prescription, administered at the Buie Clinic, Marlin, Texas, ca. 1950s. Courtesy of Dr. Neil Buie, Jr.

The pleasant relaxation of the baths is doubtless one reason for the lack of hurry, the friendliness and the lack of formality prevailing. There's simply no putting on airs, while stinging with a salt rub, you lie on a narrow cot wrapped in a dozen red-hot steaming bath towels and trussed up with blankets until you can't move anything except your eyelids and there's no sound save the chug-chug of the steam pipes and the rivers of perspiration as they fall to the floor. With your hair in strings, your rouge and powder gone where the woodbine twineth and your face the color and slightly the texture of a hot freshly boiled beet there's no caring whether the person on the cot next yours belongs to the same club you do or to no club at all, you never can quite be strangers again.[41]

A recommended bathing regimen in Marlin included drinking several glasses of mineral water upon arising in the morning and taking the baths between 8:00 and 10:30 A.M. or between 2:00 and 3:30 P.M. According to Mrs. Harris, who ran Marlin's Harris House, her boarders faithfully rose each morning, walked to the pavilion, and drank a glass of mineral water thirty minutes before breakfast so that they "didn't have any problems the rest of the day." This routine, she observed, took place every morning for the entire three-week stay, except for the later years when people came for only a week's cure.

One Marlinite described a typical reaction to the demanding bath schedule:

First, you are left in the tub of hot water until you are "hard boiled;" then you have salt rubbed into you; then oil, and are worked, rubbed and kneaded till you feel like a mayonnaise dressing (no pun intended). Making the best kind of time, a full bath with all the fixings takes about an hour, yet there are some (women mostly) who think this is too short. Some of them have even requested to be allowed to remain in the tub for an hour; evidently believing that if a little is good more is better. Many of the newcomers gush about the pleasures of bathing. "Oh, I just love the baths; I wish I could take two or three a day," they say at first. After awhile they begin to look for excuses to skip a day. Soon they are back again to wishing they could take two or three a day, but this time their reason is so they can the sooner finish their course and be through with them.[42]

The sensory, symbolic, and ritualistic dimensions of the watering experience in relation to health and well-being disclose the richness and attractiveness of this phenomenon. The power of water to evoke varied responses attests to its importance in the creation of "place." Impersonal space becomes a known place through these sensations. Consequent perceptions depend on how people evaluate the experience. Often they consider such responses symbolic of deeper levels of significance.

As the modern world began to intrude upon this practice, people wanted to spend less time in three-week-long, lengthy baths. In essence, time began to be more valued than place, and people began to lose their connections with these once-sacred places.

CHAPTER 8

Places Lost

WE CANNOT SAY that the modern world has completely eliminated mythical behaviour; but only that its field of action is changed: the myth is no
longer dominant in the essential sectors of life: it has been repressed,
partly into the obscurer levels of the psyche, partly into the secondary
or even irresponsible activities of society.

—*Mircea Eliade,* Myths, Dreams, and Mysteries

everal factors contributed to the disappearance of spas and resorts
in Texas. Fires, floods, and other natural disasters furthered the
decline of sites already waning in popularity. Government regulations about
health and hygiene also lessened the demand for watering places. In addition,
the rise of insurance coverage, the Great Depression, and World Wars I and
II influenced the way people used leisure time and money. Finally, broader
societal changes in medicine, lifestyle, and travel spelled the end of an era for
once-famous watering venues.

Fires, Floods, and More

Random occurrences such as accidents and acts of nature hastened the
end of many resorts. Although floods and fires demolished structures, no
single agent caused any one place to shut down. Some authorities, for example, attributed the decline of Sutherland Springs to the 1913 flood, after
which a more temporary structure on stilts replaced the bathhouse and sanitarium. T. C. Richardson, publisher of the town's newspaper *Health Resort* in
the 1910s, explained Sutherland Springs' decline as due to "dissatisfied parties
[who] sued the townsite company, delayed the issuance of titles to lots that
had been sold, [and] interfered with financing for further development." [1]

According to the Work Projects Administration (WPA), automobiles caused the town's collapse by channeling people to other resorts. Yet despite these speculations, the place's popularity returned even after the flood. In 1914, owner T. Williams counted 2,500 people during Fourth of July celebrations, which, he said, approached a record from two years earlier. Encouraged, he dredged out some of the mud-choked bathing pools and built a $10,000 sanitarium with fifteen rooms for guests. The teachers of Wilson County Teachers' Institute chose the revitalized facility as the site for their 1915 meeting.

According to Mrs. Fred Anderson, Williams' granddaughter, the spa attracted little mineral water business after 1917, when the U.S. Army contracted to send soldiers there to recuperate. The sanitarium operated, however, until her grandmother died in 1920 and her grandfather grew less interested in keeping up the business. Although it was the Depression that caused the town's demise in 1927, a fire several years before had burned twelve to fifteen buildings. After the fire, many people left Sutherland Springs. One physician, however, chose to remain; he operated a small sanitarium and gave sulphur baths until 1934 or 1935.[2]

Both bankruptcy and accidental fires accounted for the disappearance of Wootan Wells. The site's business flourished until about 1903, according to the founder's daughter, but because of the proximity of Marlin's hot mineral water, business gradually slacked off. By 1914, only one of four hotels remained open, and according to the daughter of a doctor who moved there to practice, "the popularity of the health resort had waned to some extent, however, many still came to drink the water and enjoy the quiet of the lovely little spot." Shortly thereafter, a number of fires finished off the town. The bottling works operated until 1926, when it also burned. Another account attributed the town's decline to a major flood in 1899, which did half a million dollars' worth of damage. Probably both its misfortunes and its proximity to competitor Marlin's hot waters had doomed the watering place.[3]

Fires indeed took their toll on many a spa's wooden structures. Among those damaged were Lampasas' Park Hotel in 1895, many of Mineral Wells' bathhouses and pavilions in 1905, the Hynson Springs Hotel in 1915, and San Antonio's Hot Wells Hotel in 1925. However, the recreational functions of these aforementioned hotels had ended well before the fires occurred. The Park Hotel had closed to customers in 1891, the Hynson Springs Hotel curtailed operations in 1905, and by 1925 Hot Wells had been serving as a schoolhouse for two years. In 1905, Mineral Wells suffered a $100,000 fire that burned "the entire Hawthorne block with the Mineral Wells bathhouse, sanitarium, west wing of the Wann house, the old Lithia pavilion and a portion of the Crazy well houses. . . . It is thought that the fire was the work of an incendiary." Four months later the Palo Pinto Bathhouse and a hotel, the Webb Cottage, also burned. The account did not specify whether arson was involved in these cases as well.[4]

Other places were simply torn down. Hilton agreed to build his hotel in Marlin if the owner tore down the Arlington Hotel so that it would not compete for business. The last owners of the Sutherland Springs' hotel razed it to provide more space for a turf farm.

Inaccessibility proved a handicap for some spas and a mark of exclusivity for others. Railroads spurred hopes for many resorts. In 1925, a physician financed a sanitarium for Hudspeth County's Hot Wells with the help of a manager of the Southern Pacific, who promised to build either a switch or a new depot. Railroads guaranteed the continued success of other spas, such as Sutherland Springs, Mineral Wells, Marlin, and Chalybeate Springs. Trains stopped regularly at Musgrove, also called Chalybeate Springs. They allowed families to travel independently; the women from Sulphur Springs, for example, could travel there during the week, while the menfolk followed on the weekend.

Those spas that the railroad bypassed were sometimes, but not always, disadvantaged. Dalby Springs, unable to secure a line, had to send hacks ten miles to DeKalb. A seven-mile distance did not adversely affect Wizard Wells' business, however; it shipped mineral water by rail, and many health-seekers continued to visit, even until the 1980s.

The automobile tended to have the same effect on spas as did the railroad; it precipitated the decline of some smaller resorts, as convenient travel allowed access to more famous resorts farther away. Midyett Springs began to decline after World War I as roads linked travelers to other places. Locals attribute its decline to the popularity of Rosborough Springs, about twenty miles away. According to a WPA report, water from Rosborough Springs was still for sale for ten cents a gallon in the 1930s, but the site's popularity by then had waned. When railroad travel sagged in Hughes Springs as automobiles grew popular, the spa lost its attraction as a resort. On the other hand, Wizard Wells, only thirty miles from the more famous Mineral Wells, enjoyed continued success after the widespread availability of the automobile.

In a few cases, such as that of Glen Rose, the springs and wells went dry. Although some people believed that Wizard Wells' decline was brought about by dry wells, the spa business here continued to operate until 1984. Apparently the proprietors had on occasion used the water faster than the aquifer could replenish it.[5]

Wars, Laws, and Regulation

Other agents that could precipitate a resort's demise included the prevailing economic climate, which also determined the amount of leisure time and money that people spent at a resort. Armed conflict and government regulations also played a role. No new spas opened during the Civil War, for example, but during that time a famous one closed its doors. The owner of the Piedmont Springs Hotel (Grimes County) went broke, and the spa's glory days quickly faded. Although the Smith Hotel at Old Sulphur Springs (Tyler County) burned down during the same period, there is little evidence that the war adversely affected other established watering places. The military conflict, in fact, likely created business. On the other hand, spa patronage did decrease during and after the two world wars. Sutherland Springs declined after World War I, although whether the war caused this decline is uncertain. The popularity of San Antonio's Hot Wells decreased during 1914–18, when the hotel housed military officers and their families. Prohibition dealt the final blow, after a school purchased the Hot Wells Hotel in 1923.

Prohibition, however, was less a hindrance than a boon for some spas. Dr. Neil Buie Jr., the son of the physician who founded the Marlin Sanitarium and the Buie Clinic in 1914, reported that the waters seemed to help "jake leg," a malady common in Prohibition times:

> Texas had its share of ignorant and unscrupulous saloons and plenty of bootleggers. Out-of-town patients came in droves for the treatment of [jake leg]. Jake leg was caused by drinking methyl (wood) alcohol rather than ethyl alcohol. There's a world of difference. Consuming ethyl can knock out your liver if you drink enough of it every day, but methyl has a different effect. Someone with jake leg had a typical walk, a sort of slinging of the legs. The condition affected a victim's nervous system and destroyed his coordination. The mineral water baths seemed to give some relief. Alcoholics also came to Marlin hoping to get "boiled out."[6]

Frank Oltorf attributed Marlin's decline to fewer clients of certain per-suasions: "Dr. Buie and Dr. Torbett [by then dead] lie reconciled in their rivalry, no longer caring that the repeal of Prohibition and the invention of penicillin destroyed the demand for their mineral water as a cure for jake leg and the malady of France." What Oltorf noted half jokingly did carry some truth. Those two common ailments, jake leg and venereal disease, contrib-uted much to Marlin's early success. Although the Depression era reportedly hurt the resort, many locals considered this the peak of spa patronage. The 150 to 200 persons who bathed daily at the sanitarium after World War II and into the 1950s amounted to about half of the bathers during Marlin's heyday twenty or thirty years earlier.[7]

Although Mineral Wells' Baker Hotel filed for bankruptcy in 1932, it didn't close its doors until 1963. Patronage declined from 1941 to 1944, how-ever, when the hotel housed military personnel. Business picked up some-what in 1945, but never increased back to prewar levels. Finally, in the 1950s, the hotel management closed down the mineral water bar, though the baths remained open. In that decade other ways of attracting business occupied the hotel's managers. The ritziness of the 1930s was gone, and the average patron stayed only a few days. One local inhabitant described the change "from poshy to patriotic to plastic."[8]

Bottlers also began to encounter problems. Increasing government pres-sure limited the types of claims printed on labels. In 1915, the Parker–Palo Pinto County Medical Society censored all labels and advertising literature for Mineral Wells' water. In addition, federal authorities confiscated waters that they claimed were "mislabeled" because the labels cited cures of ail-ments. In 1913, Star Well from Mineral Wells shipped a quantity of bottles later seized because of mislabeling—their labels claimed to cure "thousands of every ailment." The authorities also seized many bottles of adulterated mineral water in the 1910s and 1920s. In 1916, for example, the federal gov-ernment found 120 half-gallon bottles of "Crazy No. 3" contaminated with an animal substance. Around the same time, it seized Famous Mineral Wells Water and Grogan's Mineral Water from Sweetwater and declared them "adulterated and fraudulently misbranded," for they claimed to cure many diseases. In 1927, federal authorities seized "Crazy Mineral Water" bottles shipped to Louisiana because the labels gave the impression that the water cured rheumatism, constipation, cystitis, diabetes, and other complaints. The U.S. Department of Agriculture also warned bottlers of advertising "radioactive" on their waters because the radioactive emanations [what today would be called radon] began to dissipate a few days after bottling.[9]

In contrast, some professionals in the medical field seemed confident of the value of selling the waters. The *Texas State Journal of Medicine* commented: "This is revolutionary, to say the least of it, and Mineral Wells water may justly be said to have lifted itself from the patent medicine class, and become that which nature intended it should be, the legitimate therapeutic agent of the medical profession."[10]

Government pressure mounted in the following decades. At the 1933 Chicago World's Fair, authorities sponsored an exhibit at the behest of Rexford Guy Tugwell, President Franklin Roosevelt's Under Secretary of Agriculture, to promote the passage of his Pure Food and Drug Act. Amid the "quack medicines" lay the Crazy Water Crystal display, which, the government claimed, contained only Glauber's salts, a veterinary medicine no longer used on humans.[11] The negative publicity damaged the credibility of manufacturers, though not completely: Crazy Water Crystals still sold into the 1970s, although the company had by then moved from Mineral Wells.

Insurance for Our Ills

After World War II, to spend money for lengthy resort visits seemed inappropriate when insurance paid for other forms of treatment, especially the new "miracle" drugs, such as antibiotics or cortisone shots. Insurance did not cover visits to the "healing waters." Medical historian Henry Sigerist thus compared the success of European spas to the failure of American ones:

> And when, in the 19th and 20th century health insurance was introduced in one country after another, treatment in health resorts became available to large groups of wage earners. The Sickness Insurance Funds sent many patients to spas where they were treated at the expense of the Funds. In Europe, therefore, such treatments were not a privilege of the rich.
>
> The situation is totally different in America. We have no health insurance [to cover spa visits]. We have no organization that would enable us to send large numbers of people of low income to health resorts.[12]

Martha Jones, whose family ran Wizard Wells' Lone Star Bathhouse from 1942 to 1974, believed that after that spa's peak in the 1950s, clientele visited less because of the increased popularity of hospitalization insurance.

Jim Davis attempted to renovate the old Lone Star Bathhouse in the 1970s and 1980s, but in 1984 he shut down the operation. He was convinced that if Medicare and Medicaid would have paid for his clients' treatments, it would have ensured his success.[13]

Frank Oltorf attributes the failure of two bathhouses built in the 1960s in Marlin to two rival factions, neither of which bothered to check if the treatments they offered would be covered by patients' insurance:

> Marlin has always been a town that divided itself into groups. One bath rivaled the other. One bank rivaled the other. When they decided they needed a new bathhouse, each bank got a group together. . . . They both went broke. I said that if Dr. Buie had been alive, this whole thing would have been taken care of by Medicare. They thought they would qualify for Medicare without asking for an official position. They found out they didn't qualify for it. But if Dr. Buie had been alive, before they ever built it, he would have had Senator Connally or whoever have a letter from the department telling him that it was covered.[14]

Insurance coverage, the Great Depression, and World Wars I and II influenced the way people used leisure time and money, but these factors cannot fully account for the rapid disappearance of these places. It was, finally, the broader societal changes in medicine, lifestyles, and travel that paved the way for spa owners to shut their doors.

A Changing Society

Perhaps most instrumental in the disappearance of spas was the changing nature of medicine. Rebuilding hotels and bathhouses seemed inappropriate when new discoveries enabled pills to displace "taking the waters" as an avenue to better health. With the dominance of the "germ theory" and the discovery of sulfa drugs, antibiotics, and other "miracle" drugs, people perceived mineral water as less useful and more time-consuming. Remedial drug intervention, or allopathic therapy, prevailed over less intrusive therapeutics, which included the older water cures of hydrotherapy and balneotherapy.

In the early days of Texas resorts, many doctors approved water treatments. Later, however, some physicians began to eschew balneotherapy because of its faddish image. Sigerist recalled the 1890s as the time when American medicine turned "scientific." At that time Johns Hopkins Hospital and School of Medicine trained physicians in laboratories and hospitals, but since most spas were privately owned, they lacked research institutes affiliated with medical schools. In contrast with their European conterparts, American spas lacked authorities to promote balneotherapy. In fact, American medicine disregarded water therapies, as the effects from mineral water bathing were difficult to attribute to any one factor in a complicated mineral mélange. The 1890s thus marked the beginning of scientific medicine, which began to take its toll on Texas resorts in the ensuing decades.

Changes in the American lifestyle—particularly as it related to allocation of time—also contributed to the gradual demise of most spas. People were less willing to spend three weeks at a spa for a chronic ailment if pills and injections could alleviate problems more quickly. Vernon Daniels, manager of Mineral Wells' Baker Hotel from 1952 to 1962, noted that his hotel's trade started to decline when sulfa drugs came out. In the mid-1960s, Dr. Neil Buie Jr. left the Marlin clinic because it had lost so much bathing business that it was no longer profitable to operate. He felt that mineral water bathing was "out of style," but he also ascribed the decline to medical reasons:

> Steroids and other medication became available for arthritis treatment. This bathing business in Marlin was always touted as the treatment for arthritis. Business slipped—I'd say, 50 to 75 percent. It was going down, down, down. The clinic was totally dependent on the visitor trade.[15]

Richard Peacock, onetime manager of Marlin's Sanitarium and Bath House, echoed Buie's observation:

> The doctors themselves were the worst enemy of the bathhouse. . . . The young doctors after the war did not believe in the waters. The miracle drugs such as cortisone and various others that were developed during the war—a lot of the young doctors thought a needle and shots could do the same thing as the mineral waters did. And that's a mistake.[16]

Ruby Harris of Marlin also attributed the decline in her business to "rheumatism shots" that the doctors started to give, and soon they did not recommend the baths at all. Some doctors also told patients to pour Epsom salts into their bathwater, but according to Mrs. Harris, the experience at the baths was completely different from taking a bath in one's own home. Business at Marlin's Harris House, however, did not start leveling off until the late 1960s, suggesting that those with fewer financial resources either never lost their faith in the waters or could only afford that kind of treatment.[17]

In Marlin, the tradition lasted longer than at other places in Texas, partly because the medical profession appropriated the practice and transformed it into a tool of physical medicine. Nevertheless, after younger physicians stopped prescribing balneotherapy, the bathhouse business declined. Prompt relief, rather than a leisurely treatment, was what the modern doctor ordered, or, as Sigerist suggested in 1942:

> [Patients] want an operation if possible or, if this cannot be done, they want at least injections. Treatment in a health resort is an affair of several weeks, and such a lengthy treatment does not appeal to the average American patient quite apart from the costs involved. The trouble is that chronic diseases cannot be cured quickly.[18]

As the public stopped believing in the transformative powers of the waters, perceptions about these places changed along with their buildings, activities, and visitor expectations. The bathhouse yielded center stage to other venues, which generally demonstrated less concern for the qualities of waters than for the social calendar. San Antonio's Hot Wells provides a prime example. From its beginning, Hot Wells in San Antonio aimed to attract the rich and famous. It achieved a grander resort style with its zoo and hotel. Most of Hot Wells' notoriety stemmed from its gambling parlor, the Jockey Club, and the resident bookie.

As social events seduced pleasure-seekers, the standardized forms of such events allowed more flexibility in location. A dance or card game or tennis match need not be tied to a particular spring. Time, too, had become an important factor, as fewer healthseekers chose to invest several weeks at a resort. Loss of faith in the waters' healing powers dealt the final blow. When spas lost their powers to attract patrons seeking a cure, their demise was virtually ensured.

Nature's Way

In the end, one cannot reduce the treatment of disease by mineral waters to the realm of the superstitious—by pointing solely to the placebo effect or to psychotherapeutic influences—or balneotherapy would not have lasted as long as it did. Yet the view of the waters as sacred and mysterious indeed did play a large role in attracting patrons to these places. A "nature cure" may seem unsophisticated and unscientific to today's health consumer and to the medical establishment, but it represented the beliefs of the nineteenth-century Texan. Because Texas' mineral waters cannot be seen, smelled, tasted, or felt anymore, the average person cannot experience the force of nature as magic elixir, health restorer, and fountain of youth. The sensibilities of the Texan of today are different from those of the Texan of twenty or more years ago, when many people "took the cure."

Continued belief in water as sacred ensured a spa's operation. As health seemed the primary factor in the establishment of resorts in Texas, a belief in the healthful benefits of the waters accounted for the resorts' continued success and longevity. Because smaller spas such as Tioga, Wizard Wells, Sutherland Springs, and Indian Hot Springs concentrated primarily on offering health-related activities rather than social ones, these operated as successfully and, in many cases, longer than the more-developed resorts. After attitudes about the waters' sacredness diminished and their market potential decreased, however, a resort's days were numbered. Hot Wells, marketed primarily as a recreational retreat, experienced the shortest life span—twenty-five years. After Lampasas and Mineral Wells underwent similar transformations, their fame as resorts lasted only a few more years. Mineral Wells' resort business thrived in the 1930s when four hundred mineral wells were in operation, along with the new 450-room Baker Hotel, but the boom faded quickly after World War II. The Marlin Sanitarium and Bath House, the oldest bathhouse in town, operated into the early 1980s, but perception of the town as a resort seemed to die in the 1950s as fewer doctors recommended mineral water bathing. Its lingering popularity after that time was attributable to the few diehards who felt convinced that they improved after taking the baths and returned each year for the same treatments.

Surprisingly, Stovall Hot Wells, which survived almost unchanged since its construction in the early 1930s, still had a thriving business until it recently burned down. Some clients had even moved nearby to take more frequent baths. Yet there were few lodgings or social activities to accommodate them.

In other places, the pungent water still issues forth. In Marlin the odiferous brew flows unceasingly from the old fountain in the Hygeia pavilion. At San Antonio's Hot Wells, sulphur water still gushes into two of the three bathing pools, although the surrounding bathhouse is in ruins. The manager of the grounds of Rosborough Springs reports that people today come to fill

up their gallon jugs with the water. Likewise in Tioga, people still believe in
the mystery of the waters. In the early nineties a Tioga woman reported that
her husband regularly secured a four-gallon cooler of mineral water from a
local source: "We are using it for kidney infections. We like it and know
what it can do."[19]

The End of an Era?

The spa era never officially ended. After 150 years of watering experience
in Texas, a final phase is focusing on renovation and attempts to reestablish
business because of a continuing belief in the powers of the waters. Unfor-
tunately, few of these attempts have been successful. Relatives of former hotel
owners futilely hoped for the revival of Dalby Springs after the state highway
and man-made lake provided easier access and more recreational opportunities. In Mineral Wells, numerous attempts to renovate the Baker Hotel and
its bathhouse, both vacant since 1963, have failed. The large expenditure of
capital needed to renovate the 450-room hotel proved too burdensome for
developers. The mineral water business still survives to some extent in Mineral Wells, as some bottling works continue to market the water.

Other attempts temporarily succeeded. In the 1970s, a bathhouse and
bottling plant operated in Tioga. Although the bottling was a one-man operation, health food stores around Dallas, Fort Worth, and Denton distributed the water. A retired rancher rejuvenated the old Hilton Hotel and
Marlin Sanitarium in 1968 and called it the Falls Health Spa. After several
openings and closings, it closed permanently in the early 1980s. There were
also plans to renovate the dilapidated Marlin Sanitarium and Bath House
(which finally burned down in 1992).

A decade ago, a San Antonio investor seeking to redevelop the city's Hot
Wells spa courted Japanese, French, and German investors for renovation
capital for the ruined bathhouse. Although unsuccessful, he continued to
use the sulphur waters in his own health institute. Further west, people still
informally take the baths in the undeveloped springs around Indian Hot
Springs. Chinati Hot Springs, formerly Kingston Hot Springs, recently reopened after being closed and in private hands for several years.

Attraction to the waters around the state still exists in isolated pockets,
but without incorporation into a large-scale pleasure resort or backing by a

medical facility, endeavors to redevelop the spas seem doomed. Texas does not have in abundance the hot natural springs that exist in much of the West, nor the grand architecture of the East, and so incorporation into a major recreational retreat would seem the only recourse available for Texas developers, unless alternative-health therapists are willing to open local practices. Perhaps these places need an industrious promoter who could use strategies similar to those employed in earlier times. The waters then virtually sold themselves.

No one factor alone explains why these once-vibrant places have virtually disappeared, leaving few signs or relics on the landscape. Distinctive watering places disappeared for many reasons: changing circumstances, societal attitudes, and values. Daily spa life is gone, along with its slower, simpler lifestyle. Yet the waters continue to flow, waiting to be rediscovered by a modern-day Ponce de León.

Song of the Sacred Waters

From the 1830s, mineral waters—an important Texas resource—played a pivotal role in the life of many early towns. These towns, some of which have disappeared, sprang up around colorful, odiferous, or bitter waters. People worked, played, and prayed around them. Dreams fed the frenzy that oftentimes accompanied such a discovery. Throughout Texas' history, this pastime continued to attract both the weak and the strong in body. Those spas that survived the rough-and-tumble years of the Texas frontier possessed assorted advantages and opportunities—a picturesque location with a variety of natural waters, such as Sutherland Springs or Indian Hot Springs; a more isolated location but aggressive boosters and a varied choice of social activities, such as Mineral Wells; a well-publicized sanctioning by the medical establishment, such as Marlin; and finally, faithful believers in the power of the waters, such as Lampasas, Stovall Hot Wells, Kingston Hot Springs, Wizard Wells, and Tioga.

For at least 150 years these spas acquired many layers of meaning, for the waters did not constitute the totality of these places. People with similar hopes and affinities created distinct social activities in different settings. From the Piney Woods of East Texas to the desertlike Quitman Mountains of West Texas, they journeyed to partake of nature's magic elixir. Wherever they traveled in Texas, they gathered on a daily basis around pavilions, bathhouses, fountains, or boardinghouses—facilities similar to those of other spas but different from buildings in other Texas towns. They participated in local events that fostered friendships and relieved the stresses of everyday life. By sharing stories of suffering and recovery, people met on a common level. By playing together, they learned about Texas' hills, rivers, and plains. By settling in new surroundings, they grew attached to these places.

This phenomenon did not belong exclusively to well-heeled folks, as each spa offered inexpensive baths, a place to camp, and oftentimes, free drinking water. Because these places attracted the settler and the pioneer, there appeared to be few examples of grandiose resort architecture, which supports the assertion that this phenomenon shaped the common person. Only the old, abandoned Baker Hotel in Mineral Wells now stands as a lone sentinel to a lost age when dreams of attracting national celebrities, social climbers, and seasonal resort-goers were realized for a few short years. At the other watering places, a simpler lifestyle suited the Texas temperament.

Sacred and secular orientations toward the waters affected the nature of a place's activities and its consequent architecture. The "sacred" image of the waters, their possessing some power to effect bodily or spiritual healing, was the focus of most spas in their early years. The waters became a vehicle that allowed the visitor to communicate with other levels of reality. Promoters catering to this image knew its strength and consequently sought to enhance its advantages. Success in creating attachment to places was thus based on the recognition of the character or essence of these places.

The lures for healthseekers, pleasure-seekers, and settlers varied, but the underlying attraction in Texas lay in the potency of the waters, which the invalid and healthy alike considered "fountains of youth." This concept of "youth" manifested less in a sense of immortality or rejuvenated physical appearance, as it may today, and more in a simple functioning in the everyday world. "Youth" let them once again chop wood, churn butter, walk the hills, and enjoy life and all its daily bodily demands. As long as this image was operative, journeys to these places indeed became pilgrimages, sometimes necessitating travel that was painful and inconvenient. From across the state or nation, people trekked to the spas hoping to improve their health. In the early days, camp meetings at these watering holes reinforced this idea of a consecrated journey.

Time also lost its sense of urgency when a spirit of community prevailed. Sharing concerns with others during the hours between baths facilitated friendships, and this often assured the pilgrims' return in subsequent years. Diverse pastimes enhanced this sense of camaraderie. Riding to the springs for an all-day church social, playing dominoes on a boardinghouse porch, scaling nearby hills, or sitting in a pavilion chatting with companions immersed the spa-goer in a celebration of community.

People's experiences thus connected them to these places, frequently resulting in deep attachments. Although longer periods of time are usually necessary to establish such ties, the community atmosphere, along with the ready-made myths of earlier sacred times, made it easier to feel at home in the new place. Myths made sense of the mysterious nature of the waters. In addition, as the waters intimately enveloped the body with their wetness and odors, they engaged the imagination. Recognition of their symbolic value to cleanse, purify, and renew expedited the uniting of person and place, allowing each to participate in the other's nature. A person's pain also enabled this connection, opening up a willingness to accept the elusiveness of a nature cure. The rituals involved in taking the waters then allowed the health seeker to participate in the sacred, to partake of the world of dreams and symbols. The routine of taking a bath became a ritual, and, if it proved successful in alleviating pain, a strong connection with the spa and its physical location easily took hold.

Daily activities around the waters, however, depended on one's orientation. In the secular realm, they emphasized less respect for the power of the waters and all the usual activities that occurred around them. The desire for entertainment dominated this perception. Pleasure-seekers might scale nearby hills, but they probably would not sit for hours in small pavilions while drinking occasional cups of water and socializing with others. As medical therapies changed, so did the perceived need to spend weeks at a particular locale. Changing lifestyles eliminated sojourns that were too time-consuming to justify the expense. Social activities away from the waters also hastened the demise of Texas spas. Their physical structures deteriorated. Since pleasure resorts could be situated almost anywhere, these spas no longer warranted the capital needed for refurbishment or expansion.

Perhaps the most telling difference in yesteryear's perception of the waters comes from Sophia Vickrey Ard. The mineral well in Salado was something that she was taught to respect, a response not normally extended to nonliving things. People simply valued the old well:

> It seems to me that they wanted their children, including their youngest—me—to have the experience of going and waiting for a bottle to fill, and it was treated with—the old well was treated like a very old and honored man. It was a thing to be revered almost. You respected those old things, because they were of nature and still they were of service, and they were still going.[1]

Before it disappeared, "taking the waters," then, constituted a communion with nature, a harmonious relationship in step with contemporary values and beliefs. The living waters sang melodious and sometimes melancholy songs about hope, camaraderie, and renewal. They sang of lost loves celebrating new beginnings, of broken bodies yearning to dance again, of spirited places touching heart and soul. Their music reverberated throughout the state. Stand next to any Texas spring and listen closely. A faint echo can still be heard.

County List of Medicinal Wells and Springs

County	Spring/Well	Nearby Area	Possible Years of Operation
Anderson	Elkhart Mineral Wells	Elkhart	1880s–1890s
	Loretto Mineral Wells*	Elkhart	?
Angelina	Sulphur	Homer	1890s
Bee	Mineral (City)	Beeville	1870s–1880s
Bell	Isby Well	Belton	1890s
	Leon Spring	Belton	1890s
	Leonoland Spring*	Belton	1880s
	Key's Wells	Salado	1900s
	(sulphur well)	Salado	1890s–1910s
	(sulphur springs)	Salado	1850s
	Elliott Well	Belton	1930s
Bexar	Dullnig's Well	San Antonio	1880s–1900s
	Harlandale		
	Hot Sulphur Well	San Antonio	1910s
	Hot Wells	San Antonio	1890s–1920s (–1930s**)
	Terrell Wells	San Antonio	1890s–1940s
	(mineral spring)	San Antonio	1850s
Bosque	(well)	Meridian	1890s
Bowie	Boston Chalybeate	Old Boston	1890s
Bowie	Dalby Springs	Dalby Springs	1840s–1910s (–1920**)
	Farrier Spring	Dalby Springs	1870s–1900s
	Ghio Spring	Texarkana	1910s
	Ingensole Chalybeate (Ingersoll)	Redwater	1890s

* Possibly the same spring or well as the one above.
** Some evidence suggests informal use of waters—perhaps simply their consumption.

County	Spring/Well	Nearby Area	Possible Years of Operation
Bowie	Red or Jarrett Springs	Boston	1880s
(continued)	Lonestar Mineral	Texarkana	1900s–1910s
	Texarkana*	Texarkana	1900s
Brazos	Manganic Wells	Bryan	1880s–1890s
	McQueen's Well	Bryan	1880s
	Sulphur Springs	Millican	1880s–1890s
Brewster	Hot or Boquillas Springs	Big Bend	1900s–1940s (–1990s**)
Brown	(mineral well)	Brownwood	1910s
Burnet	Sulphur Springs	Marble Falls	
Caldwell	Rogers' Springs (Cardwell, Texas Sour)	Luling/Lockhart	1870s–1890s
	Burditte's Well (Burditt's, Burdette)	Luling/Lockhart	1870s–1910s
	Luling (Sour) (or Soda Springs)	Luling	1870s–1890s
	Sulphur Spring	old Atlanta	1870s
Calhoun	Vaca-Tesia Spring	Port Lavaca	1900s
Callahan	Putnam Mineral Wells	Putnam	1800s–1910s (–1930s**)
	Pecan	Little Pecan Creek	1890s
Camp	Chalybeate Mineral Spring	Pittsburg	1890s
Cass	Banguss Mineral Springs (Bogue)	Viola	1880s
	Hughes (Chalybeate)	Hughes Springs	(1860s–**) 1870s–1900s (–1930s**)
	White Sulphur Springs	Marietta/White Sulphur	1880s–1890s
	(mineral spring)	Linden	1850s
	Thrasher Springs	Linden	1910s
Cherokee	Chalybeate City Springs	Rusk	1870s–1890s
	Seven Sisters Springs	New Birmingham	1870s–1890s
	Castalian Springs	Rusk	
Colorado	Kessler Springs	Columbus	1870s–1880s
	McCroskey Springs	Alleyton	
Cooke	Mineral Wells	Burns	
Dallas	DD Duncan	Trinity Mills	1880s (–1930s**)
	Gill Well	Dallas (Oak Lawn)	1900s–1920s
Deaf Smith	Hereford Well	Hereford	1910s

County	Spring/Well	Nearby Area	Possible Years of Operation
Denton	Brock's Mineral Well	Denton	1900s (−1930s**)
De Witt	(sulphur springs)	Sandus Creek	1880s
Dimmit	Daugherty	Carrizo Springs	1890s
	Kelly-Hennigan Well*	Carrizo Springs	1890s
	Carrizo Springs	Carrizo Springs	1900s−1910s
Eastland	Mangum	Mangum	1900s−1910s (−1930s**)
	Maurice Well	Mangum	1900s−1910s (−1930s**)
	Carbon Mineral Well	Carbon	1900s
Ellis	Milford	Milford	1900s
	well	Waxahachie	1900s−1920s
Erath	Duffau's Sulphur Wells	Duffau	1880s−1910s (−1920s**)
	Southland Spring*	Duffau	1910s
Falls	Marlin	Marlin	1890s−1980s
	(spring)	Alto	1860s
Fannin	Mead Spring	Honey Grove	1890s−1900s
Fayette	Slack Well	Waelder	1890s
	Sulphur Springs	Black Jack Springs	1880s
Fisher	(mineral spring)	Roby	1890s
Frio	Sour Well	Pearsall	1890s
Galveston	High Island	High Island	1890s−1910s (−1920s**)
Gillespie	Pecan Spring	Lange's Mill	
Gonzales	Sour Spring	Harwood	1870s−1880s
	Sour Well	Gonzales	1860s−1880s
	Warm Springs	Ottine	1900s−1940s
	Walker's Springs	Wilson Creek	1860s
Grayson	Cedar Springs	Cedar Mills	1880s
	Cook's Springs	Sherman	1890s
	Tioga (inc. Simmons Well & Rains)	Tioga	1880s−1980s
	X-Ray Spring	Whitesboro	1900s
Gregg	Capp's Mineral Wells	Longview	1880s−1940s
	Phillips	Gladewater	1870s−1900s
Grimes	Kellum's (White Sulphur Spring)	Anderson	1830s−1880s
	Piedmont	Piedmont	1840s−1870s (−1880s**)

County	Spring/Well	Nearby Area	Possible Years of Operation
Hardin	Saratoga (New Sour Lake)	Saratoga	(1850s–**) 1880s–1890s
	Sour Springs or Sour Lake	Sour Lake	1830s–1900s (–1940s**)
Harris	Houston Hot Well	Cypress	1914–1950
Harrison	Hynson's Iron Mtn.	Marshall	1850s–1900s
	Rosborough Springs	Marshall	1880s–1920s (–1930s**)
	Montvale	Marshall/Harleton	1890s–1900s
Haskell	Haskell Mineral Well	Haskell	1900s
Hays	Bale's Well	San Marcos	1890s
Hill	Hubbard Hot Well	Hubbard City	1890s–1920s
	Brandon	Eastern part of county	1880s
Hood	Thorp Spring	Thorp Spring	1870s–1890s
Hopkins	Crabtree's Sour	Sulphur Springs	1880s
	Pate Sour Well	Sulphur Springs	1880s–1890s (–1930s**)
	Sour Well*	Sulphur Springs	1900s
	Weaver Well	Sulphur Springs	1880s
	Sulphur Springs	Sulphur Springs	1870s–1900s (–1930s**)
Houston	Rice Mineral Well	?	1890s
Howard	sulphur springs	Big Spring	1850s
Hudspeth	Indian Hot Springs	Indian Hot Springs	(1900s–**) 1920s–1960s
	Hot Wells	Hot Wells	1900s
Hunt	Mitchell Well	Greenville	1920s
	Mineral Wells	Campbell	1900s–1920s
Jack	Wizard Wells	Wizard Wells (Vineyard)	1880s–1980s
Jasper	Falls Spring	Browndell	
Jefferson	Sour Springs	Beaumont	1890s
	(artesian well)	Beaumont	1900s
	Port Arthur Mineral Well	Port Arthur	1900s
Karnes	(mineral spring)	?	1850s
	Kenedy Hot Wells	Karnes City	1910s–1950s
Kaufman	Crystal Spring	Terrell	1910s
Kendall	Indian Mineral	Boerne	1880s
	Kendall County*	Boerne	1900s

County	Spring/Well	Nearby Area	Possible Years of Operation
Kendall (*continued*)	Sisterdale (Kapp's Hydropathic Institute)	Sisterdale	1850s–1860s
Lamar	Bell's Mineral Wells	Blossom	1880s–1890s
	Blossom Mineral Wells	Blossom	1900s (–1930s**)
	Beauchamp Wells*	Blossom	1910s
	Carlsbad Well (Carlsbad Dyspepsia)	Blossom	1900s
	Hefner	Blossom	1910s
	Bloy's Well	Paris	1880s–1930s
Lampasas	Abney Well	Lampasas	1900s–1920s
	Chandler's Springs	Lampasas	
	Gooch Spring, Hughes Spring	Lampasas	1850s–1870s
	Hancock Springs (Great Boiling Spring)	Lampasas	1850s–1890s (–1900s**)
	Hanna Springs	Lampasas	(–1850s**) 1870s–1910s (–1930s**)
	Cooper Spring	Lampasas	1870s
	Scott (Burleson's or Lower Spring)	Lampasas	1850s–1870s
La Salle	(artesian well)	Cotulla	1890s
	Woodward Vichy Spring	Woodward or Rockbridge	1900s
Lavaca	St. Mary's Mineral Well	Hallettsville	1910s (–1930s**)
	Fuller Wells	Hallettsville	1910s
Lee	Darden	Moab	1890s
	Gum Springs	Lincoln	1890s
	Waitman Well	?	1890s
Leon	(spring)	Jewett	1910s
Limestone	Fairview Springs	Kosse	1880s
	(mineral springs)	Tehuacana	
	Kennedy Sulphur Spring	Groesbeck	1890s–1910s
McCulloch	Duke's Mineral Well	?	1890s
	Brady Well	Brady	1890s
McLennan	China Spring	China Springs	1900s
	N. Waco Artesian Well	Waco	1890s–1920s
	Eddy	Eddy	1900s
Marion	Bangus Springs and 2 wells	southeast?	1890s

County	Spring/Well	Nearby Area	Possible Years of Operation
Medina	Tschuhart	Castroville	1890s
	D'Hanis Mineral Wells	D'Hanis	1880s
Milam	Rockdale	Rockdale	1890s
	Richard's Well*	Rockdale	1890s
	Thorndale	Thorndale	1940s
Montague	Queen's Peak Medical Wells	Bowie	1880s
Montgomery	Mineral (Double) Springs	Montgomery	
	Beckworth	Dobbin	1910s
Nacogdoches	Aqua Vitae Wells	Nacogdoches	1910s
	Oil Springs	Oil City/Melrose	1890s
	Shawnee	Nacogdoches	1910s
	Weatherly's Wells (Weatherby)	Garrison	1890s–1910s (–1920s**)
	Stoker Mineral Spring	Martinsville	1910s
	sulphur spring	Chireno	1910s
Navarro	Emmett	?	1900s
Newton	Hickman Springs	Burkeville	1860s
	Myer's Well	Kirbyville	1910s
Nolan	Grogan Wells	Sweetwater	1900s–1910s
Nueces	Corpus Christi Well	Corpus Christi	1890s
Ochiltree	Grogan	northeastern part?	1900s–1920s
Palo Pinto	Mineral Wells	Mineral Wells	1880s–1960s (–1980s**)
	Orono Min. Sprg, Allison, Crystal	Oran	1900s–1920s
Panola	Midyett (Breckenridge)	Midyett	1870s–1910s
	Brown Springs (Davis Springs?)	Cozart/Gary	1870s–1900s
	(mineral spring)	Tatum	1900s
Parker	Eureka No. 2 Well	Weatherford	1910s
	Love Mineral Well*	Weatherford	1900s
	Edward's Mineral Well	Weatherford	1900s–1910s
	Sheboygan Mineral Wells	Weatherford	1900s
	Chalybeate Spring	Weatherford	1850s
	Ballou Springs	Whitt	1870s–1900s
Polk	Sulphur Springs	Corrigan	1910s
Presidio	Kingston Hot Springs	Ruidosa	1930s–1990s
Red River	Coleman Springs	Annona	1880s

County	Spring/Well	Nearby Area	Possible Years of Operation
Robertson	Overall Mineral Well	Franklin	1890s–1920s
	Wootan Wells	Bremond	1880s–1920s
	Lipscomb Well	?	1880s
	Kendrick Wells	?	1880s
	Fisher	?	1880s
Rusk	Graveyard Springs (Willow)	Chapman	
	Sulphur Springs	Henderson	1890s–1900s
	Welch	Brachfield	1880s–1890s
	(mineral springs)	Mount Enterprise	1870s
	Eulalie Springs	Caledonia	1910s
	White Oak Springs	Tatum	1910s
Sabine	Sulphur Springs	Milam	
San Augustine	(springs)	San Augustine	
San Saba	Sulphur Springs	On Colorado River near ?	1850s–1890s
Smith	Headache Springs	Tyler	1850s–1870s
	Riviere Wells	Tyler	1890s–1910s (–1920s**)
Somervell	Glen Rose	Glen Rose	1880s–1940s (–1950s**)
Tarrant	Arlington Well	Arlington	1900s–1951
Taylor	North Park Mineral Well	Abilene	1910s
Terrell	Sulphur	Independence Creek	
Titus	Red (Dellwood)	Mount Pleasant	1890s–1900s (–1920s**)
	Peterman*	Mount Pleasant	
	Roach Well	Mount Pleasant / Cook	1900s
Tom Green	Carlsbad	Carlsbad	1900s–1910s (–1930s**)
	Christoval Mineral Wells	Christoval	1910s–1980s
Travis	Santa Monica	Austin	(–1890s**)
	Fifth Street Well	Austin	1890s
	South Austin Wells	Austin	1910s
	capitol well	Austin	1860s–1990s
Trinity	(sulphur springs)	Trinity Station	
	Chalybeate	On Trinity below Whit?	1870s

County	Spring/Well	Nearby Area	Possible Years of Operation
Tyler	Sulphur	Mt. Hope	1870s–1890s
	Sulphur	Chester	–1890s
	Sulphur	Rockland	1890s
Upshur	Gunpowder Spring	Gilmer	1880s–1890s
Uvalde	Hanner Well	?	1890s
	Reagan Wells	Uvalde	1880s–1940s
Val Verde	(mineral well)	Del Rio	
Van Zandt	Myrtle	Myrtle Springs	1890s
	(well)	Wills Point / Kaufman	1910s
Victoria	Sulphur Spring	?	1890s
Walker	Salinilla	Near Trinity River	1850s
	Sulphur Springs	Bidias Creek	1850s–1860s
	Wilson's Mineral Well	Huntsville	1880s
	Wyser's Springs (Tuscaloosa) (Wisner)	Tuscaloosa	1850s–1890s
	Bath	SW Walker County	1830s–1870s**
Wharton	Bernard Sulphur	Spanish Camp	1880s
Williamson	Georgetown	Georgetown	1880s–1910s (–1920s**)
	Page's Well*	Georgetown	1890s
	Taylor artesian well	Taylor	1900s
	Round Rock well	Round Rock	1900s
Wilson	Sutherland Springs	Sutherland Springs	1840s–1930s
Wise	Alvord	North central part	1900s
Wood	Chalybeate (Musgrove)	Winnsboro	1880s–1890s
	Mineola Mineral Well	Mineola	1880s–1920s
Young	Stovall Hot Wells	South Bend	1930s–1990s
	St. Augustine		1840s
?	Glenmore Sulphur Sprgs		1890s
?	Sharp's		1890s
?	Cicero Smith		1900s
?	Davis Mineral Water		
?	Jacobs		1900s
?	Waco	On Brazos River	1850s

* Possibly the same spring or well as the one above.
** Some evidence suggests informal use of waters—perhaps simply their consumption.

Regional Guide to Texas' Medicinal Waters

Gulf Coast Area

GALVESTON COUNTY

High Island The United States Geological Survey (USGS) listed High Island as a mineral water source in its publications from 1898 to 1914. The mineral well at the Sea View Hotel was called White Doe (and later Smith's Well) because of a legend that a pregnant but ill Indian had been cured by drinking the water.

HARDIN COUNTY

Saratoga The name of these springs, which were discovered in the 1850s, derived from the famed resort of New York. *The Handbook of Texas* noted that J. F. Cotton found them around 1850, and by 1879 there were cabins for rent and a pavilion over the seven or so springs. People visited the bathhouse to treat ulcers and arthritis. According to Brune, these sulphur springs dried up around 1900 because of the development of the area's oil field.

Sour Lake In 1834, the Mexican government granted to Stephen Jackson, a friend of Stephen Austin, one thousand acres, which included the springs. In an 1837 letter to Sam Houston and Dr. Ashbel Smith, later published in the *Beaumont Enterprise,* Henry Millard, surveyor, real estate broker, and lieutenant colonel under Houston at the Battle of San Jacinto, asked if each man wanted to invest $1,000 in Jackson's Chalybeate Springs, where a "lake of Chalbeate waters covering about 2 acres of ground are formed by innumerable springs boiling up within a few feet of each other all over the lake which is generally from 18 inches to two feet deep." The purchase was never made. By 1851 the springs had become the "Sour Lake Watering Place," owned by Holland Freeman and Company, according to the *New Orleans*

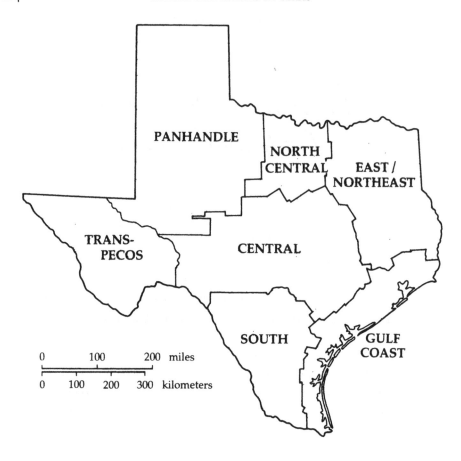

Weekly Delta. The company's ad testified to the state of enterprise at the springs at that time: "These waters for several years were in apparent obscurity, owing to the fact of no effort having been made to improve the property." Boats were to take visitors to Liberty, where carriages would finish the journey to the resort. A physician was also on duty to attend to patients.

In 1857, the *Galveston Weekly News* ran a series called "Sour Lake Letters." The writer described the lake as a "perfect circle of from 150 to 200 yards diameter" where in "dry weather, the waters entirely disappear, excepting a narrow strip on the north side and a pool of ten yards wide in the centre." The writer also noted the bathhouses on the north shore, only three of which were serviceable, and a frame building over the pool in the center of the lake. This was the ladies' bathhouse, and the proprietor was building a dry path to it at the time. There were numerous scattered springs near the lake and hidden under trees. Also noted were many guests having breakfast on the lawn of the hotel. Finally, the writer observed a "curiosity of nature" on a nearby prairie—a small depression in the soil that looked like "a dried up mudhole" with a disagreeable odor. Near this was a long pole, sharpened at one end and used to pry up a fragment of the soil. Evidently this soil was considered a mineral soap used for female complexions, and "said to be a certain enemy and destroyer of freckles, tan and sunburn, and to give an unusual brilliance and transparency to the human cuticle."

The writer noted that there were about thirty buildings on the grounds at the time (July 1857), and the proprietor, Colonel Lacy, was building a bowling saloon near the hotel. The hotel was

> beautifully located under the shade of a black-oak grove. . . . About a hundred yards to the right, under the eastern border of the grove, are ten or twelve neat log cottages, which have just been erected and furnished for the use of the guests. To the left of the hotel, as we approach, the grove becomes a forest, upon the skirt of which there are stables and carriage houses, a carpenter shop, and negro quarters. Passing through the hotel, we come to other quarters and out-houses, and then turning to the right, we discover three or four small new houses, one of which is occupied as a bar and grocery, and the others by the mechanics and laborers employed about the place.

After two weeks at the resort, the writer for the *News* did not want to detract from the healing qualities of the various springs, but he/she described in detail the practices of a temporary manager, hired since Colonel Lacy was absent. The manager thought the springs and wells needed cleaning, so he sent workers to take out the naturally percolating water, but the new water that filled in did not have the mineral strength of the old. So the manager

> thought he would assist nature to recover the tone of her system in these wells, at least so far as to restore the rich acid taste to the sulphur springs near the Lake, as it would never do to have Sour Lake water, with the "sour" left out. So he gathers up some of the sour clay lying loose upon the margin of the Lake, together with the rich deposits of the cattle at the same place and throws a portion of this delightful mixture into each of the sulphur springs. . . . Whether the effect upon the water was sufficiently acidulous to gratify his expectations, I know not; but I have seen the recollection of this experiment produce many a wry and sour face upon the invalids who still drank the sulphur waters with the hope of being restored to

health. One of the wells has since received the soubriquet of the "Cow Spring," from the liberal evidences upon its surface of having been "doctored" in the manner above mentioned.

The manager also dug a reservoir to fill barrels of water to be sold, but because he was too impatient to let nature fill it in, he drained the adjacent bathhouses of their contents. The writer ended his final letter with the observation that "all who can get away are going tomorrow, leaving behind but one invalid."

In 1866 the *San Antonio Daily Herald* noted ten wells or springs different in character. The article continued: "A use is also made of the oil which collects and floats upon the surface. The mud from the lake is frequently collected, dried, and carried away to be afterward mixed with other waters, to which it is said to convey its virtues." In 1863, while Sam Houston visited Sour Lake to bathe old wounds, he caught a cold that later developed into the pneumonia that killed him. The 1878 *Southern and Western Guide to Texas* mentioned that thirty years of experience with the twenty-seven different kinds of waters would cure "almost every disease the flesh is heir to."

By the 1880s, a Galveston businessman, J. P. Willis, built a large, 125-room plantation-style hotel (see fig. 37). He advertised well and attracted planters, businessmen, Louisiana socialites, and even poor campers. In 1897 the *Gulf Messenger* noted that there were thirty pools and wells around the greenish, bubbling lake, which had a small island in the middle, connected to it by a "rustic" bridge. Four mineral wells were under a pavilion, and the others either were unprotected and uncurbed or had smaller pavilions. Also noted were nineteen pool baths and one swimming pool. A former slave, named Bazile but commonly known as Dr. Mud (not a real physician), supposedly learned the healing properties of the mud. One visitor, as a 1936 issue of the *Houston Chronicle* recorded, remembered years later that the manager of the hotel removed Dr. Mud because he grew tired of Mud's messing up the hotel linen with his mud packs. The proprietors of Sour Lake marketed the sulphur mud and clay, called Guinea, to remove freckles.

Although Sour Lake was visited since the 1850s, it remained fairly inaccessible for forty years. In 1896 the Sour Lake Company incorporated to improve the springs. The proposed Sour Lake Springs Company planned to renovate the "run down" hotel and cottages, build a modern hotel and natatorium, connect the resort to the railroad with an electric line, and convert

37. Springs Hotel, Sour Lake, 1909. Author's postcard collection.

the salt marsh into a seventy-six-acre lake. The discovery of another resource halted any renovation plans. In 1902 the Texas Company (later Texaco) found oil, and the health business deteriorated. Scattered attempts to resurrect the business failed. In 1909 after Well #3 came in, the stream of oil cascaded down on the surrounding area, including the land around the hotel. The oil caught fire and the hotel quickly burned. In 1915 and at least through 1936, a small natatorium operated near the lake. People still used the water medicinally. Asthmatics learned how to breathe in the sulphur fumes by letting the sulphur water flow over their heads as the water entered the pool. After World War I, the proprietor found another innovative use of the water. Because automobile headlights created an undesirable glare, the owner submerged the lenses under the sulphur water to color them yellow to cut the glare. In 1928, developers envisioned a new hundred-room hotel, a golf course, a bathhouse with surgery and massage facilities, and a nightclub. These amenities never materialized, perhaps because the stock market crashed the next year. Although no substantial spa operated at Sour Lake after the turn of the century, people still recognized its beneficial resources. In 1951 the *Houston Press* reported that "letters still come into the postoffice at Sour Lake from persons who want bottles of the sulphurous mud."

Only the stories remain of this famous place. In 1938 Jesse Ziegler reported that he had seen men plaster their bald heads with the mud in hopes it would restore their hair. In addition, he thought that the place was healthful because the gases emerging from the lake killed any insects (or fish or snakes) near the waters, so that there was often a film of dead insects on top of the water.

HARRIS COUNTY

Houston Hot Well Sanitarium and Hotel, Cypress The 1914–15 *Texas Gazetteer* noted this place. According to the USGS, another well drilled in 1950 supplied a large pool, which attracted bathers for their health. Now the pool is covered over, and a gun club occupies the site.

JEFFERSON COUNTY

Sour Springs, near Beaumont The 1890–91 *Fourth Annual Report of the Agriculture Bureau* noted the springs' reputation of "being a pleasant health resort."

NUECES COUNTY

Corpus Christi The 1892 *Fourth Annual Report of the Geological Survey of Texas* noted that a well drilled to find city water instead found water heavily charged with salt and sulphates and thought to be medicinal. A Mr. Chapman, who bored the well, built a sanitarium, where he offered medicinal baths.

East–Northeast

ANDERSON COUNTY

Elkhart, one mile southeast of Elkhart The 1889 *First Annual Report of the Geological Survey of Texas* reported that a hotel was being built here and a health resort started. Some waters tasted strongly of sulphur and others of alum and iron salts. These waters probably were the same as those called Loretto Mineral Wells in 1907 by the USGS.

ANGELINA COUNTY

Sulphur Springs, fifteen miles southeast of Homer, near Rockland The 1890–91 *Fourth Annual Report of the Agriculture Bureau* noted this water as good for dropsy and general debility.

BOWIE COUNTY

Boston Chalybeate Listed as a "resort" in the 1893 USGS *Mineral Resources of the U.S.* Brune noted that from 1813 there was a stop here on the Trammel's Trace. In 1976, the springs still flowed.

Dalby Springs (and Farrier Springs)   Brune noted that in 1687 Joutel found the Upper Natchitoches tribe of Caddos living here. Later discovered around 1840 by two brothers-in-law, the various mineral springs of this area were generally known as Dalby Springs, Farrier Springs, Booth Spring, and Pirkey Spring. By 1849 a house and several cabins housed visitors who retreated to the springs particularly during summers, according to an 1849 issue of the *Clarksville Standard.* T. Bence charged man and horse $25 per month. Popular by the 1870s, the area around Farrier Springs contained an enclosure of about fifty acres, including a hotel, dancing pavilion, ballpark, and campground. In the 1880s the Pirkey Hotel and the Carter Hotel accommodated visitors. Every summer a Confederate Veterans' Reunion was held, and a dog and badger fight "entertained" spectators. In 1882 a writer for the *Standard* described the camaraderie among all classes of folks at the springs:

> I have met a variety of interesting people here—many beautiful and accomplished ladies—some young, some talented, and all agreeable. Then there are some distinguished statesmen here—Gov. Hubbard and family have rooms engaged and are now due—this their second visit this season—and then there are some others that are not distinguished, not yet statesmen; but everybody drinks Dalby water, and in this particular all meet on a common level around the springs.

The author then espoused all the activities, which included dancing, tennis, croquet, and hunting with hounds. Something for everyone, except for "that class that must needs pour the spirits down to keep their spirits up." Yet for those who could not imbibe, a local politician exclaimed that it was indeed a "blessing that this spring was discovered in a land of local option."

After the railroad bypassed the community, hopes of making Dalby Springs a first-class resort evaporated. In 1930, A. Neville noted that there were then no accommodations for visitors but that there had been a time when people in Paris made their summer pilgrimage to Dalby "as regularly as the Moslem heads for Mecca." In 1961 Frank Tolbert reported that all traces of the Black Spring had disappeared.

Ghio Springs, Texarkana   Listed by the USGS in 1911 as a mineral water source, probably for medicinal purposes. Possibly Texarkana Springs mentioned in 1907 and 1908.

Ingensole   The 1890–91 *Fourth Annual Report of the Agriculture Bureau* noted this mineral water as "recommended for rheumatism and dyspepsia."

Lonestar Mineral Well, Texarkana   It became Texarkana Lone Star Mineral Wells in 1916.

Red Springs (also Jarrett Springs), near Boston   The 1886 *USGS Bulletin* 32 called this place a resort.

CASS COUNTY

Bangus's Mineral Springs, near Viola   The 1886 *USGS Bulletin* 32 called the two springs a local "resort." By 1890, the place had fallen into disuse, according to the Geological Survey of Texas, 1890.

Hughes Springs   Brune noted that a large Caddo village existed at these springs at one time. Reese Hughes founded a town at the chalybeate spring in 1847. An advertisement in the July 6, 1882, *Austin Daily Statesman* announced the opening of the Hughes' Springs Hotel with its skating rink, billiard hall, dancing halls, hot and cold mineral baths, and a first-class band. The 1886 *USGS Bulletin* 32 called these three chalybeate springs a resort. In 1872, Dr. John McLean, a Methodist minister, preached under the brush arbor at the springs. Afterward, the Hughes family gave land for a Methodist church and the area known as Chalybeate Spring Park (see fig. 38). The park became a mecca for picnickers as the railroads brought tourists to the park and to the hotel. The 1890–91 *Fourth Annual Report of the Agriculture Bureau* noted these springs as a "well-known summer resort." By 1911 *Texas Magazine* noted that the water was still considered medicinal, but it was apparent that the springs required a good hotel person to market them.

Mineral Springs, Linden   Brune noted that around 1850 local residents perceived these springs west of Linden to be healthful.

White Sulphur Springs   The 1884 *Texas Gazetteer* reported that the town's population of seventy-five included one physician. The 1886 *USGS Bulletin* 32 called these two springs a resort ("used to a slight extent").

CHEROKEE COUNTY

The 1889 *First Annual Report of the Geological Survey of Texas* reported a large number of iron and sulphur springs in the county. Within one square mile were twelve iron springs. In one unspecified spring was a large hollow gum tree, said to be the one that General Rusk placed here fifty years earlier and to which he traveled each year from Nacogdoches County to drink the water.

Chalybeate City, five miles northeast of Rusk   There were seven or eight chalybeate and one white sulphur spring. In 1887, lots were sold. A March 1887 edition of the *Cherokee Standard* advised its readers:

38. Hughes Chalybeate Springs Park, Hughes Springs, Texas, 1990. Author photo.

There will be a slow train picnic in Chalybeate City on the 4th of July, 1887. Everybody invited and all old people especially invited. The trains will consist of ox wagons. The drivers will carry a large coarse horn and cowbells. He must blow his horn when he comes in sight of a crossroads or fork in the road and ring the bell until he passes. He must also blow and ring as he comes into the city. When all the trains get in the oldest men will be called on to tell something of "ye olden times." Basket dinner on the ground and everybody must be very polite to all the old people.

A Chalybeate Springs Hotel and Bathhouse once occupied the site. Evidently many Rusk citizens, especially the women and children who were joined by their husbands and fathers on weekends, lived in Chalybeate City during the summers. Brune reported that three tubs used for bathing were still at the site in the 1970s.

New Birmingham, three miles southwest of Rusk Seven different spring waters, called the Seven Sisters Springs, emerged from within a radius of twenty feet. The 1878 I & G.N. Railway Guide mentioned several sulphur and chalybeate springs near Rusk. In 1888, the Cherokee Land and Iron Company laid out New Birmingham to be an iron and steel center. By 1893, however, the town had significantly declined, some say due to the passage of the alien land law during Hogg's administration. This supposedly scared away the English investors, although the panic of '93 surely contributed also. At its peak, the town claimed about two thousand inhabitants, three hundred homes, and a seventy-five-room hotel. The Southern Hotel boasted billiard tables, hand-carved and polished paneling and fixtures, and dance bands "imported" from Dallas, Houston, and New Orleans. Esteemed guests included Grover Cleveland, Jay Gould, and Jim Hogg. According to Tom Finty Jr., a reporter for the *New Birmingham Times* who later became an editor for the *Dallas Morning News,* quoted in a 1980 issue of the *Sherman Democrat,* the fashion of wearing sideburns first became famous at the Southern. Efforts were made to fashion the town into a health resort. An 1889 *New Birmingham Times* article announced the formation of a company to erect hotels and bathhouses, as well as an artificial lake. In 1890 an ad sought for county agents to sell the Chalybeate Springs bottled water. The 1890–91 *Fourth Annual Report of the Agriculture Bureau* noted that the "white sulphur springs and chalybeate springs are numerous, and it is expected that this place will become a great health resort." In 1954, sixty years after it died, some Rusk citizens observed that if the nearby town of New Birmingham had pushed its mineral waters rather than its iron ore, it might have survived. One woman reported in a 1954 issue of the *Dallas Morning News* that her mother had moved there in the 1890s specifically to regain her health.

FANNIN COUNTY

Mead Springs, near Honey Grove The 1890–91 *Fourth Annual Report of the Agriculture Bureau* noted that these springs "contain iron and other mineral substance, which are recommended for chronic diseases."

GREGG COUNTY

Capp's Wells, N. Center Street, Longview Dug originally in 1885, the two wells were 125 feet deep and lined with brick. The water was sold in bottles, kegs, or drunk at the wells. The 1890–91 *Texas State Gazetteer* (cited hereafter as Texas Gazetteer) noted M. F. Capps as operator of these mineral springs. The 1890–91 *Fourth Annual Report of the Agriculture Bureau* recommended this well "as a cure for dropsy, Bright's disease, dyspepsia, biliousness, rheumatism, and kindred diseases. A qualitative analysis made by Prof. Richard, of the United States Department of Agriculture, shows it to be sulphur water, containing sulphate of iron, potash, sulphate, soda salts, and chlorides of lime and magnesia."

The USGS listed them in 1911 and 1919 as a source of mineral water, probably for medicinal purposes. The wells remained a going concern until the 1940s. Today only the well casings remain.

Phillips' Springs, Gladewater A Confederate veteran acquired the land near Union Grove and developed the springs to aid his friends' recoveries. By the 1880s the mineral water and orange-colored sediment brought people to drink and bathe in the waters. Phillips built a hotel in 1895, which was destroyed by a windstorm in 1900. People still traveled to the springs and camped out and bathed in the several bathhouses on the grounds. The Gladewater Lake infiltrated some of the springs, but a shed covers remnants of an old bathhouse, and retainer walls protect two of the springs, according to Charlotte Teske, a local citizen.

GRIMES COUNTY

The 1893 *Geological Survey of Texas* named the most important springs in the county as Kellum's and Piedmont's.

Kellum's Sulphur Springs Possibly what David Edward called Navasoto sulphur springs in 1836. Also probably what John Disturnell called the White Sulphur Spring in Montgomery County in 1855. In 1840 Francis Moore and Orceneth Fisher both placed a "celebrated" sulphur spring near the mouth of the Navasota River in northern Montgomery County. They and later chroniclers probably referred to Kellum's Sulphur Springs, which was about thirty miles northeast of Washington. De Cordova's 1849 map of Texas (and his 1858 book) reported a White Sulphur Spring ten miles north northwest of Anderson, the same place that Young's 1850 and 1852 maps indicated as Kellum's Sulphur Springs (Young placed a major trail passing through it). This spring was evidently more famous in the early years than Piedmont. (Colton's 1866 map placed a White Sulphur Spring about fifteen miles northwest of Anderson, while Johnson's 1866 and 1870 map placed Kellum's spring ten miles northwest of Anderson. Not until 1872 did Colton note Piedmont on his map.) In 1879, Homer Thrall called Kellum's Springs, "one of the finest sulphur springs in the state."

On the southeast quarter of the William Fitzgibbon league, Nathaniel Kellum built a fifty-room, two-story hotel, a bathhouse, vaults cut into the spring, and several reservoirs twenty feet in diameter and eight feet deep. A pump and pipes relayed the spring water to the hotel. For amusement, guests hunted deer and turkey, as well as danced in the second-floor parlor. In 1856 the *Galveston Weekly News* advertised the springs. It noted that there were eighteen "comfortable Cottages" that, with the main building "better adapted for comfort as a Summer house than almost any in the State or perhaps the South," could accommodate four to five hundred guests. Kellum also boasted that he would open a bowling saloon soon, but noted that they had a "first rate" school and would have ice on hand during the season. In 1858 the *Huntsville Item* carried an advertisement for Kellum's White Sulphur Springs: "Board, Lodging and Bathing, and if necessary, clothing per day, $1; fine musician on hand . . . Party every Tuesday evening." After Kellum and his wife died, the house was condemned, probably in the 1870s. In 1877 the state's medical association reported that "Kellum Sulphur Springs" had "been in repute nearly forty years for their pleasant taste and decided medical virtues" and tasted "similar to that of Congress Spring, at Saratoga, N.Y., and the White Sulphur Springs of Virginia." By 1893, the waters still possessed a local reputation of curative powers but had fallen into disuse.

Piedmont Piedmont is located on FM 3090, seven miles west northwest of Anderson in west central Grimes County. In 1843 William W. Arrington bought the site at a sheriff's sale, built bathhouses and one-room cottages, and operated a campground and health resort.

In 1858, H. Lee and C. S. Taliaferro bought the property and, in turn, sold it to Leander Cannon in 1860. By then a rock-and-wood, four-story, hundred-room hotel with broad verandas and a turreted roof accommodated visitors and contained a dining room and ballroom where Sam Houston reportedly danced the minuet. The resort attracted other famous persons as well, such as Governor Marmaduke of Kentucky. In 1861 the *Houston Weekly Telegraph* noted that the proprietor was developing the resort into a "Saratoga of Texas." The article boasted that he grew his vegetables so high that everybody should be prepared to "feed high," referring to their abundance.

In 1863 and 1864, Confederate general Magruder and thereafter General Beauregard occupied the inn. In 1865, John Walker's "Greyhound Division" of the Confederate Army, eager to drink the sulphur water upon their return from the war, camped at the springs for six days.

In 1871, John K. Spears purchased the property for $5,940 at a bankruptcy sale, but he did not do much with it except use it as a camping ground. The inn deteriorated and was eventually torn down.

There were three springs of sulphur water, named for the strength of

39. Piedmont Springs, Texas, 1990. Author photo.

minerals in the water. In 1877 the state's medical association called them "celebrated all over Texas for their rare medical properties." Today the springs still flow (see fig. 39). One of deep blue sulphur is curbed. A reservoir still keeps the other spring waters trapped for the daring bather to test.

HARRISON COUNTY

Hynson Springs In 1851, the *Texas Republican* described this place, then known as Marshall Springs, as "intended for the habitation of the muses." The owner had three bottles of spring water analyzed and they were found to be medicinal. The proprietors planned to build ten cabins by summer. An advertisement in the 1878–79 *Texas Business Directory* noted that Hynson Springs were "open all the year to Invalids and other Visitors," at rates of $2 per day. Also known as Iron Mountain Springs, these springs—some reports say more than a hundred springs emerged from the hillside—were especially noted as a summer resort. Because of the high elevation, the nineteenth-century populace fled here from the mosquito-ridden lowlands. During the Civil War three hundred men used the water from fifty springs to tan leather for the Confederacy. In 1860 Colonel Hynson bought the

40. Hynson Springs, Texas, ca. 1900. Author's postcard collection.

springs, built a house, and fifteen years later marketed the place by hiring a stage, carriages, and hacks to make daily trips to the springs from Marshall (see fig. 40). In 1890 Charlie Randall bought the springs and built a 120-room hotel, noted for its veranda, which was more than a mile long. Hotel Randall's mailing card boasted "no malaria, no mosquitoes, 120 all outside rooms, resident physician in attendance, pool, billiards and other amusements, hacks meet all trains." Around 1905, the Inter-State Investment Company sought to market Hynson Springs as a townsite, but had no success. The hotel closed in 1905 and burned down in 1915.

Montvale Springs, near Marshall The 1890 *Geological Survey of Texas* called Montvale a newly organized place of resort, lying on the Marshall and Northwestern Railway, about sixteen miles from Marshall. Brune noted that the railroad served the springs in 1882.

Rosborough Springs, near Marshall A 1859 deposition of John Chisum, assistant surveyor of this tract of land eight miles south of Marshall, mentioned the "noted spring on the Roland Survey—situated near the Trammel Trace," and stated that the spring was "shaded with a grove of Pine timber." Chisum mentioned a family murdered by the Indians at the spring

41. Rosborough Springs, Texas, n.d. Patrons can still fill their jugs from the well under the shed. The pavilion and pool are in the background. Author photo.

in 1838 and a cabin, called Roland cabin, within sight of the spring. In 1884, W. J. Rosborough Sr. purchased the tract that then became Rosborough Springs. In 1897, the *Marshall News Messenger* noted that a two-story hotel and cottages were open to the public, and eighteen different spring waters emerged within a radius of eighteen feet on the grounds. By 1911 the hotel was leased to different management, five springs were under a large pavilion, and the water was shipped. In 1924 David and Willis Driskell purchased the springs, rebuilt the hotel, and added a swimming pool, tennis courts, dance pavilion, and twenty cottages (see fig. 41). In 1933 the hotel burned. Brune noted that the foam from some water was used for skin problems, and other waters supposedly had birth-control powers. The pavilions still stand, and the water continues to flow. While the author was there in 1990, she saw people come to fill their jugs.

HOPKINS COUNTY

Crabtree's Sour Wells, Sulphur Springs Brune noted that more than one hundred springs bubbled up onto the "spring lot," which became a popular camping ground. The mineral springs were known for their medicinal effects by the time the railroad came to town in 1872. Dr. Patton used the water to make his Sour Well Eye Salve. T. Glasscock operated a bathhouse in his resort hotel, and the local Hoskins House offered baths. The 1886 *USGS Bulletin* 32 called two acid, chalybeate wells a "resort" where water was sold. The 1890–91 *Gazetteer* noted that J. W. Crabtree, O. M. Pate, and J. A. Weaver operated mineral "springs" here. Possibly same as Sour Well listed in 1919 (three quarters of a mile west of post office).

HOUSTON COUNTY

Rice Mineral Wells   The 1890–91 *Fourth Annual Report of the Agriculture Bureau* recommended these wells for malaria and rheumatism.

HUNT COUNTY

Campbell Mineral Wells   There were at least three wells in Campbell, including the one in the city park, where the pavilion became the site of social gatherings. A Campbell citizen, Mr. Garrett, dug a water well and found the water to be mineralized. Mr. John Beasley also dug several wells and organized the Campbell Mineral Wells and Park Company in 1907, according to James Conrad, East Texas State University archivist. It operated until the 1920s.

Mitchell Well, Greenville   In 1923, the USGS reported mineral water sold from here. A local resident, Mr. Zack Ryan remembered the well being south of town in a section called Mineral Heights before 1920. He called the free water "better than Tylenol."

KAUFMAN COUNTY

Crystal Spring, Terrell   The USGS listed this spring in 1911 as a source of mineral water, probably for medicinal purposes.

LAMAR COUNTY

Bells Mineral Wells (Blossom Mineral Wells), near Blossom   The 1886 *USGS Bulletin* 32 called the four saline springs a "resort" and "to some extent [used] commercially." The waters were possibly the same as the Carlsbad Dyspepsia Spring noted in 1907. The 1911 USGS Water Supply Paper 276, by C. Gordon, reported that "a well 117 feet deep put down near the depot several years ago yields a small supply of mineralized water which is regarded locally as having valuable mineral properties." Possibly the same as Hefner Wells listed in 1919 (one-quarter mile west of post office) and/or the Beauchamp Wells reported by the 1923 USGS report on mineral waters.

Bloys' Well, Paris   In 1932 A. Neville noted that this well had been famous for fifty or more years, and that young folks used to walk out to the well for an afternoon jaunt. A mile east of the well, I. Bernstein dug a well and bottled its water. His son used to drive a tank wagon around the city to sell the water. According to Neville, some people joked that Bernstein had "doctored" the water because it tasted so horrible.

MARION COUNTY

Bangus Springs, southeast of county, near Louisiana The 1890–91 *Fourth Annual Report of the Agriculture Bureau* noted these springs.

MONTGOMERY COUNTY

Mineral Springs (Double), 3.1 miles south of Montgomery Brune noted that people often stayed a month to partake of the one fresh and one mineral spring.

NACOGDOCHES COUNTY

Aqua Vitae Wells, Nacogdoches The USGS listed these wells as the source of mineral water in 1911 and 1919. When they first opened in 1909, the promoters had dug two wells, erected a pavilion, and made improvements to the park surroundings. Although the railroad had promised to bring customers, a proposed bathhouse, hotel, and other improvements never materialized.

Shawnee Mineral Springs, 9.3 miles south of Nacogdoches on Southland Paper Company land Brune noted the Indian mounds nearby and the stories from nearby residents that people used to camp at the springs for health reasons.

Stoker, 4.3 miles west of Martinsville The 1914 USGS Water Supply Paper 335 called this spring a "local resort."

Sulphur Spring, fourteen miles southeast of Nacogdoches Probably Oil Springs. The 1890 *Second Annual Report of the Geological Survey of Texas* indicated that the property was improved by the building of a pavilion and a wall around the spring: "Visitors formerly came in wagons with their families and camped out for several days."

Weatherly Spring (also spelled Weatherby in some sources), Garrison The 1890 *Second Annual Report of the Geological Survey of Texas* reported that the property was "recently improved" by building a circular wall three feet in diameter and an octagonal wooden pavilion thirty feet in diameter. A company, partly financed by the city, organized to build a hotel. The 1914 USGS Water Supply Paper 335 called this "white spring" a "local resort." Ed Weatherly, proprietor, placed an ad in the 1914–15 *Texas Gazetteer* call-

---

Weatherly Well
-- WATER --
ED. M. WEATHERLY, Proprietor

A specific for all forms of Stomach
and Kidney Troubles.

PRICE — First Case of twelve one-half
gallon bottles, $2.75; Crates refilled, $1.00.
Refund on Crate, $1.75.

GARRISON, TEXAS

---

42. Weatherly Well advertisement, *Texas State Gazetteer,* 1914–15. Courtesy of Center for American History, University of Texas at Austin.

ing his water "a specific for all forms of stomach and kidney troubles" (see fig. 42). The directory noted that large quantities of water were shipped to all points. In 1923 the USGS reported that a hotel here could accommodate fifty guests. In 1966 the Garrison Lions Club planned to "rejuvenate" the old well by recurbing, cleaning it, and making the water useable.

NEWTON COUNTY

Myers Mineral Well, Kirbyville   In 1911 the USGS listed this well as a source of mineral water, probably for medicinal purposes.

PANOLA COUNTY

Brown Springs, near Cozart   According to the 1914 USGS Water Supply Paper 335, this spring was "noted as a neighborhood resort for about 35 years, and recently a few temporary cabins have been erected for the accommodation of visitors."

Midyett (originally known as Breckenridge Springs), sixteen miles from Carthage   In 1870 D. Richardson noted that "Breckinridge Spring [*sic*] [was] one of the most valuable mineral springs in Texas or the South." The spring, although recognized in the 1850s, was developed as a health resort in the 1880s. Big Jack Midyett curbed and improved it around 1885. According to the 1890–91 *Fourth Annual Report of the Agriculture Bureau,* the spring was believed "to possess medicinal properties of great value" and was especially "recommended for kidney and liver troubles." The village then thrived until after World War I. Mrs. Nugent, daughter of Jack Midyett, remembered the arched bridge covering the marshy area that the spring

43. Midyett, Texas, 1990. Note the covered shed with benches and the cover over the well. Author photo.

formed as it flowed freely. Her mother said that on Sunday afternoons the ladies in their long dresses, hats, and umbrellas would parade across it in a procession. The summer resort town had a hotel, saloon, school, church, and three stores. In 1979 the Midyett family rebuilt the spring shed as accurately as they remembered it, with the exception of the benches that used to extend all the way around the interior (see fig. 43). Mrs. Nugent remembered the springs fondly: "It was a community gathering place. It added something to the value of life that we have lost."

RED RIVER COUNTY

Coleman Springs, six miles southeast of Annona   According to the 1886 *USGS Bulletin* 32, these three chalybeate and sulphureted springs were used to some extent as a "resort."

RUSK COUNTY

In 1879, Homer Thrall, an early Methodist minister, mentioned several springs in the county: "One near Mt. Enterprise, which is considered very valuable and is much resorted to by invalids for its healing qualities . . . another southeast of Mt. Enterprise, some four or five miles distant, considered good in cases of dropsy and other diseases" (now on Temple-Inland Lumber Company property).

Mineral Spring, 0.75 miles east of the old town of Eulalie, 1.9 miles north of Caledonia The 1914 USGS Water Supply Paper 335 called this spring a "local resort."

Welch's Spring, near Brachfield In 1904 artd again in 1905, camp meetings took place here. According to Brune, one of the seven springs here contained sulphur and iron. People gathered here on Sundays, and some came to camp or stay in the hotel.

White Oak Spring, Tatum The 1914 USGS Water Supply Paper 335 said that the iron and sulphur water of this 70° F spring was used medicinally. Brune noted that only seeps remained.

SMITH COUNTY

Headache Springs, Tyler Because of a Civil War blockade, a surgeon from Virginia erected a pharmaceutical laboratory in a frame building here to manufacture medicines and liniments. In brainstorming why the spring was called "headache," Dallas newspaperman Frank Tolbert surmised that it was because of the busthead whiskey produced during the war. Tolbert suggested that it was due to the aspirin-like taste of the water, since aspirin was not invented until 1893. It is assumed that people drank this water since the mid-1800s because it was believed healthful.

Riviere Wells 1, 2, and 3, Tyler In 1911 and 1919 the USGS listed these wells as sources of mineral water, probably for medicinal purposes. After Richard Riviere moved to his homestead on Bois D'Arc Street in 1896, he sank a well and decided to bottle his newly discovered mineral water. The Riviere Company also bottled Coca-Cola and later Dr Pepper.

TITUS COUNTY

Red Mineral Springs, Mount Pleasant In the 1890s, Jessie Reed began to develop the springs as a resort by building some "camp houses." The 1890–91 *Texas Gazetteer* noted Reed's Red Springs in its business directory (see fig. 44). In 1907 Reed sold the property to the Red Springs Mineral Development Company. In 1908 the company opened the Dellwood Hotel on a hill by the springs (see fig. 45). The hotel, in the shape of the letter "Y," contained seventy rooms, a dining room, a barbershop, a parlor, and steam baths. In the lobby were fountains where clear, blue, and red water flowed. The company also built a shed around the springs, a pavilion, a pool, and a bathhouse. A mule car running on wooden rails carried passengers from the

44. Red Mineral Springs, Mount Pleasant, Texas, early 1900s. Author's postcard collection. The camp houses date to the 1890s.

45. The Dellwood, Mount Pleasant, Texas, 1909. Author's postcard collection.

town to the park. In 1911 the USGS listed these springs as a source of mineral water, probably for medicinal purposes. In the summer of 1910 a Confederate soldiers' reunion was held in the park. The hotel then closed that year, and after brief stints as a boys' prep school and a boardinghouse, the building burned down in 1925. Local historian Traylor Russell lists the primary reasons for the failure of the resort as a lack of advertising and transportation inadequacies. Brune noted that the springs no longer flowed but were contained in a tank in the park.

Roach Well, near Mount Pleasant   In 1908 and 1919 the USGS listed this well as a source of mineral water, probably for medicinal purposes.

TRINITY COUNTY

Alford's Bluff   The 1878 I & G.N. Railway Guide mentioned the Chalybeate springs at Alford's Bluff, as well as the Sulphur springs near Trinity Station, possibly formerly Bath.

TYLER COUNTY

Mineral Spring, near Mount Hope   In 1879 Homer Thrall commented that this sulphur spring "would be an excellent watering place if conveniently fitted up and attended to properly."

Sulphur Springs, northeast of Chester   The Alabamas and Coushattas reportedly used the spring for curative value. Before 1890, Dr. S. P. Willson operated a sanitorium here. Phoebe Armstrong in her book about this area mentioned that by the 1890s there was no hotel or sanitorium, but it was reported that people still came for their health and stayed in a small house. Brune noted in 1978 that the springs were largely buried in sand.

Sulphur Spring, near Rockland   The 1890–91 *Fourth Annual Report of the Agriculture Bureau* called this a "fine sulphur spring." Brune found the spring to be dry.

VAN ZANDT COUNTY

Myrtle Springs, 2.5 miles northeast of Hooks   On November 19, 1891, an article in the *Herald* contended that the springs "must" become a health resort, asserting that a hotel and infirmary would soon be established. It further stated:

> The chalybeate water is an excellent tonic, and speedily builds up and gives tone to the run down system. So strongly are these waters impregnated with minerals that horses refuse to drink of them. The record is unbroken by a single failure. Invalids come to the springs and leave healed. Our claim is based on demonstration. We challenge the oval Earth, 25,000 miles in

circumference, to produce a mineral water that can give speedier, more thorough, and lasting effects than the sulpho-saline of Myrtle Springs . . . the Ferro-Manganese waters of Myrtle Springs is the best tonic in the world.

Brune noted that a park and lake with gondolas also graced the site, originally called Holden Springs but changed to Myrtle Springs because of the abundance of crepe myrtle grown here.

WALKER COUNTY

Carolina (earlier known as Bath)   Young noted the settlement of Bath on his 1836 map. According to William Bollaert, Carolina, lying in a prairie behind the 150-foot-high bluffs on the Trinity River, had around twenty deserted buildings in 1844. Carolina was noted on De Cordova's 1849 map and on Johnson's 1863 and 1870 maps as well.

Salinilla Springs   In 1855 Disturnell located these white and salt sulphur springs by the Trinity River. These might be the sulphur springs noted on the 1866 Colton map as eleven miles northwest of Huntsville (and on Johnson's 1859 and 1870 maps between Nelson and S. Bidias Creeks). If this assumption is correct, in 1858 J. De Cordova called this a "very fine spring supersaturated with magnesia and possessing all the healing property that can be expected." He also placed this spring near the Bedais [*sic*].

Tuscaloosa Springs (also Wyser's Bluff)   Situated on the Trinity, ten miles north of Huntsville and thirty miles south of Crockett. On his 1849 map De Cordova noted its location at the mouth of Mill Creek. In 1858 a stage stop with accommodations operated at these red, black, and white sulphur springs. The 1860 Census reported G. A. Wyser as hotelkeeper. In 1866 the *San Antonio Daily Herald* noted it as a "very strong sulphur spring." The springs evidently still operated until 1870, as Johnson noted it on his map. The 1886 *USGS Bulletin* 32 said that locals used this sulphureted spring.

WOOD COUNTY

Chalybeate Springs (earlier called Musgrove Springs), three miles east of Winnsboro   The 1886 *USGS Bulletin* 32 called this chalybeate spring a "resort." The 1890–91 *Fourth Annual Report of the Agriculture Bureau* stated that it was recommended for diseases of the blood. Although established as a health resort in 1866 by L. M. Musgrove, Walker Fore built a twenty-seven-room, two-story hotel in the 1880s, which operated until 1895. The hotel-turned-private-residence was torn down in the 1930s. The village once contained a post office, a depot, general stores, a school, and other businesses, which no longer survive. According to Winnsboro radio commentator Bill Jones, this was a favorite retreat for Sulphur Springs folks. Mothers would arrive by train during the week, followed by the fathers on Saturday for a party, often feted by a cornet band concert and lit up with Japanese lanterns. Guests would descend stairs on the hillside to drink from the spring, which poured into a concrete trough, covered by a gazebo. Some even say that a conveyor belt brought water buckets up to the hotel for consumption.

Mineola The 1884 *Texas Gazetteer* noted several mineral springs in town. The Texas and Pacific engineers had stopped here to replenish their water supply. In 1892 a drilling crew, looking for salt, instead found mineral water. Henry Baird drilled the first well. A chemical analysis determined that the water had curative properties, as reported in a 1941 issue of the *Dallas Morning News*. In 1893 the USGS noted that Mineola Mineral Wells was a place of resort. A 1913 issue of *Texas Magazine* noted that "in the center of the city is a well 1,400 feet deep, flowing a rich lithia water free to all and highly recommended by leading physicians. Many gallons of water have been shipped to neighboring towns annually." The *Mineola Monitor* noted in 1936 that the mineral water well in the town square was lost because of bad piping.

North Central

CALLAHAN COUNTY

Putnam Mineral Well, Putnam In 1911 the USGS listed this well as a source of mineral water, probably for medicinal purposes. A 1912 prospectus entitled "Putnam—the Great West Texas Health and Pleasure Resort," put together by the Putnam Commercial Club and the Putnam Mineral Water Company, boasted how since 1910 the town had made improvements such as "the new Carter-Holland Hotel (American plan, low rates, modern equipment)" and "a new up-to-date Mineral Bath House, adjoining hotel and a bottling plant" (see fig. 46). With one thousand business and residential lots for sale and on the main line of the Texas and Pacific, the town had advantages to be advertised: "Putnam Mineral Waters are Dame Nature's own prescription for suffering humanity. They have no equal." In the same brochure hawking the investment potential of "inexhaustible fertile soils and rich deposits of oil, gas, coal, copper, silver and gold" was an analysis of the

46. The Carter-Holland Hotel and adjoining mineral bathhouse, Putnam, Texas, 1911. Author's postcard collection.

three mineral wells by a Houston chemist, the medicinal value of the water as proclaimed by a Fort Worth City Health Officer, and numerous testimonials by professional people around the state. Trains stopped at the hotel for meals, allowing passengers to sample the waters. In addition, the brochure boasted that the resort was listed in the schedule of health and winter resorts by every road in the Southwestern Passenger Association. Testimonials usually included a comparison to other waters. One man, a state labor commissioner, wrote that he received more benefit for his rheumatism from the water of Well No. 2 than he did from that of "Marlin Wells, Mineral Wells, and Hot Springs." After oil was discovered nearby, the town neglected the resort business. Dr. R. G. Milling, a rubbing doctor, turned the hotel into a sanitarium that operated until about 1918. He was described as a "handsome man with a distinguished air about him" who "wore a frock-tailed coat and his long hair reached to his shoulders." Evidently his treatments were quite an affair—an orchestra even furnished background music. John Berry wrote in his article for the *West Texas Historical Association Yearbook* that for Saturday night dances, people from nearby Baird would hire a coach, hitch the coach on a freight train to Putnam, and then leave the coach on the switch until the one o'clock train would come through and take them home. After the discovery of oil in the area, the company ceased to function as people pinned their hopes on the new liquid treasure. Locals remembered that the water was still being consumed through the 1960s, when the interstate highway came through, resulting in the demolition of the hotel and the covering up of the wells.

DALLAS COUNTY

Gill Well, Dallas   Dr. J. G. Mills and J. D. Aldredge piped water from a well drilled near Reverchon Park in 1903 to a bathhouse and natatorium. This well operated until the Depression, when residue stopped the flow of water in the pipes.

DENTON COUNTY

Brock's Mineral Well, near Denton   The USGS listed this well in 1908, 1911, and 1919 as a source of mineral water, probably for medicinal purposes.

EASTLAND COUNTY

Carbon   Gene Fowler mentions a mineral water bathing establishment here in the early 1900s.

Mangum   Halfway between Cisco and Carbon on the Houston Texas Central Railway line (later the MKT), promoters of Mangum advertised eighteen wells. Pete Mangum discovered the water in 1902 and started the Mangum Mineral Water Company. The Switzers built the Don Carlos Hotel about 1908, and R. W. Mancill ran a split-log bathhouse behind the hotel. There was a distinct advantage to its being a railroad town, besides the fact that it was an eating station for two trains. Its waters were shipped around Texas and to adjoining states. A chemist said the waters resembled those of New York and the Sheboygan waters of Wisconsin. By the late 1910s only the Maurice and Mangum wells operated. The Don Carlos Hotel lasted until the late 1930s.

ELLIS COUNTY

Milford Mineral Wells, Milford   In 1908 the USGS listed these wells as mineral water sources (see fig. 47).

ERATH COUNTY

Duffau's Sulphur Wells, Duffau   The 1886 *USGS Bulletin* 32 called these seven wells a "resort." One well, one mile east of Duffau, gained a reputation as a spa after the discovery of mineral water in 1882. Several bathhouses and a hotel served those who came to bathe and drink the water, and a hack met train passengers at Hico. The 1914–15 *Texas Gazetteer* mentioned the Duffau Mineral Wells Development Company as a business enterprise.

47. Milford Resort, Texas, 1908. Author's postcard collection.

GRAYSON COUNTY

Cedar Springs near Cedar Mills The 1886 *USGS Bulletin* 32 noted that these five sulphureted and chalybeate springs were once a resort.

Cook's Springs The 1892 *Texas Gazetteer* noted this town, 5.5 miles northeast of Sherman on the MKT line, as a health resort.

Tioga In 1881 the Texas and Pacific Railroad reached this site, where the workmen stopped to drink water from a well dug almost twenty years earlier. Three years later a local blacksmith supposedly noticed that the burn on his hand healed more quickly when he bathed it in the water from a spring behind his shop. He and his brother thereafter marketed a mineral water salve and shipped the water from his mineral spring located west of the railroad. Other entrepreneurs marketed the water as Atlas Water, Radium mineral water, and Star Condensed mineral water. In 1903 the *Texas and Pacific Quarterly* noted that the Bradley Cottage was the only hotel, but there were numerous private boardinghouses accommodating guests (see fig. 48). Around 1900, 150 to 200 people stayed at the Bradley Cottage in Tioga. The only two states not represented in the register supposedly were Vermont and Oregon, and the proprietor offered a free meal to anyone from those states. According to the 1914–15 *Texas Gazetteer,* Tioga boasted of several mineral

48. Rains Mineral Wells and Bradley Cottage, Tioga, Texas, ca. 1910s. Author's postcard collection.

wells "noted for their medical virtues, including the Tioga Sanitarium and Water Co. and the Bradley Cottage, and the Samuel Wilson Hotel and mineral well" (see fig. 49). Around the Depression, the resort lost much patronage. In 1947 fire destroyed one of the main bathhouses and shut down the wells. Then a new proprietor took over the old Wilson Hotel and replaced the old bathhouse. In 1965 another bathhouse opened for business and continued operating into the 1970s, along with a small bottling operation. By the 1980s the mineral water was no longer marketed (see fig. 50). Yet in 1991, according to Mrs. Corine Tolleson, a local citizen, people still got the water from two private homes for medical use. She used it herself for kidney infections. She claimed that people called her from as far away as California to find out if the baths were still given here.

X-Ray Spring, Whitesboro Mentioned by USGS in 1908.

HOOD COUNTY

Thorp Spring In 1871, Captain Sam Milliken came to the Thorp Spring, already noted for its waters, and built a springhouse and bathing rooms. The summer resort soon lost favor as more resorts became established in West Texas. In 1969 Lake Granbury covered up the springs.

JACK COUNTY

Wizard Wells The social column in the January 27, 1883, *Vineyard County Guide Post* noted: "Mr. Kirk, wife and daughter of Montague County are camping here and using the water. Mrs. Kirk has tapeworm." The pro-

```
————— DRINK —————
TIOGA MINERAL WATER
" Good for What Ails You "
————— CURES —————
Rheumatism, Constipation,
Indigestion, Liver, Stomach and
Kidney Troubles
Owned. Bottled and Shipped By
TIOGA SANITARIUM & WATER COMPANY
TIOGA, TEXAS
```

49. Tioga advertisement, *Texas State Gazetteer,* 1914–15. Courtesy of Center for American History, University of Texas at Austin.

motional edition also advised that "persons locating here and persons too poor to pay this tax will be allowed to use the water free of all charge." After G. W. Vineyard dug the well, the water was noted to have the purgative power of castor oil. Around 1880, after Vineyard found relief for eye and leg infections, people from Oklahoma and North Texas began to camp around Bean's Creek. Eventually a school, churches, a newspaper office, a post office, a general store, hotels, and bathhouses dotted the landscape. The town of Vineyard was platted in 1882, but the name eventually changed to Wizard Wells in 1915, to suggest some magical powers of the waters. In an early brochure, "beautiful Wizard Wells" was billed as the "modern health resort." A three-story Mountain-View Hotel and Bathhouse (opened in 1909), the Wizard Bathhouse, and the Crystal Bathhouse, later called the Lone Star Bathhouse, accommodated healthseekers. In 1964, when Frank Tolbert visited, the Wizard Bathhouse was standing abandoned. In 1964 journalist Jerry Flemmons interviewed seventy-year-old Tom Ware, who said, "I seen people come to this town by the thousands. I seen the time when there's a camp under every tree big enough to make shade in the summer. The hotels would start in early morning giving baths as fast as they could all day long." Wolf hunter Bill De Long told of several hot baths that reduced the swelling caused by a rattlesnake bite. By the 1960s the town was only a ghost of its

50. Banner Well, Tioga, Texas, 1990. Author photo.

51. Wizard Well, Texas, 1990. Author photo.

former self; it officially closed in 1968, but was revived again in the 1970s by Jim Davis of Jacksboro. Davis said his treatments would clear out the body and rid it of parasites. After the twenty-one-day treatment, he and his guests would celebrate by having a crutch burning. He said that Pepsi-Cola had been interested in putting a bottling plant there but did not. The seven vacant apartments still standing by the first well (commemorated by a historical marker—see fig. 51) opened in 1917, and the Lone Star Bathhouse took its first bather in 1929. The hotel was added in 1949.

The hotel/bathhouse finally shut down to the public in 1984. A ghostly wall sign barely revealing the words HOT MINERAL BATHS, and the old well are the only visible reminders of past days of resort glory.

MONTAGUE COUNTY

Queen's Peak Medical Wells, Bowie An April 2, 1950, *Dallas Morning News* article quoted from an 1883 booklet titled "The Little Wonder of the West": "Queen's Peak Medical Wells—so justly celebrated for medicinal water and salubrious atmosphere, scenery, and pretty women are situated about four and one half miles due north of this place (Bowie). As a health resort, it rivals Aitken, South Carolina."

Mineral Wells See chapter 5.

Oran In 1905 there was a well gaining fame for its medical value. Dr. J. M. Patterson owned it at the time and soon erected a two-story hotel. Thirty-five years later, the *Palo Pinto County Star* boasted that the waters at the time were as good as those at Mineral Wells. Later, the paper continued its report: "The mineral waters of the place are becoming quite popular and to accommodate the visitors a 16 room hotel has been erected and is opened to the public a few days since by F.M. Bailey, a public spirited citizen of the town. . . . Ten or twelve wells will soon be sunk, and the little town is expected to soon become a thriving city." In 1907 (and again in 1911), the USGS mentioned the Allison, Crystal, and Patterson Springs as sources of mineral water. The 1914–15 *Texas Gazetteer* noted the Read and Bailey Mineral Waters in its business directory. The wells were abandoned around the 1920s.

Eureka No. 2 Well, East Weatherford In 1911 the USGS listed this well as a source of mineral water, probably for medicinal purposes. Possibly also Love Mineral Well mentioned in 1907, and/or Edward's Well, mentioned in 1908.

Sheboygan Mineral Wells, near Weatherford In 1908 the USGS listed these wells as mineral water sources.

Glen Rose In 1885 a letter reprinted in the *Glen Rose Citizen* noted that "in the village there are about 40 perpetually flowing artesian wells of pure white sulphur water and as many freestone flowing wells as people desire. From Dallas to this Texas Nile and the eternal fountains of health." The hills and bluffs around the Paluxy River proved to be popular for camping: "A large number of families have visited the Glen this summer and the cosy cheerful camps, merry laugh and jovial abandon have enlivened the umbrageous groves along the enchanted valley almost continually since the first of June. On the bluff near Mr. Jackson's glorious fountain of life, health and joy, are six from Hill County." Not all seemed enchanted, however, for in September another account noted that "all of them complained of the hog nuisance, and many of them left earlier than they intended on that account." In 1903 the first of many sanitariums opened in Glen Rose. A variety of healers here, some of whom gave mineral water baths, included chiropractors, magnetic doctors, and massage therapists.

In its early days Glen Rose lacked facilities to greet visitors. In 1886 Glen Rose claimed forty-five to fifty artesian wells of white sulphur water along one and a quarter miles of the Paluxy River, and although campers populated the area, "the accommodations [were] wholly insufficient—that people in quest of rest, recreation or health at a summer resort desire such change and entertainment as is not offered in Glen Rose." The locale's popularity as a spa was hampered, however, by its not being on a railroad line and being a day's ride by hack from Cleburne. A 1918 article in the *Christian Courier* described this town:

> But the great value and drawing card of Glen Rose is its mineral waters. The whole country about not only abounds in the beauties of nature, rugged cliffs, boulders, overhanging rocks, hills and woodland parks, and picturesque scenes, but gushing springs and fountains. Deep wells have been bored and capped and there gushes out a stream of sulphur or iron water. Hundreds and thousands of people come every season to drink this water and to rest and recreate. Hundreds of automobiles will come in from Cleburne, Fort Worth, Dallas and other towns and cities, tents are stretched everywhere in the parks, boarding places are crowded—hundreds to whom this water proves a boon and a cure to the "ills that flesh is heir to."

A 1925 brochure noted two hundred flowing white sulphur wells. The water had many uses. According to one local in a book about the legends of Glen Rose, it kept the mites off birds and chickens and made good whiskey. In 1938 the *Dallas Morning News* reported that the town of 1,500 had nine parks, three sanitariums, and two bathhouses to serve its reported 250,000 visitors. From the Stump Well gushed four different kinds of mineral waters.

The distinct sulphur odor of the waters began to disappear in the early 1960s. The Stump Well was torn out in the 1950s, and the springs and wells eventually stopped flowing.

TARRANT COUNTY

Arlington Mineral Well   In 1892 the town drilled a well and struck mineral water. At first only the horses drank it, but after 1900 someone found a medicinal value to it. A sanitarium operated from 1904 to 1910, and a plant utilized the water for crystals in the 1930s. A favorite initiation for college freshmen was to make them drink the water, according to a 1972 article in the *Citizen Journal*. After being capped in 1952 because it obstructed traffic

52. Arlington Mineral Well, Arlington, Texas, ca. 1930s. Author's postcard collection.

in the center of downtown, the water was piped to the library (see fig. 52). In 1984, after pesticides were found in the water, city officials substituted city water in the fountain.

YOUNG COUNTY

Stovall Hot Wells Close to the small town of South Bend and ten miles from Graham, this place was one of the last operating spas in Texas. In drilling for oil on his plantation in 1929, Mr. E. C. Stovall discovered the hot, oily water, which seemed to cure a skin disease of some Mexican workers. He erected a hotel and provided a cafe, a barbershop, a bathhouse, cottages, playgrounds, croquet, tennis courts, and skeet shooting grounds. Weekly community sings took place in the lobby. The skeet grounds were famous in the 1930s, and "skeet artists of the nation" shot there each week. In the early 1990s the painted tin siding, reminiscent of the old CHEW MAIL POUCH TOBACCO signs, still proclaimed BOIL OUT THE POISON and BATHE YOUR WAY TO BETTER HEALTH. Interest did not wane in the 101° sulphurous water until the complex burned in the summer of 1994. One of the last owners, Judy and Roy King, reported a loyal following; for example, 221 pilgrims bathed there in February 1991. Investors may possibly rebuild this historic resort.

Central

BELL COUNTY

Isby Well, near Belton The 1890–91 *Fourth Annual Report of the Agriculture Bureau* recommended this well and Leon Spring for general debility and rheumatism.

Salado Mineral Wells Possibly same as Key's Wells, listed by USGS in 1911 as mineral water source, probably for medicinal purposes. The 1901 USGS *Twenty-first Annual Report* included a report from a local resident commenting on the seven wells within a six-mile radius, four miles east of the town, all having strong sulphur water. However, this report could instead have targeted the sulphur springs, three miles east/northeast of Salado. A 1925 *Dallas News* article spoke of the "wonderful cures which have been effected by the well" and the fact that "the women of Salado once contributed a fountain to go over the well" but it had fallen away. The 1900 annual of Thomas Arnold High School included analyses of two wells. Well 1 was supposed to cure indigestion and stomach problems and was located in front of the present Stagecoach Inn (northeast of the entrance but west of the road). Patricia Barton, a local citizen, noted that the bathhouse at Well 2, near the Main Street crossing of Salado Creek, washed away in the flood of 1921.

BEXAR COUNTY

Dullnig's Well The 1897 *Geology of the Edwards Plateau* located this well six miles southeast of the Bexar County Courthouse. In 1907 the USGS reported its use. Although Austrian immigrant George Dullnig could never make a go of his resort, his mineral water won the highest award at the St. Louis Exposition in 1905 for the best display of mineral waters at the exposition. The various waters from eleven wells drilled around 1886 on his ranch were more famous than the resort. Dullnig shipped the iron water and also dispensed it at his downtown store and bank. After Dullnig died in 1908, Herbert Gregory took over the ranch house and created the Dullnig Wells Hotel and Bathhouse. Guests stayed in this two-story structure while taking baths in the nearby bathhouse. Cottages also housed guests, as the wells were sufficiently far from town. The 104° F sulphur water emerged from 2,205 feet. The enterprise closed around 1925 and the structures were torn down in 1935.

Harlandale Hot Sulphur Well, three miles south of San Antonio, on Corpus Christi Boulevard In 1911 the *Light* announced plans to build a bathhouse at the new wells: "The baths will be entirely for curative purposes and will be conducted in the same manner as other great watering places of America and Europe." It also noted that there would not be a large swimming pool since many people objected to one because of the "unnecessary noise." The baths were arranged in successive order—showers first, then pools of 100°F, a room of 150°F, a mud bath, an electric bath, and finally, cold plunges. An ad for the resort in the 1911 *Light* declared that the business, open every day from 7 A.M. to 7 P.M., was "endorsed by hundreds of San Antonio's leading citizens who have already taken our luxurious baths." The bathhouse offered Turkish, Russian, Roman, electric, and mud baths, steam and vapor rooms, reception rooms, cooling and massage rooms and a barbershop and hair salon. The resort closed around 1920, and the property eventually became part of the Harlandale Independent School District.

Hot Wells, San Antonio   See chapters 5 and 6.

Mineral or Indian Springs, southeast of San Antonio on Calaveras Creek   Brune noted that Indians valued these waters and that early settlers held camp meetings here. The springs no longer flow.

Terrell Wells, five miles south of San Antonio, on Pleasanton Road   The 1897 *Geology of the Edwards Plateau* located this well in the suburb of San Jose. Around 1895, Dr. Frederick Terrell drilled for oil but found hot sulphur water instead. He first built a public swimming area, then a bathhouse, and finally a hotel. When he sold it to a Missouri investment company, they built a trolley line to the establishment. The completed sanitarium grounds contained five acres of a parklike setting, including a sixty-room hotel, a covered passageway to the bathhouse, and "camp houses" (see fig. 53). A 1910 brochure bragged that the well contained radium and made a ludicrous pronouncement: "Now if a body could be charged with radium, say once in five years, there is no reason why we could not live forever." The wells closed sometime around the 1940s.

BOSQUE COUNTY

Mineral Well, near Meridian   The 1890–91 *Fourth Annual Report of Agriculture Bureau* endorsed this water for rheumatism, neuralgia, and dysentery.

BRAZOS COUNTY

Manganic Wells, three miles northwest of Bryan   The McQueen mineral well reported in 1890 by the Agriculture Bureau is the same well. In 1883 improvements consisted of a one-story building, a row of cottages for boarders, several bathhouses, and a latticed summer house over the principal

53. Terrell Wells, San Antonio, Texas, ca. 1920s. Author's postcard collection.

well, which was seventy-five feet deep. Another well supplied water for the bathhouses. McQueen, the proprietor, delivered the water to Bryan each day and shipped it across the state, according to the *Texas Prairie Flower* in 1883. The 1893 *Fourth Annual Report* of USGS called this a health resort. In the 1892 *Texas Gazetteer*, C. Parsons advertised that the proprietor was now prepared to receive and accommodate guests here at the "wonderful healing waters" of Manganic Wells, "nature's own remedy and infallible health restorer." Also pictured is a small pavilion over the well (see fig. 54). There were three separate wells located half a mile west of the Houston and Texas Central Railway.

Sulphur Springs, Millican The 1886 *USGS Bulletin* 32 called these eight springs a resort. One of these springs may possibly be the Boiling Spring reported in the 1893 *Fourth Annual Report* of USGS as a health "resort." This spring emerged from the west bank of the Navasota River on the J. Gray headright.

BROWN COUNTY

Well, Brownwood According to the Texas Water Development Board, A. C. Snyder drilled a well in 1916 to check for oil. The Jane Johnson Clinic later used this water from the Ellenburger Aquifer.

Wonderful Healing Waters.

"Manganic Wells."

NATURE'S OWN REMEDY
AND

INFALLIBLE HEALTH RESTORER.

SURE, SPEEDY, SAFE.

Situated near Bryan, Texas, ½ mile west of H. & T. C. Ry.

The Best Mineral Waters Yet Discovered.

PROPERTIES : A I. Tonic, Appetizer, and Blood Purifier, Alterative, Laxative, Astringent, Diuretic, Diaphoretic, Antiperiodic, Etc.

Especially Pre-eminent in allaying Inflammation in any Part of the System,

Already developed are three separate and distinct wells, each affording a different mineral water of incalculable value, and possessing wonderful medicinal and healing properties. Most miraculous cures of various diseases, malignant and of long standing, have been effected by the use of these waters, in a remarkably short time, the effect usually being permanent and lasting, as attested by numerous certificates in possession of the proprietor, who is now prepared to receive and accommodate guests at extremely moderate rates. The rooms at this watering place are elegantly furnished, well ventilated, and erected with a special view to the comfort of guests, who are assured of every reasonable care, polite and courteous attention, good, substantial diet, well cooked and prepared.

☞ Special and prompt attention given to shipment of MANGANIC WATER to all points.
☞ For full Descriptive Pamphlet containing Analysis of Waters, Certificates of Cures, Rates, etc.,

Address

(See also page 912.)

C. C. PARSONS, Proprietor,
BRYAN P. O., TEXAS.

54. Manganic Wells advertisement, *Texas State Gazetteer,* 1892. Courtesy of Center for American History, University of Texas at Austin.

CALDWELL COUNTY

Burdette's Wells (also Burditt's Wells)   The 1886 *USGS Bulletin 32* called this saline spring a "resort," used commercially. The 1876 Galveston, Harrisburg, and San Antonio Railway's *Description of Western Texas* mentioned Dr. Burditt's sour well as "much resorted to by invalids." Although supposedly discovered in the 1850s, in 1876 the well, a hotel suitable for seventy-five people, and temporary cottages accommodated visitors. In an 1879 San Antonio newspaper, Dr. Burditt advertised his mineral water establishment: "[T]his water and plenty to eat is the uniform prescription, and the Tonkaway Balsam for coughs, colds, consumption, and sometimes a little medical aid in nervous diseases, constitutes the medical treatment of the place." Walker's Exchange in San Antonio sold the water at five cents a glass, fifty cents a gallon, and five gallons at $2. The resort became a "whistle stop" and spur on the San Antonio and Aransas Pass Railroad. In 1877 the *Galveston Daily News* reported that twenty boarders, five of whom hailed from Galveston, were at the well (see fig. 55). One produced a glowing testimonial—"The hair and whiskers of that veteran Galvestonian S. Vansickle, are turning from gray to black under the influence of the waters."

The management changed hands in 1895 and again in 1908. Around 1911, the Burdette Mineral Wells and Hotel Company set out to create a first-class resort. The company's investment brochure, "Burdette Wells: Where the Water Fairy Dwells," noted that "already a $5,000 modern bottling plant, a $5,000 amusement pavilion and a twenty-room hotel and cottages are now installed." The prospectus projected a new $40,000 hotel and bathhouse, cement sidewalks, and a cotton gin. Of the platted one thousand business and residential lots, half sold. The resort stopped attracting patrons by the 1920s, according to one local citizen.

Caldwell Springs (also Cardwell Springs) In 1877 the state medical association noted that this watering place and Burditt's "have acquired considerable reputation for their curative properties, and a large number of persons from all portions of Texas and some from other States, have visited them this summer." Located three miles from Burditt's, the springs and a hotel accommodated about thirty boarders in August 1877 and as many campers. By 1908 the name had changed to Rogers' Springs. Mr. Rogers distilled and evaporated the water to produce mineral salts, said to resemble those of Kentucky's Crab Orchard Spring. Brune noted that only seeps remained in the 1970s.

Sour Springs, around seven miles northeast of Luling The 1886 *USGS Bulletin* 32 called these thirty acid springs a "resort," whose waters were also used commercially. These were probably the same springs that the 1878 *Southern and Western Guide to Texas* called Luling Springs. The guide mentioned the large numbers of visitors from the North and East who flocked to the resort and said also that the water was shipped around the country. Brune visited the site in 1975 and noted the limonite concretions present in the sand, the sodium carbonate in the water (thus, called soda), and the decreased flow from thirty years earlier.

Sulphur Spring This spring near the unincorporated town of Atlanta was noted in the *Lockhart Morning Courier* in 1908. According to Brune, the spring was dry in the 1970s, and only a cemetery marked the place.

Dr. H. N. Burditt's

❧SOUR WELL❧

Near Luling, Caldwell County, Texas.

This Card is intended as a general and (as nearly as possible) definite reply to the various inquiries respecting the SOUR WATER, its efficacy, etc., that reach me in a constant flow of correspondence.

A QUALITATIVE ANALYSIS

Of the Sour Water, made by Prof. GEORGE H. KALTEYER, of San Antonio, Texas, gives the following results:

Sulphate of Lime,
Sulphate of Magnesia, in large quantities,
Chloride of Sodium,
Chloride of Potassium,
Carbonate of Iron, in less quantity,

Phosphate and Chloride of Lime, small quantity,
Sulphate of Alumina, Baryta, Strontia, and Silica, a trace,
Free Sulphuric Acid, in large quantity.

The Water is acid and astringent in taste; it acts on the Liver, Bowels, Kidneys, and Skin; it increases the Blood, Appetite and Digestion; cures Liver and Spleen derangement, Bilious Fever, Hectic Fever, Debility, Rheumatism, Erysipelas, Scurvy, bad Ulcers, Skin Eruptions, Dropsy, Dyspepsia, Yellow Jaundice, Bowel and Female Complaints, Piles, Cramps, Colic, Vomiting, Sour Stomach, Constipation, Cholera Infantum, Indigestion, and various diseases instituted and perpetuated by a vitiated condition of the biliary secretions.

All Venereal Diseases, Acute or Chronic Consumption

In the early stage, where recuperative action is sufficient.

It would require strong language and forcible words to establish the virtues of this wonderful water if it were dependent on cards and circulars alone; but the afflicted go their way and tell the great things that happen at the Mineral Well. For further particulars, address,

Dr. H. N. BURDITT,
Luling, Texas.

55. Burditt's Well advertisement, *Texas Business Directory*, 1878. Courtesy of Center for American History, University of Texas at Austin.

FAYETTE COUNTY

Sulphur Springs, near Black Jack Springs, 9.3 miles southwest of La Grange   The 1886 *USGS Bulletin* 32 called these three springs a "resort."

GONZALES COUNTY

Harwood   The 1876 Galveston, Harrisburg, and San Antonio Railway's *Description of Western Texas* mentioned a well about two miles from Harwood. In the 1878 *Texas Business Directory,* Henry Butler advertised his "Great Sour Water of Texas" specifically "for the healing of the nations." He built a hotel half a mile from the depot at Harwood, sank a number of wells, and erected bathhouses near some wells (see fig. 56).

Mineral Springs   In 1867, physician Gideon Lincecum visited Dr. Walker (perhaps T. S. Walker) and his medicinal springs on Wilson's Creek. This was probably the spring noted in an 1866 article in the *San Antonio Daily Herald* as resembling "Sour Lake in taste and general appearance."

Ottine   In 1909 a Houston oil company drilled for oil but ran into a layer of rock. After using a drill bit designed by Howard Hughes, the company cut through the rock but found only 106° F artesian water from 3,400 feet deep. Evidently this abandoned well flooded the surrounding country

56. Harwood Mineral Well advertisement, *Texas Business Directory,* 1878. Courtesy of Center for American History, University of Texas at Austin.

for years, "developing a rustic spa," according to the *Gonzales Inquirer* in 1953. In the 1930s the Civilian Conservation Corps built a concrete rim around the water well. In 1941 the Gonzales Warm Springs Foundation for Crippled Children opened here in the present Palmetto State Park to cater to crippled children. A spring of hot mineralized water flowed into a large circular tank on the grounds and into the swimming pool. Because of corrosion of the pipes, the management stopped using the mineral water in the inside bathing tubs in the 1950s and then in the swimming pool in 1965. Now the Warm Springs Rehabilitation Hospital only uses the water to cut down on water heating costs.

HILL COUNTY

Hubbard Hot Well, Hubbard In 1894 local citizens contributed money to drill for a domestic water source, but they found highly mineralized water. At first a shed covered the site. By 1907 the Hubbard Hot Well Bathhouse, a one-story wooden structure with thirty-six tubs, began operations. John and Willie Woods opened a sanitarium next to the bathhouse. At one time Governor W. Hobby loaned money for the well, according to the *Hubbard City News* in 1981. Hubbard's peak years of growth, 1900 to 1920, can largely be attributed to the mineral water patronage. In 1911 the USGS listed this well as a source of mineral water, probably for medicinal purposes. Sometime around 1926 the bathhouse closed because of corrosion in the pipes, and it burned in 1934. Attempts to dig another well fell through.

KENDALL COUNTY

Kendall County Mineral Springs, three miles west of Boerne The 1886 *USGS Bulletin* 32 called this saline, chalybeate, and sulphureted spring a "resort." The 1890–91 *Fourth Annual Report of Agriculture Bureau* noted the spring's local reputation for treatment of liver and consumption problems.

Sisterdale In 1849 German refugee and geographer Dr. Ernst Kapp settled in Sisterdale with his family and established his Hydropathic Institute, using spring water from a nearby creek. Hermann Lungwitz rendered a pen-and-ink sketch of the various treatments. Frederick Law Olmsted noted that "the delicious brook water has been turned to account by him for the cure of disease, and his house is thrown open to patients." In 1862 Kapp and members of his family closed the institute and returned to Germany.

Park Hotel and Cottages
HANCOCK SULPHUR SPRINGS.

The finest bathing in the world. 202 large and elegantly furnished rooms in a beautiful grove and on a high elevation. Electric Bells in every room.

HENRY HOLTON, Manager. **$2.00 to $3.00 per Day.**

CERTIFICATE OF ANALYSIS OF THE HANCOCK SPRINGS,

By E. WALLER, Ph. D., of New York.   **LAMPASAS, TEXAS.**

Per U. S. Gallon of 231 Cubic Inches.

INGREDIENTS.	GRAINS.
Chloride of sodium	49.836.
Bromide of sodium	traces.
Bi-carbonate of lithia	0.186.
Bi-carbonate of lime	24.282.
Bi-carbonate of iron	0.052.
Chloride of magnesium	18.265.
Chloride of calcium	9.040.
Sulphate of potassa	2.024.
Sulphate of lime	2.462.
Alumina	0.059.
Silica	0.496.
Organic matter	trace.
Total	106.701.

ELWYN WALLER, Ph. D. New York, August 28, 1883.

57. Park Hotel advertisement, *Texas State Gazetteer*, 1890–91. Courtesy of Center for American History, University of Texas at Austin.

LAMPASAS COUNTY

Lampasas   The only mention of this place being called White Sulphur Springs was in an advertisement in J. De Cordova's 1858 *Texas: Her Resources and Her Public Men.* He mentioned several springs in Lampasas:

1. Hancock's or the Great Boiling Spring.
2. Chalybeate, one hundred yards above the Boiling, containing no iron.
3. Scott's Spring, one mile below the Boiling, containing sulphureted hydrogen, rose from a bog.

He called the bathing here "fine." He mentioned a family, all with sore eyes, who visited in 1855 and left relieved after a month of bathing three times daily.

In 1866 the *San Antonio Daily Herald* called these springs "widely celebrated for their medical virtues." It mentioned Hancock Springs for bathing and the other springs, including Scott's Spring, for drinking. The 1878 *Southern and Western Guide to Texas* mentioned that these springs were as celebrated in the Southwest as Saratoga's Congress Springs were in the North (see figs. 57 and 58). See chapters 5 and 6 for the rest of the story.

Hanna Sulphur Springs and Baths

YOUNG MEN'S BUILDING AND LOAN ASSOCIATION,

PROPRIETORS.

LAMPASAS, - - TEXAS.

58. Hanna Sulphur Springs advertisement, *Texas State Gazetteer*, 1890–91. Courtesy of Center for American History, University of Texas at Austin.

LAVACA COUNTY

Fuller Wells, near Hallettsville Listed by USGS in 1911 as source of mineral water, probably for medicinal purposes.

St. Mary's Mineral Well, near Hallettsville Listed by USGS in 1911 as source of mineral water. The 1914–15 *Texas Gazetteer* carried an ad for St. Mary's Mineral Wells, "Greatest Medium to Restore Health and Strength in the Human System" (see fig. 59).

LIMESTONE COUNTY

Kennedy (sulphur) Spring, three miles west of Groesbeck The 1890–91 *Fourth Annual Report of the Agricultural Bureau* called this a popular summer resort for pleasure-seekers and invalids.

Tehuacana Springs, eight miles south of Tehuacana The only mention that this author could find about any possible medicinal value of these springs was in the 1877 *Transactions* of the Texas State Medical Association, by Sam R. Burroughs.

MCLENNAN COUNTY

Waco Hot Water Wells By 1890 there were five artesian wells, two of which were near the public square. The *Geyser City Record* in that year noted that it was hoped that the waters would also bring settlers to the city: "The invalid restored and charmed by the social, educational and manifold advan-

ST, MARY'S MINERAL WELLS

Greatest Medium to Restore Health and Strength in the Human System

ANALYSIS JUNE 1901, BY PROF. H. H.
HARRINGTON:

Sulphate of Calcium	37.3 grains to gallon
Bicarbonate of Calcium	31.13 grains to gallon
Calcium Chloride	190.2 grains to gallon
Magnesium Chloride	40.4 grains to gallon
Sodium Chloride	133.7 grains to gallon
Sodium Bicarbonate	78.7 grains to gallon
Total Mineral	511.4 grains to gallon

It has proven to be the best remedy for such disorders as Stomach and Liver Trouble, Rheumatism, Lumbago, Female Ailments, Heart, Kidney and Bladder Troubles, Impurities of the blood, Running Sores, Ulcers, Eczema, all kinds of Skin Diseases and a Great Restorer of HUMAN VITALITY.

A Trial of this water will be given to anyone wishing to try its curing powers.

A. STANKIEWICZ, Prop., Hallettsville, Texas

59. St. Mary's Mineral Wells advertisement, *Texas State Gazetteer*, 1914–15. Courtesy of Center for American History, University of Texas at Austin.

tages of the city, will cease to be the visitor and become the citizen." In 1893 a Chicago physician wrote that Waco, the "Geyser City of Texas," offered water comparable to that of Hot Springs, Arkansas. The 1898–99 city directory attested that "the Hot Wells, yielding curative waters at a temperature of 103° F, the fame of which has extended around the entire world, continue to attract invalids from the four corners of the earth. Hotels and natatoriums have been built for the accommodation of health seekers at the Waco spas" (see fig. 60). He testified that the water had reduced the death rate in the population since its discovery four years earlier. Padgitt's Park Natatorium and the Natatorio-Sanitorium offered hydrotherapy with its mineral water baths.

MCCULLOUGH COUNTY

Brady Well The 1892 *Fourth Annual Report of the Geological Survey of Texas* reported a well at Brady whose mineral water had been used by invalids "with beneficial results."

Duke's Mineral Well The 1890–91 *Fourth Annual Report of the Agriculture Bureau* noted that this well had a local reputation as a resort for the afflicted.

MEDINA COUNTY

D'Hanis Mineral Wells, D'Hanis In 1883 an advertisement ran in the *Texas Prairie Flower* for hot and cold baths at these wells half a mile from the [train] station.

Tschuhart Mineral Wells, three miles east of Castroville The 1890–91 *Fourth Annual Report of Agriculture Bureau* noted these wells.

60. Natatorium, Hot Well Bathhouse, Waco, Texas, 1910. Author's postcard collection.

MILAM COUNTY

Thorndale In 1929 the Crazy Crystal Mineral Water Company drilled a well to 2,231 feet to the Fredericksburg Group, which supplied highly mineralized (10,500 mg/l), hot (120°F) water that was then evaporated to produce crystals. In 1990 the water flowed into a ditch. A legal dispute ensued about whose duty it was to cap the well—the owner's or the water commission's.

ROBERTSON COUNTY

Overall Mineral Well, Franklin The 1890 *Texas Gazetteer* advertised this place as "the best mineral water now known in the world," at least according to I. R. Overall, the proprietor (see fig. 61). The 1914 USGS Water Supply Paper 335 called this the Overall Mineral Well.

Wootan Wells, three miles west of Bremond The town was founded by Francis Marion Wootan, who moved to Texas from Alabama in 1873. In 1878 Wootan dug a seventy-five-foot well to supply his farmstead with water, which subsequently turned his plates yellow and his clothes red. After learning of the high mineral content from a chemist, he distributed the water freely until in 1880 he formed a partnership with T. W. Wade to bottle the

═══════OVERALL═══════
MINERAL WELLS
FRANKLIN, TEXAS.

The Best Mineral Water now known in the World.

It is the only water that is insured to cure Dyspepsia, Indigestion, General Debility, Flux, Cholera Morbus, Catarrh, Chronic Diarrhœa, Nervous or Sick Headache.

Taken in doses from a wine glass to an ordinary milk glass, after each meal, will cure either of the above diseases. By bathing the parts affected,when practicable, or by injection when you cannot bathe two or three times per day, it will cure the following diseases, viz: Inflammatory, Chronic or Granulated Sore Eyes, Chronic Sore Throat, Scald Head, Tetter, Ringworm, Erysipelas, Warts, Piles, Gonorrhœa, or any Skin Disease, and is particularly adapted to the cure of many of the Diseases of Ladies, such as Whites, Flooding, Ulcerated or Inflammation of the Womb. If the water fails to do what I claim for it above, I will refund the money paid for water,—parties making affidavit of the same.

I. R. OVERALL.

61. Overall Mineral Wells advertisement, *Texas State Gazetteer,* 1890–91. Courtesy of Center for American History, University of Texas at Austin.

water and market the property as a health resort. In 1881 three more wells were dug and four hotels were built. A mule-drawn train transported visitors and bottled water between the resort and the Houston and Texas Central depot south of Bremond. The developers then built two rows of cottages, a dance pavilion, and bathhouses. F. M. Wootan became the first postmaster, and the post office operated from 1883 until 1919. By 1890 the resort had two hundred permanent and two thousand summer residents, including occasional guests James S. Hogg and his daughters. In 1898 it was reported that Buffalo Bill Cody participated in a shooting match on the grounds.

Before 1900 there were thirty businesses, including six physicians' offices, a school, opera house, billiard hall, wagon maker, blacksmith, dairy, gristmill, cotton gin, two general stores, three churches, and Western Union and Wells Fargo stations. Droughts and an 1899 flood damaging buildings and destroying roads added to the company's financial problems. In 1909 the company that managed the resort was auctioned for $10,000. In 1915 the *Texas State Gazetteer* listed a population of 150 persons, a hotel, store, blacksmith, and cotton gin. A 1916 fire destroyed cottages and hotels, but the bottling works operated until it burned in 1926, finishing off the resort.

SAN SABA COUNTY

Sulphur Springs, on the Colorado River, south of San Saba   The 1886 *USGS Bulletin* 32 called this spring a "local resort." *The Handbook of Texas* noted that in 1855 N. S. Rector and Dr. R. B. Pumphrey promoted the resort. J. De Cordova's 1858 *Texas: Her Resources and Her Public Men* called this spring on the southwestern bank of the river the "Great Colorado Sulphur Spring." Forming the head of the spring, the water was clear as crystal and "the escaping gas gives it a most beautiful, sparkling, silvery appearance." He spoke of the "extraordinary cures from the water" and said that it was so "impregnated with sulphur that the olfactory nerves will detect it at least a mile from the spring." At that time no improvements had been made, but he asserted that the spot would become "the great watering-place of the South." Later in the century, a crude bathhouse was the only improvement.

TOM GREEN COUNTY

Carlsbad After townspeople drilled for a public water supply and found mineral water, they changed the name of the newly founded town of Hughes to Carlsbad, after the famed European resort. The Perry Mason Land Company built a bathhouse in the center of the plaza on a hill overlooking the North Concho River valley. The company also built a pavilion, and a lady named Ma Goodwin operated the Carlsbad Inn, according to the *Dallas Times Herald* in 1969. In 1912 a sanitorium was built about a mile from town.

Christoval By 1964 only one bathhouse, the Rawls Bathhouse, operated in town, and it accommodated about thirty-five people a day. The Christoval Bathhouse, constructed in 1915, closed in 1990 after a forty-five-year practice of mineral water therapeutics and chiropractics (see fig. 62). In 1926 Dr. Thomas Percifull acquired the bathhouse and after changing the name of the building, he practiced in the Percifull Chiropractic Sanitarium, where no drugs or surgery was allowed. Dr. R. Rawls, who had apprenticed under Dr. Snyder in Glen Rose, dug a well to the sulphur-water stratum and built a bathhouse, which Dr. Jenkins later acquired.

TRAVIS COUNTY

Capitol A well drilled in 1858 contained water impregnated with hydrogen sulphide. In 1877 the state medical association noted in *Transactions* that "at one time it was common for the citizens to go morning and evening and drink of the waters." In 1890 an artesian well was drilled deeper after the earlier well went dry, and in 1893 it became the fad to take morning rides and walks to the well. In 1928 a fountain was erected over the well but is now not functioning.

Fifth Street Well, near San Jacinto Street, Austin This well, drilled in 1899, was half a mile southeast of the Capitol. An advertisement in the

62. Christoval Bathhouse, Texas, 1913. Author's postcard collection.

1900 *Austin Statesman* extolled the popularity of this "resort," where a bathhouse was open for hot and cold vapor baths. The 1901 USGS *Twenty-first Annual Report* said the sulphur water from this well was comparable to those waters of Kentucky's Blue Lick Springs, Lampasas' Hanna Springs, and Harrogate, England. According to the Texas Water Development Board, a barbershop on the site used this sulphur water from the Paluxy Aquifer for bathing. The well later was covered over with a steel plate.

Santa Monica In 1877 the state medical association noted these sulphur springs, fifteen miles above Austin (now covered by Lake Austin), where previous to the Civil War, families spent "a part or the whole of the summer season at these springs, and derived benefit from the use of their waters." In 1840 Bonnell called them Agua Fria. According to the Austin Board of Trade of 1890, in 1541 Coronado's party made chisel marks in the rock to trace the source of gold found in the river sand.

South Austin Wells, South Austin In 1911 the USGS listed these wells as a source of mineral water, probably for medicinal purposes.

WILLIAMSON COUNTY

Georgetown   In the 1880s Page's Mineral Well Steam Bath operated for about ten years in Oak Grove Park. Around this time also, H. Burkhardt opened Georgetown Mineral Wells and Sanitarium in San Gabriel Park and shipped water for five cents a gallon. The 1890–91 *Fourth Annual Report of the Agriculture Bureau* noted five mineral wells in the suburbs of this community. Dr. Edgar Everhart of the University of Texas compared the water favorably "with the most noted mineral waters of Europe and America."

Taylor   The 1901 USGS *Twenty-first Annual Report* reported that the water from four wells at Taylor was not suited to use in boilers but was "considered medicinal and splendid for bathing."

South

BEE COUNTY

Mineral City   W. Morris originally dug a well to obtain water for his sheep, but the sheep refused to drink the water he retrieved. He sold the land to John and R. Sanford, who thereafter dreamed of a vast treasure to be found in the abandoned well. They sent a sample of water to be analyzed and found that it contained sixteen minerals. In 1879 Sanford built an eight-room hotel and bathhouse nearby. About ten years later the well was abandoned, as it was shallow and digging a deeper well contaminated the mineral water with fresh water. Between then and 1934 several attempts were made to rediscover the water, all to no avail.

CALHOUN COUNTY

Vaca-Tesia Spring, Port Lavaca   In 1907 the USGS mentioned this spring as a source of mineral water.

DIMMIT COUNTY

Carrizo Springs   The 1890–91 *Fourth Annual Report of the Agriculture Bureau* noted the Kelly-Hennigan well, whose water was recommended for "general debility, catarrh, and cutaneous eruptions." While the springs were not known specifically for their medicinal value, town promoters once had dreams of developing them as a health resort. There were other mineral wells in the area. The 1896–97 *Texas Gazetteer* carried an ad for the Daugherty Mineral Water from Carrizo Springs, "the most wonderful natural remedy

DAUGHERTY MINERAL WATER
FROM CARRIZO SPRINGS,
DIMMIT COUNTY, TEXAS.
The most wonderful natural remedy on earth for Chronic Constipation,
Indigestion, All Catarrhal, Stomach, Liver, Blood and Skin Diseases.

Containing the enormous quantity of **1396.3** grains of Solid Mineral Matter per gallon. Compounded in nature's own laboratory, fresh from the bowels of Mother Earth.

"Daugherty Mineral Water," from Carrizo Springs, Texas, submitted to me by you:

Solid Contents—U. S. gal. 231 cub. in.1395.72 Grs.	Potassium Bi-carbonate	60.92 Grs
Sodium Chloride............ .... 725.207 "	Magnesium Bi-carbonate	194.737 "
Sodium Bi-carbonate................. 122.621 "	Magnesium Sulphate............ ...	4.231 "
Potassium-Chloride....... .... 37.025 "	Lime Bi-carbonate	185.785 "

Respectfully, T. P. BARBOUR.

H. H. ALVORD, Sole Agent,
258 Main Street, · · · · DALLAS, TEXAS.

63. Daugherty Mineral Water advertisement, *Texas State Gazetteer,* 1896–97. Courtesy
of Center for American History, University of Texas at Austin.

on earth for chronic constipation, indigestion, all catarrhal, stomach, liver,
blood and skin diseases" (see fig. 63). In 1913 and again in 1915 there were
notices of reviving interest in the wells. In the former year, some New Orleans capitalists who owned a well here considered building a resort hotel
and further advertising the water. In 1915 J. McCaleb leased the well "east
of town on the Asherton road," repaired the building, and tried to "revive
the interest formerly displayed through the South in this efficaceous natural
remedy." Many plans announced by local media never materialized. One, as
reported by the *Javelin* in 1918, proposed to make Carrizo Springs a popular
spa to rival Colorado and Southern California as a health resort:

> The New Orleans capitalists who control the mineral water well here are
> now considering the establishment of a large resort hotel in this town, and
> the beginning of a national campaign of advertising for the exploiting of
> the mineral water. It has a wide use at the present time, but it is their
> intention to push the sales to the maximum limit.

FRIO COUNTY

Sour Well, near Pearsall The 1890–91 *Fourth Annual Report of the
Agriculture Bureau* noted this well's reputation for curative powers.

KARNES COUNTY

Kenedy Hot Wells, Kenedy A hotel and sanitarium utilized the waters
accidentally discovered in 1915. The waters continued in use until 1954.

LA SALLE COUNTY

Artesian well, Cotulla The 1890–91 *Fourth Annual Report of the Agriculture Bureau* noted that this well was recommended for dyspepsia.

Woodward Vichy Spring, Rockbridge Listed by USGS in 1908 and 1911 as a source of mineral water, probably for medicinal purposes.

UVALDE COUNTY

Hanner Well The 1890–91 *Fourth Annual Report of Agriculture Bureau* noted this well, twenty-five miles from the railroad, as recommended for dyspepsia and debility.

Reagan Wells In 1885 Harvey Hammer dug the first well, which he later sold to John Reagan. Reagan subsequently built a two-story hotel, with bathhouse. B. W. Briggs then bought the site and built cabins. Finally, in 1916, Y. D. Taylor's large bathhouse business thrived until his death in the early 1940s and his wife's death in 1945. Bathing was then discontinued.

VAL VERDE COUNTY

Sulphur Mineral Well, Del Rio In 1891 the *Texas Sanitarian* published an analysis done by E. Everhart, chemistry professor at the University of Texas. He noted that this water possessed "all the qualities of a first-class water, and that is one found in Del Rio, belonging to Mr. Mason. This water stood for over six weeks in my laboratory without losing, appreciably, any of its properties . . . and is probably equal to any found elsewhere in the world."

Panhandle / Plains

NOLAN COUNTY

Grogan Wells Sanitorium, Sweetwater At the turn of the century Dr. W. R. Grogan established the sanitorium to take advantage of the hot springs for baths and treatments. A pavilion and the Grogan Wells Hotel also accommodated healthseekers (see fig. 64). In 1914 a new owner operated it as the Grogan Wells and Boone Institute of Massage, which continued to offer mineral water treatments as well as massage, according to the *Sweetwater Weekly Reporter.*

TAYLOR COUNTY

North Park Mineral Well, Abilene In 1911 the USGS listed this well as a source of mineral water, probably for medicinal purposes.

64. Grogan Wells Sanitarium, Sweetwater, Texas, 1907. Author's postcard collection.

Trans-Pecos

BREWSTER COUNTY

Hot Springs (Boquillas)   J. O. Langford moved to Hot Springs in 1909 because he hoped the hot springs would improve his malarial condition. Apparently they did; he and his family stayed to make a going concern of his resort operation until border trouble forced them to move in 1913. They returned in 1927 and stayed until 1942, at which time they sold the land to the state, which gave it to the nation for the establishment of Big Bend National Park. In 1929 Langford improved the bathhouse, built tourist courts and a store with post office. Lovie, Langford's daughter, remembered that many visitors who bathed in the springs did so on their physician's recommendation. Langford used to tell the story of a man from East Texas who each year visited the springs on foot (seven hundred miles). Her father tried to get him to carry water to the next water hole, a distance of twelve miles, but the man refused, saying it was too far to carry the water (Porterfield). According to the Hot Springs register from 1937 to 1940, most visitors were from the local area—Valentine, Alpine, Marathon, El Paso, and Mexico.

Others undertook the odyssey from Houston, San Antonio, Anadarko, New Mexico, San Diego, and Seattle (Big Bend Archives).

HUDSPETH COUNTY

Hot Wells, southeast of Sierra Blanca In 1907 the Southern Pacific Railroad drilled a well to one thousand feet and encountered water at about 104° F. A 1925 article in the *Mountain Eagle* mentioned W. D. Fisher's bathhouse, which a number of people visited each year, and a doctor from Fort Worth who wanted to built a sanitarium in Hot Wells. In 1926 plans for the sanitarium were materializing, and the Southern Pacific spokesman promised to build a switch and a new depot. In 1964 a local resident spoke of a "gift from God, our Hot Mineral Well." She had taken the baths years earlier for rheumatism, and she believed that "this valuable water was not brought to the surface of this earth to flow down a stinking, filthy little creek and no one benefit from its use!" She was strongly suggesting that the town could benefit by again developing this resource.

Indian Hot Springs Listed in the National Register of Historic Places. Frank Tolbert was fascinated with this place. His many columns about it placed it on the other side of nowhere, yet a perfect sanctuary for re-creating one's health. Mary Lee, who managed it for owner H. L. Hunt from 1970 till Hunt died in 1974, told a story of a woman she knew whose pilgrimage to the springs could have been her last:

> There's a little girl, a friend of mine, Mary Jo Brown, in El Paso. About ten years ago, her husband drove up on a Sunday afternoon. Her feet were so swollen that she didn't even have socks on. Her hands were swollen. She hadn't worn jewelry or shoes in five years. He had documented evidence from doctors all over the world. Cancer. They had just left Houston and gave her two weeks to live. We put her in the baths Sunday night. Bill went back to El Paso because he had to go back to work. By Thursday Mary was up in the kitchen helping us dry dishes. She had put shoes on. Today she works in a shopping mall in El Paso. She had only two weeks to live, and if you had seen her, you would have believed it. Her cancer was in the pancreas, liver, colon. Monday we put her in there three times. We'd gradually put her in ten minutes and test the water to be sure she could stand it. We'd put her out on sweat tables and wrap her in blankets. By Thursday all the swelling was down. That's a miracle within itself. We saw that. We called Mr. Hunt, and got documented evidence of it.

In the 1960s there were nine hot springs and one cool soda spring. The Squaw Springs, used by local women, supposedly cured female complaints

65. Kingston Hot Springs, Texas, 1990. Author photo.

and was good for the complexion. Two "bleaching springs" took off freckles, according to Jewel Babb, who used to operate the springs. Pat Ellis (Taylor) Littledog who had interviewed Babb years ago about her curanderism, in 1986 made another journey to the springs for renewal: "We were sick, like hospital patients, and I wanted nothing, really, but a hospital bed, getting up to take baths three times a day and drink hot spring water, nothing more required, not even the stress of company, while the body cleared."

The Chief Springs, where the strongest water flowed, much to the bene-fit of older men, so the story goes, used to have a stone trough supposedly carved by Indians. It was later covered up with a bathhouse. Stump, Mexi-can, Dynamite, and Fishing Hole Springs are other springs. In 1968 Tolbert wrote of some celebrities who visited the springs: heavyweight boxing champ Gene Tunney; E. Holub, linebacker for the Kansas City Chiefs; and Cam-eron Mitchell, star of the television series *High Chaparral.*

It is difficult to distinguish fact from the mythology that has colored accounts of the springs' history. Some say Geronimo frequented the springs, while others say Victorio, of the Mimbres band of Apaches, was more likely to use the springs. Other stories include Rockefeller's visiting the springs in the 1920s, when a resort was built, and the latest was Billy Porterfield's column in the *Austin American-Statesman* mentioning that Vanderbilts once used it as a spa, although this author has never come across that name associated with this place. It closed during World War II and reopened again under Hunt's ownership. It is presently in private hands.

PRESIDIO COUNTY

Chinati Hot Springs, formerly Kingston Hot Springs (Ruidosa Hot Springs), seven miles north of Ruidosa in the Chinati Mountains According to Brune, the Mendoza-López Expedition may have camped here in 1684, and also Captain Joseph Idoyaga in 1747. Kingston was a small commercial resort developed around the 118°F mineral spring. In 1898 Annie Kingston bought 1,200 acres so that her brother-in-law's arthritic condition might improve with bathing. She piped the water to three adobe bathhouses. Later, in 1937, the Kingston family built seven cabins for accommodations. Members of the Kingston family still owned the springs until 1990, when it closed to the public. At that time there were three individual soaking tubs in individual rooms in the bathhouse. The Pauls' (Bea's grandmother was Annie Kingston), who operated the resort before it closed, said that during their best season, September to June, they had visitors from Kentucky, Michigan, Pennsylvania, Canada, and Germany every year to partake of the waters. Jack Paul estimated that approximately one thousand people visited each year (see fig. 65). It closed for a few years and is now under new ownership.

$\mathcal{N}otes$

1. TAKING THE WATERS

1. Hiroshi Nohara, "Penetration of Mineral Water Constituents," in Sidney Licht, ed., *Medical Hydrology* (Baltimore: Waverly Press, 1963), p. 127.

2. Terrell Well Company, "We Want to Tell You about the Terrell Hot Well: The Well that Contains Radium" (San Antonio: Terrell Well Company, 1910; Center for American History, University of Texas at Austin).

3. "Health and Pleasure at Mineral Wells: The Famous Texas Resort," pamphlet, ca. 1911, in Mineral Wells Vertical File, Rosenberg Library, Galveston.

4. Ross Estes and Robert Duncan, eds., *I Remember Things: An Informal History of Tioga, Texas* (Quanah, Tex.: Nortex Press, 1977), p. 5.

5. Pat Remick, "Mineral Wells to Celebrate 100th Anniversary Next Week," *Dallas Morning News*, 11 September 1982.

6. *Lockhart Morning Courier*, 5 October 1908; *Galveston Daily News*, 26 June 1877.

7. Richard Peacock, manager of Marlin Bathhouse, interview with author, 3 February 1991; Mary Lee, manager of Indian Springs, interview with author, 5 June 1990.

8. J. M. Willis, "Report of the Committee on the Mineral Waters of Texas," in *Transactions of the Sixteenth Annual Texas State Medical Association* (Fort Worth: Texas State Medical Association, 1884), p. 202.

9. "Common Sense Concerning Mineral Waters," *Texas State Journal of Medicine* 3 (1907): 206; "Read What Physicians Say about Mineral Wells, Texas: The Famous All-the-Year-Round Health Resort," pamphlet, ca. 1908, in Mineral Wells Vertical File, Rosenberg Library, Galveston.

10. J. H. Eastland, "Mineral Wells: Its Climatology and the Therapeutic Value of Its Waters," *Texas State Journal of Medicine* 5 (December 1909): 306.

11. Richard Kovacs, "The Problem of American Spas," *Journal of the American Medical Association* 127 (14 April 1945): 977.

2. HISTORIC WATERING TRADITION

1. Vladimir Krízek, "History of Balneotherapy," in Sidney Licht, ed., *Medical Hydrology* (Baltimore: Waverly Press, 1963), pp. 131–143, 149.

2. William C. Hirsch, "Historical Springs," *Current Literature* 34, no. 3 (March 1903): 297–298; and Frederick Alderson, *The Inland Resorts and Spas of Britain* (Newton Abbot: David and Charles, 1973), p. 17.

3. William Addison, *English Spas* (London: B. T. Batsford, 1951), p. 3.

4. Carl Bridenbaugh, "Baths and Watering Places of Colonial America," *William and Mary Quarterly* 3, no. 2 (April 1946): 150–152.

5. Herman L. Kamenetz, "History of American Spas and Hydrotherapy," in Licht, *Medical Hydrology*, pp. 165–166.

6. Jefferson Williamson, *The American Hotel* (New York: Knopf, 1930), pp. 228–233.

7. Bridenbaugh, "Baths and Watering Places of Colonial America," p. 173.

8. Henry W. Lawrence, "Southern Spas: Source of the American Resort Tradition," *Landscape* 27, no. 2 (1983): 3–4.

9. Ibid.

10. Kamenetz, in Licht, *Medical Hydrology*, pp. 168–169.

11. Perceval Reniers, *The Springs of Virginia* (Chapel Hill: University of North Carolina Press, 1941), pp. 28–30.

12. Katharine Dos Passos, "Sweet Waters of the South," *Woman's Home Companion* 65 (1938): 21, 144.

13. Harrison Rhodes, "American Holidays: Springs and Mountains," *Harper's Monthly Magazine* 129 (September 1914): 539.

14. Earl Pomeroy, *In Search of the Golden West: The Tourist in Western America* (New York: Knopf, 1957), pp. 17–22.

15. Billy M. Jones, *Health-Seekers in the Southwest, 1817–1900* (Norman: University of Oklahoma Press, 1967), pp. 151–165.

16. Stephen Powers, *Tribes of California* (Berkeley: University of California Press, 1877), as cited in Kim Charnofsky, "California Mineral and Hot Springs: Historical and Geographical Considerations in Their Perception, Location, and Development" (master's thesis, University of California at Berkeley, 1989), pp. 15, 23.

17. Jones, *Health-Seekers in the Southwest*, p. 102.

18. Winslow Anderson, *Mineral Springs and Health Resorts of California* (San Francisco: Bancroft, 1892), p. xxx.

19. Charles R. Reynolds, "American Health Resorts: The Importance of Health Resorts and Their Facilities in Medical Preparedness," *Journal of the American Medical Association* 123, no. 13 (27 November 1943): 832–836; and Frank H. Krusen, "American Health Resorts: The Place of Health Resorts in Rehabilitation Following Injuries," *Journal of the American Medical Association* 125 (29 July 1944): 907.

20. A. C. Peale, "Mineral Springs of the United States," in *USGS Bulletin,* no. 32 (Washington, D.C.: Government Printing Office, 1886), p. 137.

21. W. Pepper and H. Bowditch, "Report of the Committee on Sanitaria and on Mineral Springs," in American Medical Association, ed., *Transactions* 31 (1880): 537–565; Peale, "Mineral Springs of the United States," p. 137.

22. Peale, "Mineral Waters," pp. 772–794.

23. Mamie Wynne Cox describes such a "season," during which she met her physician husband, in *A Love Story of Mineral Wells* (Mineral Wells: Index, 1932).

3. TEXAS' RESORTS

1. Much of the information concerning the classification of springs comes from late-nineteenth-century and early-twentieth-century USGS reports and from Gunnar Brune, *Springs of Texas,* vol. 1 (Fort Worth: Branch-Smith, 1981).

2. Alexander Deussen, "Southeastern Texas Coastal Plain," USGS Water Supply Paper 335, 1914.

3. Christopher D. Henry, *Geologic Setting and Geochemistry of Thermal Water and Geothermal Assessment, Trans-Pecos Texas and Adjacent Mexico* (Austin: Bureau of Economic Geology, University of Texas at Austin, 1979).

4. Some governmental sources, including USGS reports on sales of bottled water, never pinpointed the exact location of certain medicinal waters. Not all mineral wells and springs mentioned in Appendix A appear on the map in Figure 6, as many places, particularly those mentioned by the USGS, never included county names, so their location is unknown. Since little documentation exists on some "resorts," they were probably so small or such short-term affairs that they are also not included on the map.

5. "Digging of Hubbard Hot Well—Wood's Hospital—Midwife, Bertha Shanklin," *Hubbard City News,* November 1981, special edition commemorating Hubbard's 100th birthday.

6. For reminders of once-popular springs, see Brune, *Springs of Texas.*

7. "A History of Sour Lake and Legend of Its Origin," *Houston Daily Post,* 2 July 1903; "Sour Lake: One of the Wonders of the World," *Gulf Messenger* 10, no. 5 (May 1897): 232.

8. Ruth Garrison Scurlock, "Sour Lake: Spa of the Big Thicket," in Francis E. Abernethy, ed., *Tales from the Big Thicket* (Austin: University of Texas Press, 1967), p. 170.

9. Lovie Whitaker, taped interview with Teresa Whittington, Archives of the Big Bend, Bryan Wildenthal Library, Sul Ross State University, Alpine.

10. George Bonnell, *Topographical Description of Texas* (Austin: Clark, Wing, Brown, 1840), p. 24.

11. C.D.M., "Sour Lake Letters," *Galveston Daily News,* 14 July 1857.

12. "Piedmont Sulphur Springs," advertisement in *Texas Almanac* (Dallas: A. H. Belo, 1859).

13. F. M. Cross, *A Short Sketch-History from Personal Reminiscences of Early Days in Central Texas* (Brownwood, Tex.: Greenwood, 1912), p. 30.

14. J. P. Blessington, *The Campaigns of Walker's Texas Division* (Austin: Pemberton Press, 1968), p. 302; Inter-State Investment Company, "A Realty Talk," ca. 1905, p. 6, typewritten copy in Hynson Vertical File, Marshall Historical Museum Archives; Frank X. Tolbert, "Headache Springs Park Is Still a 'Headache,'" *Dallas Morning News,* 30 August 1971.

15. Thomas T. Ewell, *History of Hood County* (Granbury, Tex.: Frank Gaston, 1895; reprint, Granbury, Tex.: Junior Woman's Club, 1956), p. 114.

16. "Our 'Mineral Waters' and 'Places of Resort,'" *Texas Medical and Surgical Record* 2 (August 1882): 350–351.

17. Houston and Texas Central Railroad, *Points of Interest to Tired People,* Center for American History, University of Texas at Austin, ca. 1900.

18. J. W. Register, "Mineral Wells, Famous Resort," *Texas Magazine* 2, no. 3 (July 1910): 63–64; Marlin Chamber of Commerce, "Marlin: It's in Texas. The Oasis of Health" (N.p., n.d.), in Center for American History, University of Texas at Austin.

19. *Mineral Wells Daily Index,* 6 May 1907.

20. "Texas' Carlsbad," *Texas and Pacific Quarterly* 8, no. 3 (July 1905): 27, 31–34. The magazine sprinkled many pictures of Mineral Wells throughout several issues, despite the fact that those issues carried no articles on the town. For pictures of Lovers' Retreat, Donkey Rides, McDonald's Park, Smith and Barber Lake, motoring up East Mountain, "Love in a Cottage," and an 1881 picture of the first well, see the April 1903, October 1905, and October 1907 issues.

21. *Lampasas Leader,* 26 August 1904.

22. *Marlin Ball,* 26 May 1905.

23. "Mineral Wells of Texas," *Texas Health Journal* 5, no. 12 (June 1893): 315; Putnam Commercial Club, "Putnam—The Great West Texas Health and Pleasure Resort," prospectus, 1911; Scrapbook of Mangum, Texas, 1905–1927, in Centennial Memorial Library, Eastland.

24. "Health and Pleasure at Mineral Wells: The Famous Texas Resort," pamphlet, ca. 1911, in Mineral Wells Vertical File, Rosenberg Library, Galveston.

25. "Texas' Carlsbad," pp. 32–33.

26. Scrapbook of Mangum.

27. Johnna Reed and Monte Williams, "Sweetwater: Once Site of Health Center," *Big Country* 3 (1979): 44; Gene Fowler, *Crazy Water: The Story of Mineral Wells and Other Texas Health Resorts* (Fort Worth: Texas Christian University Press, 1991), pp. 143–149; J. Marvin Hunter, "A Texas Town That Faded," *Frontier Times* 18, no. 1 (October 1940): 13–14.

28. Glenn Willeford, "Closing of Kingston Hot Springs Leaves Public Questioning Its Future," *Presidio International,* 21 June 1990.

4. PLACES LIVED

1. This excerpt is an abbreviated version of the longer one from a local Lampasas newspaper of 17 February 1931, reprinted from an older (unnamed) paper. In "The Origin of Lampasas Springs," Lampasas County Historical Commission Scrapbook, Lampasas County Courthouse.

2. Lewis Nordyke, "That Crazy City: Mineral Wells," *Texas Parade* (March 1952): 23–24.

3. Walter Prescott Webb, ed., *The Handbook of Texas* (Austin: Texas State Historical Association, 1952), p. 782; *Sherman Democrat,* 19 September 1948; Corine Tolleson to author, 14 March 1991; Frank X. Tolbert, "Artists and Deer 'Haunt' the Wells," *Dallas Morning News,* 15 February 1964.

4. *Hot Sulphur Baths* (San Antonio: Guessaz and Ferlet, 1902), p. 3, in Center for American History, University of Texas at Austin.

5. The initial quote appears in "Tioga, Texas," *Texas and Pacific Quarterly* 15, no. 4 (October 1912): 56, while the subsequent quotes come from "Rosborough Springs," *Marshall News Messenger,* August 1897, typewritten copy in Rosborough Springs Vertical File, Marshall Historical Museum Archives, and from J. W. Torbett Sr., *The Doctor's Scrapbook* (Dallas: Wilkinson, 1947), p. 101.

6. W. M. Yandell, "The Climate of Trans-Pecos Texas, Compared with That of Other Parts of the State, with Special Reference to a Suitable Climate for Consumptives," *Texas Sanitarian* 5, no. 8 (June 1896): 25–32; J. W. Carhart, "Lampasas as a Health Resort," *Texas Sanitarian* 3, no. 4 (February 1894): 135–141.

7. Putnam Commercial Club, "Putnam—The Great West Texas Health and Pleasure Resort," 1911, p. 14.

8. Mineral Wells Commercial Club, "Quarterly Guide," brochure, 1909, in Mineral Wells Vertical File, Rosenberg Library, Galveston; Inter-State Investment Company, "A Realty Talk," ca. 1905, pp. 1–3, typewritten copy in Hynson Vertical File, Marshall Historical Museum Archives.

9. "The Fountain of Youth," pamphlet, ca. 1910, in Center for American History, University of Texas at Austin; *Hot Sulphur Baths,* p. 20.

10. "The Hot Well," *Marlin Democrat,* 29 February 1908.

11. Letter from W. A. Clark to editor of *Sutherland Springs Health Resort,* 6 December 1910; "Lampasas, Texas: Its Mineral Springs," pamphlet (Chicago: Poole, ca. 1888; reprint, 1972).

12. Frank X. Tolbert, "Notes on Apaches' 'Fountains of Youth,'" *Dallas Morning News,* 14 May 1970; Frank X. Tolbert, "Not Just Legend at Indian Springs," *Dallas News,* 25 September 1967.

13. W. F. Bookman, "Dramatic Struggle of Nature, Far Underground, Closely Intertwined with History of Sour Lake," *Houston Chronicle,* 21 June 1936; *Myrtle Springs Herald,* 19 November 1891.

14. W. A. McDonald, "The Fountain of Youth," *Tioga Herald,* 21 November 1919.

15. "History of Harrison County, Texas," *Texas Pioneer Magazine* 5, no. 4 (1880): 224.

16. "Mineral Wells, Palo Pinto County, Texas," *Texas Prairie Flower* 2, no. 3 (September 1883): 118.

17. James J. Bell, Jr., "Testimonials," collection of Mary Lee, Fort Worth.

18. The first visitor's remarks appeared in *Sutherland Springs Health Resort,* 31 January 1911; *Sutherland Springs Western Chronicle,* 7 September 1877.

19. "Sour Lake: One of the Wonders of the World," *Gulf Messenger* 10, no. 5 (May 1897): 228.

20. M. Whilldin, ed., *A Description of Western Texas* (Galveston: Galveston, Harrisburg, and San Antonio Railway, 1876), pp. 6–7.

21. David B. Edward, *The History of Texas* (Cincinnati: J. A. James, 1836), pp. 89–90.

22. In the 1892 *A New Medical Dictionary,* George Gould, M.D., defined *miasma* as "a term loosely applied to the floating germs of any form of microbic life, especially those generating in marshy localities." This theory had dominated medical thought for centuries.

23. Edward, *History of Texas,* p. 90.

24. "A Day in Lampasas," *Lampasas News,* 28 July 1905.

25. Mineral Wells Commercial Club, "Quarterly Guide."

26. Cephas Shelburne, "The Hidden City," *Christian Courier,* 18 April 1918, typewritten copy, Glen Rose Vertical File, Glen Rose Library.

27. Midyett Marker File, Texas Historical Commission.

28. Shelburne, "The Hidden City."

29. *Vineyard City Guide Post* 1, no. 5 (27 January 1883), collection of W. W. "Bill" Dennis, Jacksboro.

30. Andrew Morrison, "Sour Lake Mineral Springs: The Texas Sanitarium," *City of Houston* (Engelhardt Series: American Cities, 1891), p. 123.

31. Meg A. Fone, "Bathhouse Row," *Marlin Democrat,* 11 March 1908.

32. William J. Maltby, *Captain Jeff or Frontier Life in Texas with the Texas Rangers* (Colorado, Tex.: Whipkey, 1906), p. 143.

33. C.D.M., "Sour Lake Letters."

34. "What Others Say about Mineral Wells Waters: Testimonials (with Analyses)," pamphlet, ca. 1911, in Mineral Wells Vertical File, Rosenberg Library, Galveston; letter from Tolleson to author.

35. *Lampasas Daily Times,* 18 June 1878.

36. Johnnyrae Luker Fite, ed., *Hughes Springs, Texas, Histories* (Naples: Sesame Literary Club and the Printing Factory, 1986); and W. E. Penn, *Life and Labors of Major W. E. Penn: "The Texas Evangelist"* (St. Louis: C. B. Woodward, 1896), pp. 172–174.

5. DAILY SPA LIFE

1. Diary of James Billingsley, Center for American History, University of Texas at Austin.

2. *Lampasas Dispatch,* 26 July 1877. The account that follows has been gleaned from both the *Dispatch* and the *Lampasas Daily Times,* primarily from editions in summer 1878.

3. *Lampasas Dispatch,* 26 July 1877.

4. *Lampasas Daily Times,* 4 June 1878.

5. Ibid., 2 August 1878.

6. Mrs. W. H. Moses, "Park Hotel, Hancock Park Dominated Local Scene in 1898," *Lampasas Record*, 19 December 1963. The *Lampasas Record* must have misprinted the date in the title because the author in the article noted that the hotel burned in 1895.

7. *Lampasas Leader*, 11 May 1889.

8. *Austin Daily Statesman*, July and August 1883; and "Lampasas, Once a Famous Health Resort in Texas, Retains Much of Its Early Day Quaintness," *San Antonio Express*, 5 July 1936.

9. "Lampasas, Once a Famous Health Resort"; *Lampasas Leader*, 1 June 1889; 23 and 30 April 1892; Jonnie Ross Elzner, *Lamplights of Lampasas County* (Austin: Firm Foundation, 1951), p. 123.

10. *Lampasas Leader*, 6 October 1888.

11. James P. Cole, "A History of Lampasas County: 1882–1895" (master's thesis, Sam Houston State College, 1968); and Elzner, *Lamplights of Lampasas County.*

12. "A Day in Lampasas," *Brownwood Bulletin*, reprinted in *Lampasas News*, 28 July 1905.

13. *Lampasas Leader*, 15 July 1904.

14. "Lampasas, Once a Famous Health Resort"; Clint Pace, "Lampasas Thrives upon Soil Prosperity," *Austin American-Statesman*, 8 February 1948.

15. J. H. Baker, "Diary Excerpts," 1881, reprinted in *Palo Pinto County Star*, 26 April 1940.

16. H. M. Berry, "A Brief History of Mineral Wells," reprinted in *Palo Pinto County Star*, 12 and 17 April 1942.

17. Ibid., 1 and 8 May 1942.

18. *Mineral Wells Daily Index*, 6 May 1907; and "Mineral Wells, Palo Pinto County, Texas," *Texas Prairie Flower* 2, no. 3 (September 1883): 119.

19. Mineral Wells Commercial Club, "Hotel Guide for Visitors to Mineral Wells," brochure, 1909, in Mineral Wells Vertical File, Rosenberg Library, Galveston; and Sara Hartman, "Mineral Wells," *Gulf Messenger* 6 (1893): 293.

20. Mamie Wynne Cox, *A Love Story of Mineral Wells* (Mineral Wells, Tex.: Index, 1932), p. 31; and "Texas' Carlsbad," *Texas and Pacific Quarterly* 8, no. 3 (July 1905): 27; and Lewis Nordyke, "That Crazy City: Mineral Wells," *Texas Parade* (March 1952): 23.

21. "Texas' Carlsbad," p. 31.

22. Effie N. Birdwell, "Famous Mineral Water Company," 1989, in Marker File, Texas Historical Commission; *Mineral Wells Daily Index*, 6 May 1907.

23. J. W. Register, "Mineral Wells, Famous Resort," *Texas Magazine* 2, no. 3 (July 1910): 63; and "Mineral Wells," *Texas and Pacific Quarterly* 10, no. 3 (July 1907): 13–14.

24. "Health and Pleasure at Mineral Wells: The Famous Texas Resort," pamphlet, ca. 1911, in Mineral Wells Vertical File, Rosenberg Library, Galveston.

25. "Mineral Wells, the 'Carlsbad' of Texas," *The Bohemian* 4, no. 4 (1903/1904): 83.

26. "Texas' Carlsbad," pp. 29–30.

27. Mineral Wells Commercial Club, "Quarterly Guide," pamphlet, 1909, in Mineral Wells Vertical File, Rosenberg Library, Galveston.

28. *Palo Pinto County Star*, 21 June 1940.

29. "The Baker . . . a Baker Hotel," pamphlet, n.d., in Rosenberg Library, Galveston; Crazy Water Hotel Company, "Here—May You Find All That You Seek of Health, Comfort, and Satisfaction," pamphlet, 1930, in Mineral Wells Vertical File, Rosenberg Library, Galveston.

30. Nordyke, "That Crazy City," p. 21.

31. Cameron Quinn, interviewed by Randy Eli Grothe, "A Golden Past and a Broken Present," *Dallas Morning News*, 5 December 1976.

32. Richard Peacock, telephone interview, Bryan, 3 February 1991; "The Baker Hotel," State-

ment of Significance, National Register of Historic Places Inventory File, Texas Historical Commission.

33. "The Tramp and the Barrel," *Marlin Democrat*, 11 March 1908.

34. Clarita Buie, "The Booster Days," in Marlin Chamber of Commerce, ed., *Marlin: 1851–1976* (Marlin: Chamber of Commerce and Bicentennial Heritage Committee, 1976), pp. 62–63.

35. Frank Calvert Oltorf interview, Marlin, 16 February 1990.

36. Ruby Harris interview, Marlin, 6 March 1991.

37. *Marlin Democrat*, 3 January 1909.

38. J. W. Torbett Sr., *Hot Air Verses from the Hot Water Town* (Marlin: Byrne Color Press, 1914), p. 61.

39. Hale's comments appear in *Houston Post,* 14 April 1971; Harris interview.

40. Meg A. Fone, "The Pavilion," *Marlin Democrat*, 4 March 1908.

41. The initial quote came from William Schuyler Frost, ed., *Review Marlin* (Quanah: Nortex Press, 1909), p. 3; the latter quote is from *Marlin Democrat,* 9 December 1908. See also Rosella H. Werlin, "Forever Amber," *Dallas Times Herald,* 9 December 1962.

42. *Marlin Democrat*, 21 June 1911 and 26 March 1910.

43. Oltorf interview.

44. Frost, *Review Marlin,* pp. 8, 15; and "Follow the Road to Good Health," pamphlet, n.d., in Marlin Vertical File, Center for American History, University of Texas at Austin; *Marlin Democrat,* 29 February 1908.

45. Torbett, *The Doctor's Scrapbook* (Dallas: Wilkinson, 1947), p. 101; "Follow the Road to Good Health."

46. Oltorf interview.

47. Ibid.

48. Mary Ann Kreps, "Falls Hotel Investors File for Bankruptcy," *Waco Tribune-Herald,* 8 January 1986.

49. Tom Belden, "Town Taps Past for Modern Cure," *Dallas Morning News,* 5 April 1978.

50. M. J. Sullivan, ed., *International Blue Book Publication* (San Antonio: M. J. Sullivan, 1912), p. 16.

51. "Through the Hot Wells Hotel," *San Antonio Light,* 8 July 1902. For a more recent study, see Anne A. Fox and Cheryl Lynn Highley, *History and Archaeology of the Hot Wells Hotel Site,* Archaeological Survey Report no. 152, 41 BX 237 (San Antonio: Center for Archaeological Research, University of Texas at San Antonio, 1985), pp. 8–11.

52. Southern Pacific Line, *San Antonio: The Mission City* (Houston: Southern Pacific Line, 1916), pp. 12–13; "Terrell Wells: A Modern Health and Rest Resort," ca. 1926, in Vertical File, San Antonio Conservation Society; *San Antonio Light,* 8 October 1907.

53. Fox and Highley, "History and Archeology of the Hot Wells Hotel," p. 9.

6. MARKETING THE WATERS

1. "Prospectus of the Proposed Sour Lake Springs Company of Texas," ca. 1898, p. 1, Sour Lake Vertical File, Rosenberg Library, Galveston. Other promotional quotes appeared in Sutherland Springs Development Company, "Why Not Know Why?" prospectus, ca. 1909, Center for American History, University of Texas at Austin, p. 16; Inter-State Investment Company, "A Realty Talk," ca. 1905, typewritten copy, Hynson Vertical File, Marshall Historical Museum Archives, pp. 4–6; Putnam Commercial Club, "Putnam—The Great West Texas Health and Pleasure Resort," prospectus, p. 14.

2. Inter-State Investment Company, "A Realty Talk," p. 2.

3. Ibid., p. 4; Bob Forrest, "Historic Hynson Springs Strewn with Debris, Covered by Growth," *Marshall News Messenger,* 9 June 1974.

4. J. K. Crook, *The Mineral Waters of the United States and Their Therapeutic Uses* (New York: Lea, 1899), p. 454.

5. "Cardwell Springs," *Galveston Daily News,* 23 August 1877.

6. *Lockhart Morning Courier,* 5 October 1908.

7. Maudling Land Company, "Burdette Wells: Where the Water Fairy Dwells," prospectus, Center for American History, University of Texas at Austin.

8. George W. Bonnell, *Topographical Description of Texas* (Austin: Clark, Wing, Brown, 1840), p. 94; Francis Moore, Jr., *Map and Description of Texas* (Philadelphia: H. Tanner, 1840), p. 49.

9. J. B. Polley, *Sutherland Springs Western Chronicle,* 20 April 1877.

10. *Sutherland Springs Western Chronicle,* 3 August 1877.

11. *Wilson County Journal,* 21 April 1909.

12. *Sutherland Springs Health Resort,* 3 January 1911.

13. Ibid., 28 February 1911.

14. Henry W. Lawrence, "Southern Spas: Source of the American Resort Tradition," *Landscape* 27 (1983): 9. Lawrence's article includes a site plan of a resort in the "national style" from an 1865 edition of *Frank Leslie's Illustrated Newspaper.*

15. "Wootan Wells," *Texas Prairie Flower* 2, no. 4 (October 1883): 184–185.

16. "Lampasas, Texas: Its Mineral Springs," pamphlet (Chicago: Poole, ca. 1888; reprint, 1972).

17. "A Mineral Water from Gonzales," *Texas Sanitarian* 2, no. 1 (1892): 24.

18. W. A. McDonald, "The Fountain of Youth," *Tioga Herald,* 21 November 1919. The preceding proclamations appeared in *Lockhart Morning Courier,* 5 October 1908; "Rosborough Springs," *Marshall Morning Star,* May 1894, in Marshall Historical Museum Archives; Scrapbook of Mangum, Texas, 1905–1927, in Centennial Memorial Library, Eastland; and "Hot Sulphur Baths" (San Antonio: Guessaz and Ferlet, 1902), p. 7, in Center for American History, University of Texas at Austin.

19. *Mineral Resources of the U.S.* (Washington, D.C.: GPO and USGS, 1905, 1907), pp. 1305, 779; *Texas Almanac* (Dallas: Dallas News and A. H. Belo, 1929), p. 278. The 1907 USGS report noted that more than half of the output came from Mineral Wells, but it also implied that some establishments that reported sales were not necessarily resorts.

20. *Sutherland Springs Western Chronicle,* 3 August 1877; *San Antonio Herald,* 5 December 1879; and *Sutherland Springs Health Resort,* 4 April 1911.

21. "Water That Puts Pepper into Plodders Brought a Bonanza to Mineral Wells," *Dallas Times Herald,* 16 July 1978.

22. Hill Houston interview, Marlin, 16 February 1990.

23. *Myrtle Springs Herald,* 19 November 1891.

24. Frank X. Tolbert, *Tolbert's Texas* (New York: Doubleday, 1983), pp. 139–140; "Prospectus of the Proposed Sour Lake Springs Company of Texas."

25. Ross Estes and Robert Duncan, eds., *I Remember Things: An Informal History of Tioga* (Quanah, Tex.: Nortex Press, 1977), p. 56.

7. THE EXPERIENCE OF BATHING

1. Lovie Langford Whitaker, taped interview by Teresa Whittington, 30 August 1976, Archives of the Big Bend, Bryan Wildenthal Library, Sul Ross State University, Alpine, Texas.

2. Fannie Darden to *Sutherland Springs Western Chronicle*, 7 September 1877.

3. Pat Ellis Taylor, *The God Chaser* (Austin: Slough Press, 1986), p. 115. The author now calls herself Pat Littledog.

4. George E. Walton, *The Mineral Springs of the United States and Canada* (New York: D. Appleton, 1883, 1892), p. 24; François Françon et al., "Classification of Therapeutic Mineral Waters," in Sidney Licht, ed., *Medical Hydrology* (Baltimore: Waverly Press, 1963), p. 391.

5. C.D.M., "Sour Lake Letters," *Galveston Daily News*, 14 July 1857.

6. W. E. Fitch, ed., *Mineral Waters of the United States and American Spas* (Philadelphia: Lea and Febinger, 1927), pp. 30–41.

7. "Lampasas, Texas: Its Mineral Springs," pamphlet (Chicago: Poole, ca. 1888; reprint, 1972).

8. *Lampasas Daily Times*, 28 June 1878.

9. *Sutherland Springs Western Chronicle*, 26 January 1877.

10. C.D.M., "Sour Lake Letters."

11. Walton, *The Mineral Springs of the United States and Canada*, pp. 22–23. Derivation of color is considered a more complex process today. Physical characteristics generally depend upon the predominant chemicals or contaminants. Some waters may appear opalescent—white from sulphur, blue from the decomposition of alkaline sulphurs, or red from irons. Organic material from decaying vegetation may produce a yellow or brown color. If deep brown, the water may have passed through peat or lignite. Generally, more colored waters occur in areas of abundant vegetation. See François Françon et al., "Classification of Therapeutic Mineral Waters," and John D. Hem, "The Geochemistry of Water," in Licht, *Medical Hydrology*, pp. 391, 44–45.

12. J. De Cordova, *Texas: Her Resources and Her Public Men* (Philadelphia: Lippincott, 1858), pp. 274–275.

13. Traylor Russell, *History of Titus County, Texas* (Waco: W. M. Morrison, 1965), pp. 239–240.

14. Glen Rose Chamber of Commerce, "Glen Rose, Texas: The Famous Health and Pleasure Resort," pamphlet, 1925, Center for American History, University of Texas at Austin; John Henry Brown to editor of *Dallas Herald*, reprinted in *Glen Rose Citizen*, 10 September 1885; and De Cordova, *Texas: Her Resources and Her Public Men*, p. 258.

15. Josephine Polley Golson, *Bailey's Light: Saga of Brit Bailey and Other Hardy Pioneers* (San Antonio: Naylor, 1950), p. 105.

16. Frank X. Tolbert, "The Black Spring Wouldn't Freeze," *Dallas Morning News*, 29 August 1961.

17. "Sour Lake: One of the Wonders of the World," *Gulf Messenger* 10, no. 5 (May 1897): 229; Robert Cotner, *James Stephen Hogg: A Biography* (Austin: University of Texas Press, 1959), pp. 547–548.

18. *Myrtle Springs Herald*, 19 November 1891.

19. Woods Hutchinson, "Taking the Waters: The Humbug of Hot Springs," *Everybody's Magazine* 28, no. 2 (February 1913): 160.

20. Aline Thompson Rothe, "Texas 'Fountain of Youth,'" *Houston Chronicle*, 10 April 1949. The geologist A. R. Roessler also predicted that huge quantities of oil underlay the area, a fact confirmed twenty-five years later. Today it is generally considered that sodium chloride will impart a salty taste, magnesium sulfate a bitter taste, and carbon dioxide an acid taste.

21. "Sam Crane on Marlin," *Marlin Democrat*, 29 February 1908.

22. Charlotte B. Teske to author, 30 June 1990; and *Mineral Wells Daily Index*, 6 May 1907.

23. A. F. McKay, "Waco: The Geyser City of Texas," *American Climates and Resorts*, 1893; reprint *Waco Heritage and History* 3, no. 3 (Fall 1972).

24. Richard Peacock interview, 3 February 1991.

25. Harris interview; Phoebe Young Armstrong, *From the Forks of Turkey Creek* (privately printed, 1987), p. 26.

26. *Lampasas Dispatch*, 23 May 1878.

27. *Lampasas Daily Times*, 29 August 1878.

28. De Cordova, *Texas*, p. 258.

29. *Sutherland Springs Western Chronicle*, 24 August 1877.

30. Mamie Wynne Cox, *A Love Story of Mineral Wells* (Mineral Wells, Tex.: Index, 1932), p. 8.

31. Mineral Wells Commercial Club, "Quarterly Guide," brochure, 1909, Mineral Wells Vertical File, Rosenberg Library, Galveston.

32. Whitaker interview by Whittington.

33. *Mineral Wells Daily Index*, 6 May 1907; A. F. Weaver, *Time Was in Mineral Wells: A Crazy Story but True* . . . (Mineral Wells: Mineral Wells Heritage Society and Houghton-Bennett, 1975), pp. 56, 129.

34. William Schuyler Frost, ed., *Review Marlin* (Quanah, Tex.: Nortex, 1909), p. 8.

35. Oltorf interview.

36. Marlin Chamber of Commerce, "Modern Bath Houses, Clinics and Sanitariums," pamphlet, ca. 1940, Marlin Vertical File, Center for American History, University of Texas at Austin; Evelyn Andress, "The South's Greatest Health Resort," n.d., in WPA Falls County Scrapbook, Center for American History, University of Texas at Austin; Peacock interview.

37. Anne A. Fox and Cheryl Lynn Highley, *History and Archaeology of the Hot Wells Hotel Site*, Archaeological Survey Report no. 152 (San Antonio: Center for Archaeological Research, University of Texas at San Antonio, 1985), p. 14. Other details on the Hot Wells Bathhouse appear in *San Antonio Express*, 9 February 1902.

38. "Lampasas, Geographical Center," *Texas Magazine* (November 1910): p. 71.

39. Meg A. Fone, "Bathhouse Row," *Marlin Democrat*, 11 March 1908.

40. Velva White interview, Mineral Wells, 6 June 1990.

41. Grace Catherine Calvin, "Marlin Wells: Pride of Brazos Valley," clipping, ca. 1929, in "Texas Cities and Towns," Texas Scrapbooks, Houston Public Library.

42. *Marlin Democrat*, 11 March 1908.

8. PLACES LOST

1. T. C. Richardson, *Autobiography of the Rambling Longhorn* (Oklahoma City: Farmer-Stockman, 1959), p. 59.

2. Mrs. Fred Anderson interview, Austin, 16 October 1990, and Lillian Masters interview, Floresville, 24 February 1991.

3. Fay B. Allbritton to James Turner, 26 November 1968; Flora Eaves to Lottie May Walker, 20 April 1956, both in Scrapbook of Susan Bass, Bremond, Texas; J. W. Baker, "Wootan Wells, a Cen-Tex Ghost Town," *Waco Tribune-Herald*, 23 November 1969.

4. "35 Years Ago," *Palo Pinto County Star*, 3 July and 13 November 1940.

5. Helen M. Carter and Pat B. Randolph, eds., *Legends and Memories of Glen Rose, Texas* (Dallas: Randolph Publishing, 1987), p. 8; Jim Davis, telephone interview, Hitchcock, Texas, 3 November 1990. For a list of many springs that did dry up, see Gunnar Brune, *Springs of Texas*, vol. 1 (Fort Worth: Branch-Smith, 1981).

6. Neil Buie Jr., interview, Galveston, 14 June 1990. Dr. Buie ran the bathhouse from 1946 to 1966.

7. Frank Calvert Oltorf, *The Marlin Compound: Letters from a Singular Family* (Austin: University of Texas Press, 1968), p. 266; Buie interview; Richard Peacock, telephone interview, Bryan, 3 February 1991. Some journalists recorded that the Depression particularly hurt business. See Jack Flanders, "Marlin's Magic Mineral Water an Attraction," *Waco Tribune-Herald,* 20 July 1974; and Judy Williamson, "Marlin: A Texas Town's Mineral 'Rites,'" *Dallas Morning News,* 12 December 1982.

8. Cameron Quinn, as quoted in Randy Eli Grothe, "A Golden Past, and a Broken Present," *Dallas Morning News,* 5 December 1976.

9. Arthur J. Cramp, ed., *Nostrums and Quackery* (Chicago: American Medical Association, 1921); American Medical Association, *Mineral Waters* (Chicago: American Medical Association Bureau of Investigation, 1934), pp. 9, 12–13, 25; Harvey W. Wiley and Anne Lewis Pierce, "The Mineral Water Humbug," *Good Housekeeping* 59 (1914): 108.

10. "Mineral Wells Advertising to Be Censored," *Texas State Journal of Medicine* 7 (May 1915): 5–6.

11. Gene Fowler, *Crazy Water: The Story of Mineral Wells and Other Texas Health Resorts* (Fort Worth: Texas Christian University Press, 1991), pp. 46–48.

12. Henry E. Sigerist, "American Spas in Historical Perspective," *Bulletin of the History of Medicine* 11, no. 2 (February 1942): 138–139.

13. Martha Jones, telephone interview, Wizard Wells, 8 September 1990; Jim Davis, telephone interview, 3 November 1990.

14. Frank Calvert Oltorf, interview, Marlin, 16 February 1990.

15. Neil Buie Jr., interview, Galveston, 14 June 1990.

16. Richard Peacock, telephone interview, Bryan, 3 February 1991.

17. Ruby Harris, interview, Marlin, 6 March 1991; Vernon Daniels, telephone interview, Mineral Wells, 6 June 1990.

18. Sigerist, "American Spas in Historical Perspective."

19. Martha Hand, interview, Rosborough Springs, 7 August 1990; Corine Tolleson to author, 14 March 1991.

9. POSTSCRIPT: SONG OF THE SACRED WATERS

1. Sophia Vickrey Ard, quoted in Patricia L. Barton to Janet Valenza, 28 March 1991.

$\mathcal{B}ibliography$

$\mathcal{G}eneral$

Addison, William. *English Spas.* London: B. T. Batsford, 1951.

Albanese, Catherine L. *Nature Religion in America.* Chicago: University of Chicago Press, 1990.

Alderson, Frederick. *The Inland Resorts and Spas of Britain.* Newton Abbot: David and Charles, 1973.

American Medical Association. *American Medical Directory.* Vol. 1. Chicago: American Medical Association, 1906.

————. *Mineral Waters.* Chicago: American Medical Association Bureau of Investigation, 1934.

Amory, Cleveland. *The Last Resorts.* New York: Harper, 1952.

Anderson, Winslow. *Mineral Springs and Health Resorts of California.* San Francisco: Bancroft, 1892.

Armstrong, Samuel T. "Waters, Mineral." In *Reference Book of Practical Therapeutics,* vol. 2. Edited by Frank P. Foster. New York: D. Appleton, 1897.

"An Association of Medical Hydrology: The Great Need of Immediate Action, Popularize Our American Spas." *Journal of American Medical Hydrology* 1, no. 1 (January 1932).

Baker, D. W. C., ed. *A Texas Scrap Book Made Up of the History, Biography, and Miscellany of Texas and Its People.* Austin: Steck, 1935.

Baudisch, Oskar. "Magic and Science of Natural Healing Waters." *Journal of Chemical Education* 16 (September 1939): 440–448.

Baur, John E. *The Health Seekers of Southern California 1870–1900.* San Marino, Calif.: Huntington Library, 1959.

Bell, A. N. *Climatology and Mineral Waters of the U.S.* New York: William Wood, 1885.

Bell, John. *The Mineral and Thermal Springs of the United States and Canada.* Philadelphia: Parry and McMillan, 1855.

Bemelmans, Ludwig. "How I Took the Cure." *Holiday* 25 (1959): 64–65.

Bolton, Herbert Eugene. *Texas in the Middle Eighteenth Century: Studies in Spanish Colonial History and Administration.* Austin: University of Texas Press and Texas State Historical Association, 1970.

Bonnell, George W. *Topographical Description of Texas.* Austin: Clark, Wing, Brown, 1840.

Bracht, Viktor. *Texas in 1848.* Translated by Charles Frank Schmidt. San Antonio: Naylor, 1931.

Braman, D. E. E. *Braman's Information about Texas.* Philadelphia: J. B. Lippincott, 1857.

Breckinridge, Anne. "Health Resorts." *Hygeia* 15 (1937): 728–730.

Bridenbaugh, Carl. "Baths and Watering Places of Colonial America." *William and Mary Quarterly* 3, no. 2 (April 1946): 150–181.

Brown, Dee. *The American Spa.* Little Rock: Rose, 1982.

Bruce Jr., Dickson D. *And They Sang Hallelujah.* Knoxville: University of Tennessee Press, 1974.

Brune, Gunnar. *Springs of Texas.* Vol. 1. Fort Worth: Branch-Smith, 1981.

Bryan, Kirk. "Classification of Springs." *Journal of Geology* 27 (1919): 522–561.

Buie, Neil. "The Modern Spa: Health or Hokum." *Texas State Journal of Medicine* 58 (May 1962): 323–324.

Burkhalter, Lois. *Gideon Lincecum.* Austin: University of Texas Press, 1965.

Burroughs, Sam R. "Report of Committee on Indigenous Medical Resources of Texas." *Transactions.* Marshall: Texas State Medical Association, 1877.

Cassedy, James H. *Medicine and American Growth, 1800–1860.* University of Wisconsin Press, 1986.

Charnofsky, Kim. "California Mineral and Hot Springs: Historical and Geographical Considerations in Their Perception, Location, and Development." Master's thesis, University of California at Berkeley, 1989.

Coleman, James M. *Aesculapius on the Colorado: The Story of Medical Practice in Travis County to 1899.* Austin: Encino Press, 1971.

Collins, W. D. "Mineral Waters." In *Mineral Resources of the U.S. for 1920,* pp. 161–163. Washington, D.C.: United States Geological Survey (USGS) and Government Printing Office (GPO), 1920.

"Common Sense Concerning Mineral Waters." *Texas State Journal of Medicine* 3 (1907): 206.

Cramp, Arthur J., ed. *Nostrums and Quackery.* Chicago: American Medical Association, 1921.

Crook, J. K. *The Mineral Waters of the United States and Their Therapeutic Uses.* New York: Lea, 1899.

De Cordova, J. *Texas: Her Resources and Her Public Men.* Philadelphia: J. B. Lippincott, 1858.

Demars, Stanford E. "British Contributions to American Seaside Resorts." *Annals of Tourism Research* 6 (1979): 285–293.

Deussen, Alexander. "Geology and Underground Waters of the Southeastern Part of the Texas Coastal Plain." USGS Water Supply Paper 335. Washington, D.C.: GPO, 1914.

Dieter, Melvin E. *The Holiness Revival of the Nineteenth Century.* Metuchen, N.J.: Scarecrow Press, 1980.

Disturnell, John. *Springs, Water-Falls, Sea-Bathing Resorts and Mountain Scenery of the U.S. and Canada; Giving an Analysis of the Principal Mineral Springs, with a Brief Description of the Most Fashionable Watering-Place, Mountain Resorts . . .* New York: Disturnell, 1855.

Dole, R. B. "Mineral Water Concentration in Relation to Therapeutic Activity." In *Mineral Resources of the U.S.,* pp. 1175–1192. Washington: USGS and GPO, 1911.

Dos Passos, Katharine. "Sweet Waters of the South." *Woman's Home Companion* 65 (1938): 21, 144.

"The Drinking of Mineral Waters." *Texas State Journal of Medicine* 2 (1915): 241.

Duffy, John. *The Healers: The Rise of the Medical Establishment.* New York: McGraw-Hill, 1976.

Dumble, E. T., ed. *First Annual Report of the Geological Survey of Texas, 1889.* Austin: State Printing, 1890.

Dunlap, E. Dale. "Tuesday Meetings, Camp Meetings, and Cabinet Meetings." *Methodist History* 13 (October 1974): 85–106.

Eastman, Max. "Healing at the Shrine." *Texas Review* 6 (June 1915): 120–135.

Edward, David B. *The History of Texas.* Cincinnati: J. A. James, 1836.

Eliade, Mircea. *The Sacred and the Profane: The Nature of Religion.* San Diego: Harcourt Brace Jovanovich, 1957.

Ellis, Arthur J. "Mineral Waters." In *Mineral Resources of the U.S.,* pp. 463–510. Washington, D.C.: USGS and GPO, 1917.

Fisher, Orceneth. *Sketches: Texas in 1840.* Springfield, Ill.: Walters and Weber, 1841. Reprint, Austin: Texian Press, 1964.

Fitch, W. E., ed. *Mineral Waters of the United States and American Spas.* Philadelphia: Lea and Febinger, 1927.

Fowler, Gene. *Crazy Water: The Story of Mineral Wells and Other Texas Health Resorts.* Fort Worth: Texas Christian University Press, 1991.

Fox, Daniel E. *Traces of Texas History: Archaeological Evidence of the Past 450 Years.* San Antonio: Corona, 1983.

Frazier, J. M. "Hydrotherapy." *Texas State Journal of Medicine* 3 (1907): 92–95.

Fuller, Myron L. "Mineral Waters." In *Mineral Resources of the United States,* pp. 1285–1312. Washington, D.C.: USGS and GPO, 1905.

Fuller, Robert C. *Alternative Medicine and American Religious Life.* New York: Oxford University Press, 1989.

Geological Survey of Texas. *Second Annual Report of the Geological Survey of Texas, 1890.* Austin: State Printing, 1891.

Gordon, C. "Geology and Underground Water of Northeastern Texas." USGS Water Supply Paper 276. Washington, D.C.: USGS and GPO, 1911.

Gould, George M. *A New Medical Dictionary.* Philadelphia: P. Blakiston, 1892.

Greenhouse, Steven. "Fading of a Spa: Incurable? Or Will a Face Lift Do?" *New York Times,* 25 July 1988.

Haggard, Howard W. "American Health Resorts: The Historical Background of Resort Therapy." *Journal of the American Medical Association* 123, no. 16 (18 December 1943): 1037–1042.

Haywood, J. K., and B. Smith. *Mineral Waters of the United States.* Bureau of Chemistry Bulletin 91. Washington: U.S. Department of Agriculture, 1905.

Hendrix, John M. "Livin' Water." *The Cattleman* 33 (December 1946): 25–28, 102–105.

Henry, Christopher D. *Geologic Setting and Geochemistry of Thermal Water and Geothermal Assessment, Trans-Pecos Texas.* Austin: Bureau of Economic Geology, University of Texas at Austin, 1979.

Hepburn, Andrew. *Great Resorts of North America.* New York: Doubleday, 1965.

Hill, R. T. "Geography and Geology of the Black and Grand Prairies, Texas." In *21st Annual Report.* Washington, D.C.: USGS and GPO, 1901.

Hinsdale, Guy. "American Mineral Springs: With Special Reference to the Thermal Springs of Virginia and Methods Employed in Their Use." *International Clinics* 2 (1916): 37–41.

Hirsch, Judith Brode. *The Spa Book.* New York: Putnam, 1988.

Hirsch, William C. "Historical Springs." *Current Literature* 34, no. 3 (1903): 297–298.

Hollon, W. Eugene, and Ruth L. Butler, eds. *William Bollaert's Texas.* Norman: University of Oklahoma Press, 1956.

Houston and Texas Central Railroad. *Points of Interest to Tired People.* Houston: Houston and Texas Central Railroad, ca. 1900. Center for American History, University of Texas at Austin.

Hutchinson, Woods. "Taking the Waters: The Humbug of Hot Springs." *Everybody's Magazine* 28, no. 2 (February 1913): 159–172.

Illich, Ivan. *H₂O and the Waters of Forgetfulness.* Dallas: Dallas Institute of Humanities and Culture, 1985.

Jackson, John Brinckerhoff. *The Southern Landscape Tradition in Texas.* Fort Worth: Amon Carter Museum, 1980.

Johnson, Charles A. "The Frontier Camp Meeting: Contemporary and Historical Appraisals, 1805–1840." *Mississippi Valley Historical Review* 37, no. 1 (June 1950): 91–110.

Jones, Billy M. "A Burden on the Southwest: Migrant Tuberculars in the Nineteenth Century." *Southwestern Social Science Quarterly* 47, no. 1 (1966): 59–67.

———. "Health Seekers in Early Anglo-American Texas." *Southwestern Historical Quarterly* 19 (1966): 287–299.

———. *Health-Seekers in the Southwest, 1817–1900.* Norman: University of Oklahoma Press, 1967.

Kennedy, William. "Report on Grimes, Brazos, and Robertson County." *4th Annual Report of the USGS.* Washington, D.C.: GPO, 1893.

Kisch, E. Heinrich. *Balneology and Crounotherapy.* Vol. 9. Translated by A. Eshner. Philadelphia: P. Blakiston's Son, 1902.

Kovacs, Richard. "The Problem of American Spas." *Journal of the American Medical Association* 127 (April 14, 1945): 977.

———. "Springs of Health." *Travel* 77 (1941): 32–34.

Krusen, Frank H. "American Health Resorts: The Place of Health Resorts in Rehabilitation Following Injuries." *Journal of the American Medical Association* 125, no. 13 (July 29, 1944): 905–910.

Lawrence, Henry W. "Southern Spas: Source of the American Resort Tradition." *Landscape* 27, no. 2 (1983): 1–12.

Levin, Alexandra. "Taking the Waters." *Early American Life* (August 1988): 10–13, 79.

Licht, Sidney, ed. *Medical Hydrology.* Baltimore: Waverly Press, 1963.

Loam, Jayson, and Gary Sohler. *Hot Springs and Hot Pools of the Southwest.* Berkeley: Wilderness Press, 1985.

Lone Star Guide: Description of Counties on the International and Great Northern Railroad of Texas. St. Louis: Woodward, Tiernan, and Hale, 1878.

Lowenthal, David. "Tourists and Thermalists." *Geographical Review* 52 (1962): 124–127.

Matson, George Charlton. "Mineral Waters." In *Mineral Resources of the U.S.*, pp. 921–54. Washington, D.C.: USGS and GPO, 1910.

McClellan, Walter S. "Spa Therapy." *The Interne* (October 1946): 671–677.

McLoughlin, William G. *Revivals, Awakenings, and Reform.* Chicago: University of Chicago Press, 1978.

"Mineral Waters in Malarial Diseases." *Daniel's Texas Medical Journal* 2, no. 7 (1887): 284–285.

"Mineral Wells Advertising to Be Censored." *Texas State Journal of Medicine* 7 (May 1915): 5–6.

Moore Jr., Francis. *Map and Description of Texas.* Philadelphia: H. Tanner, 1840.

Moorman, J. J. *Mineral Springs of North America, How to Reach Them and How to Use Them.* Philadelphia: J. B. Lippincott, 1873.

"Our 'Mineral Waters' and 'Places of Resort.'" *Texas Medical and Surgical Record* 2, no. 8 (August 1882): 350–352.

Parker, Charles A. "The Camp Meeting on the Frontier and the Methodist Religious Resort in the East—Before 1900." *Methodist History* 18 (1980): 178–192.

Peale, A. C. "Mineral Springs of the United States." In *USGS Bulletin*, no. 32, pp. 124–128. Washington, D.C.: GPO, 1886.

Pepper, W., and H. Bowditch. "Report of the Committee on Sanitaria and on Mineral Springs." In American Medical Association, ed., *Transactions* 31 (1880): 537–565.

Pomeroy, Earl. *In Search of the Golden West: The Tourist in Western America.* New York: Knopf, 1957.

Potts, Charles S. *Railroad Transportation in Texas.* Bulletin of the University of Texas, no. 119. Austin: University of Texas, 1909.

Reniers, Perceval. *The Springs of Virginia.* Chapel Hill: University of North Carolina Press, 1941.

Reynolds, Charles R. "American Health Resorts: The Importance of Health Resorts and Their Facilities in Medical Preparedness." *Journal of the American Medical Association* 123, no. 13 (November 27, 1943): 832–836.

Rhodes, Harrison. "American Holidays: Springs and Mountains." *Harper's Monthly Magazine* 129 (September 1914): 536–547.

Richardson, D. *Texas as Seen in 1870.* Shreveport: Caddo Gazette, 1870.

Richardson, T. C., and Dabney White, eds. *East Texas: Its History and Its Makers.* New York: Lewis Historical, 1940.

Roberts, O. M. *A Description of Texas, Its Advantages and Resources.* St. Louis: Gilbert, 1881.

Rock, James, and W. I. Smith. *Southern and Western Texas Guide for 1878.* St. Louis: A. H. Granger, 1878.

San Antonio Daily Herald, 26 October 1866.

Sanford, Samuel. "Mineral Waters." In *Mineral Resources of the U.S.,* pp. 1165–94. Washington, D.C.: USGS and GPO, 1906.

Sears, John F. *Sacred Places: American Tourist Attractions in the Nineteenth Century.* New York: Oxford University Press, 1989.

Shuler, Ellis W. "The Influence of the Shore Line, Rivers, and Springs on the Settlement and Early Development of Texas." *Texas Geographic Magazine* 4, no. 2 (1940): 26–31.

Sigerist, Henry E. "American Spas in Historical Perspective." *Bulletin of the History of Medicine* 11, no. 2 (February 1942): 133–147.

Simons, A. M. "American Health Resorts: Economic Aspects of Health Resort Therapy." *Journal of the American Medical Association* 124, no. 1 (January 1, 1944): 33–35.

Smith, D. H. "The Value of Mineral Springs in the Treatment of Certain Ailments." *Journal of American Medical Hydrology* 1, no. 1 (1932): 22–23.

Snyder, Eldon E. "The Chautauqua Movement in Popular Culture: A Sociological Analysis." *Journal of American Culture* 8, no. 3 (Fall 1985): 79–82.

Starr, Paul. *The Social Transformation of American Medicine.* New York: Basic Books, 1982.

Stiff, Edward. *The Texas Emigrant.* Waco: Texian Press, 1968.

Texas Agriculture Bureau. *Fourth Annual Report of Agriculture Bureau, 1890–91.* Austin: Henry Hutchings, 1892.

Texas Almanac. Dallas: Dallas News and A. H. Belo, 1859, 1904, 1912, 1929, 1941–1942, 1945–1946, 1949–1950.

Texas Business Directory. Austin: Texas Directory Company, 1878.

Texas State Gazetteer and Business Directory. Detroit: R. L. Polk, 1884–1885, 1890–1891, 1892, 1896–1897, 1914.

Texas State Medical Association. *Transactions.* Austin: Draughon and Lambert, 1885.

Thrall, Homer S. *A Pictorial History of Texas from the Earliest Visits of European Adventurers, to A.D. 1879.* St. Louis: N. D. Thompson, 1879.

United States Geological Survey. "Mineral Waters." In *Mineral Resources of the U.S.,* pp. 680–687. Washington, D.C.: USGS and GPO, 1887.

———. "Mineral Waters." In *Mineral Resources of the U.S.,* pp. 623–29. Washington, D.C.: USGS and GPO, 1888.

———. "Mineral Waters." In *Mineral Resources of the U.S.,* pp. 601–10. Washington, D.C.: USGS and GPO, 1891.

———. "Mineral Waters." In *Mineral Resources of the U.S.,* pp. 823–33. Washington, D.C.: USGS and GPO, 1892.

———. "Mineral Waters." In *Mineral Resources of the U.S.,* pp. 772–94. Washington, D.C.: USGS and GPO, 1893.

———. "Mineral Waters." In *Mineral Resources of the U.S.*, pp. 1025–44. Washington, D.C.: USGS and GPO, 1895.

———. "Mineral Waters." In *Mineral Resources of the U.S.*, pp. 747–69. Washington, D.C.: USGS and GPO, 1898.

———. "Mineral Waters." In *Mineral Resources of the U.S.*, pp. 521–35. Washington, D.C.: USGS and GPO, 1899.

———. "Mineral Waters." In *Mineral Resources of the U.S.*, pp. 899–905. Washington, D.C.: USGS and GPO, 1900.

———. "Mineral Waters." In *Mineral Resources of the U.S.*, pp. 961–66. Washington, D.C.: USGS and GPO, 1901.

———. "Mineral Waters." In *Mineral Resources of the U.S.*, pp. 1–30. Washington, D.C.: USGS and GPO, 1903.

———. "Mineral Waters." In *Mineral Resources of the U.S.*, pp. 751–79. Washington, D.C.: USGS and GPO, 1907.

———. "Mineral Waters." In *Mineral Resources of the U.S.*, pp. 755–87. Washington, D.C.: USGS and GPO, 1908.

———. "Mineral Waters." In *Mineral Resources of the U.S.*, pp. 1093–1131. Washington, D.C.: USGS and GPO, 1912.

———. "Mineral Waters." In *Mineral Resources of the U.S.*, pp. 176–221. Washington, D.C.: USGS and GPO, 1914.

———. "Mineral Waters." In *Mineral Resources of the U.S.*, pp. 307–40. Washington, D.C.: USGS and GPO, 1915.

———. "Mineral Waters." In *Mineral Resources of the U.S.*, pp. 307–44. Washington, D.C.: USGS and GPO, 1916.

———. "Mineral Waters." In *Mineral Resources of the U.S. for 1918*, pp. 495–528. Washington, D.C.: USGS and GPO, 1918.

———. "Mineral Waters." In *Mineral Resources of the U.S. for 1919*, pp. 115–45. Washington, D.C.: USGS and GPO, 1919.

———. "Mineral Waters." In *Mineral Resources of the U.S. for 1923*, pp. 109–23. Washington, D.C.: USGS and GPO, 1923.

———. "The Natural Mineral Waters of the United States." In *Fourteenth Annual Report*, pp. 49–88. Washington, D.C.: USGS and GPO, 1894.

———. "The Production of Mineral Waters." In *Mineral Resources of the U.S.*, pp. 1–34. Washington, D.C.: USGS and GPO, 1902.

———. "The Production of Mineral Waters in 1904." In *Mineral Resources of the U.S.*, pp. 1–32. Washington, D.C.: USGS and GPO, 1904.

Vance Jr., James E. "California and the Search for the Ideal." *Annals of the Association of American Geographers* 62 (June 1972): 185–210.

Vollmer, Ryan. *Affordable Spas and Fitness Resorts*. Chapel Hill: Ventana Press, 1988.

Walton, George E. *The Mineral Springs of the United States and Canada*. New York: D. Appleton, 1883, 1892.

Webb, Walter Prescott, ed. *The Handbook of Texas*. Austin: Texas State Historical Association, 1952.

Weber, F. Parkes, and Guy Hinsdale. *Climatology: Health Resorts—Mineral Springs*. Philadelphia: P. Blakiston, 1901.

Whilldin, M., ed. *A Description of Western Texas*. Galveston: Galveston, Harrisburg, and San Antonio Railway, 1876.

Wiley, Harvey W., and Anne Lewis Pierce. "The Mineral Water Humbug." *Good Housekeeping* 59 (1914): 107–111.

Williamson, Jefferson. *The American Hotel.* New York: Knopf, 1930.

Willis, J. M. "Report of Committee on the Mineral Waters of Texas." In *Transactions,* pp. 199–212. Fort Worth: Texas State Medical Association, 1884.

Wilson, John. *Health and Health Resorts.* Philadelphia: Porter and Coates, 1880.

Yandell, W. M. "The Climate of Trans-Pecos Texas, Compared with That of Other Parts of the State, with Special Reference to a Suitable Climate for Consumptives." *Texas Sanitarian* 5, no. 8 (June 1896): 25–32.

———. *A Winter Health Resort.* El Paso: Times Publishing, 1884.

Young, James Harvey. *The Toadstool Millionaires: Social History of Patent Medicines in America before Federal Regulation.* Princeton: Princeton University Press, 1961.

Zlatkovich, Charles P. *Texas Railroads: A Record of Construction and Abandonment.* Austin: University of Texas at Austin, Bureau of Business Research and Texas State Historical Association, 1981.

Texas Spas

ARLINGTON MINERAL WELLS (TARRANT COUNTY)

"Backward Glimpses." *Arlington Daily News,* 7 June 1976.

Joyner, Arista. *Arlington, Texas: Birthplace of the Metroplex.* Arlington: Arlington Bicentennial/Centennial Celebration Committee, 1976.

"Mineral Well Site Downtown due City Commemoration." *Arlington Citizen-Journal,* 24 March 1976.

"Rich Mineral Water Lies below Arlington Streets." *Arlington Citizen-Journal,* February 1972.

Stein, Michelle. "It's the Water." *Fort Worth Star-Telegram,* 15 June 1986.

BELL COUNTY'S WATERS

Atkinson, Bertha. "History of Bell County." Master's thesis, University of Texas at Austin, 1929.

Barton, Patricia L. Letter to Janet Valenza, 28 March 1991.

Dallas Morning News, 15 July 1925.

Tyler, George W. *History of Bell County.* San Antonio: Naylor, 1936.

BEXAR COUNTY'S WATERS

Advertisement for Harlandale Baths. *San Antonio Light,* 1 October 1911.

Beare, Virginia. "At the Old Dullnig Wells Hotel and Bath House." *San Antonio Reporter,* 11 August 1977.

Burkett, Lynnell. "Plans Are Underway to Restore Hot Wells Hotel." *North San Antonio Times,* 6 December 1979.

"The Cincinnati Reds Arrive in the City." *San Antonio Daily Light,* 17 March 1906.

De Vierville, Jonathan. San Antonio. Interview, 21 April 1989.

Diehl, Suzanne. "San Antonio's Ostrich Farms." *San Antonio Express,* 14 February 1971.

Dullnig, Sue. "George Dullnig and San Antonio . . . A Partnership." Manuscript, San Antonio Conservation Society, 1979.

"Dullnig's Chalybeate or Iron Water." San Antonio: Guessaz and Ferlet, 1897. Center for American History, University of Texas at Austin.

Durand, Herbert. *The City of Missions: San Antonio, Texas.* St. Louis: Woodward and Tiernan, 1894.

"Fire Damages Former Hot Wells Hotel." *San Antonio Express,* 18 January 1925.

Fox, Anne A., and Cheryl Lynn Highley. *History and Archaeology of the Hot Wells Hotel Site.* Archaeological Survey Report no. 152. San Antonio: Center for Archaeological Research, University of Texas at San Antonio, 1985.

"French Eye $50 Million Resort of Hot Wells." *San Antonio Express-News,* 12 June 1987.

"Gloria Swanson to Visit S.A." *San Antonio Express,* 12 September 1980.

Haines-Saine, Renee. "Former San Antonio Spa Nearing Rebirth." *Houston Chronicle,* 23 August 1985.

"Harriman Spends Quiet Day in Camp." *San Antonio Express,* 20 February 1909.

Hot Sulphur Baths. San Antonio: Guessaz and Ferlet, 1902. Center for American History, University of Texas at Austin.

"Hot Sulphur Wells Opening." *San Antonio Daily Express,* 5 September 1900.

"Hot Wells," Mission Parkway File, National Register of Historic Places, Texas Historical Commission, n.d.

Johnson, David R. "Early Tourists Came for Health." *San Antonio Light,* 20 October 1985.

Kase, Kathryn. "Hot Wells Gets County Boost." *San Antonio Light,* 11 September 1985.

Missouri Pacific Railway Company. *San Antonio as a Health and Pleasure Resort.* St. Louis: Woodward and Tiernan, ca. 1901.

Muncy, Mary E. "San Antonio." *Gulf Messenger* 7, no. 4 (1894): 450–451.

"The New Bath House." *San Antonio Daily Express,* 11 June 1893.

Noonan-Guerra, Mary Ann. *The Story of the San Antonio River.* San Antonio: San Antonio River Authority, 1978.

"Palm Sunday at the Resorts." *San Antonio Express,* 1 April 1901.

Phillips, Susie. "Historic Baths Need Cash Flow." *San Antonio Express-News,* 17 June 1985.

Sisk, K. Mack. "Hot Wells Looking for Cool Million." *San Antonio Light,* 7 May 1975.

Shaffer, David J. "Hot Wells Hotel Could Get Japanese Investors." *San Antonio Light,* 11 November 1987.

Southern Pacific Line. *San Antonio: The Mission City.* Houston: Southern Pacific Line, 1916.

Spencer, Gayle. "Hot Wells Hotel Drew Celebrities for Sulphur Cure." *Paseo del Rio Showboat,* February 1979.

Sullivan, M. J., ed. *International Blue Book Publication.* San Antonio: M. J. Sullivan, 1912.

"Terrell Hot Wells Figure in Plans for Famous 'Spa': Hotel and Buildings to Cost $1,000,000." *San Antonio Light,* 13 February 1910.

Terrell Well Company. "We Want to Tell You about the Terrell Hot Well: The Well that Contains Radium." San Antonio: Terrell Well Company, 1910. Center for American History, University of Texas at Austin.

"Terrell Wells: A Modern Health and Rest Resort." ca. 1926. Terrell Wells Vertical File, San Antonio Conservation Society.

"Through the Hot Wells Hotel." *San Antonio Light,* 8 July 1902.

Watkins, Sharon. "Swanson's Still Very Much a Star." *San Antonio Light,* 16 September 1980.

Wood, Jim. "S.A. Group to Court Japanese Funds." *San Antonio Express-News,* 11 November 1987.

CALDWELL COUNTY'S WATERS

Biggs, Willie. Luling. Telephone interview, 15 March 1991.

Galveston Daily News. 1877, 1883.

Galveston, Harrisburg, and San Antonio Railway. *Western Texas as a Winter Resort.* N.p., 1878.

Lockhart Register, 19 November 1900.

Maudling Land Company. "Burdette Wells: Where the Water Fairy Dwells." San Antonio: N.p., ca. 1911. Center for American History, University of Texas at Austin.

Lockhart Morning Courier, 5 October 1908.

San Antonio Herald, 5 December 1879.

Wilson, Francis. "Burditt's Well: Caldwell County, Texas." *Plum Creek Almanac* 5, no. 2 (1987): 113.

CAMPBELL (HUNT COUNTY)

Conrad, James. Letter to Janet Valenza, 1990.

CAPP'S WELL (TYLER COUNTY)

Teske, Charlotte B. *Longview: From Then . . . Til Now.* Longview: Self-published, 1987.

CARLSBAD (TOM GREEN COUNTY)

Hunter, J. Marvin. "A Texas Town That Faded." *Frontier Times* 18, no. 1 (October 1940): 13–14.

———. "Lusty Carlsbad Once Noted Health Resort." *San Angelo Standard Times,* 29 August 1954.

CARRIZO SPRINGS (DIMMIT COUNTY)

"Carrizo Springs Future as a Health Resort." *Carrizo Springs Javelin,* 2 August 1913.

Carrizo Springs Javelin.

CHALYBEATE (MUSGROVE) SPRINGS (WOOD COUNTY)

Bolding, Charles D. "Musgrove Springs or Chalybeate Springs." 7 December 1989. Marker File, Texas Historical Commission.

Jones, Bill. "Tales of Chalybeate Springs." Transcript of radio broadcast over KWNS-FM Stereo, 4 July 1984. Marker File, Texas Historical Commission.

CHALYBEATE CITY (CHEROKEE COUNTY)

"East Texas Boom Town Left to Ghosts." *Sherman Democrat,* 13 June 1980.

"East Texas Town Died Because of Bad Choice." *Dallas Morning News,* 4 April 1954.

New Birmingham Times. 1889 and 1890.

Rusk Cherokeean, 31 August 1972.

CHRISTOVAL (TOM GREEN COUNTY)

"Christoval: Once Known as Mineral Spa, It Still Claims Popularity." *San Angelo Standard-Times,* 23 August 1964.

"Christoval's Life Comes from River." N.p., n.d. Tom Green County Library, San Angelo.

"From Baths to the River." N.p., n.d. Tom Green County Library, San Angelo.

DALBY SPRINGS (BOWIE COUNTY)

Clarksville Standard, 12 July, 4 August 1849.

"Dalby Springs." *Clarksville Standard,* 22 September 1882.

McWilliams, Margaret. "Ghost Town of Red Gold." *Junior Historian* 18, no. 2 (November 1957): 8–10.

Neville, Alexander White. *Backward Glances.* Paris, Tex.: Wright Press, 1985.

Tolbert, Frank X. "The Black Spring Wouldn't Freeze." *Dallas News,* 29 August 1961.

DEAF SMITH COUNTY (HEREFORD)

Ratcliff, J. D. "The Town without a Toothache." *Collier's,* 19 December 1942.

Tolbert, Frank X. "Hereford Exports City Tap Water." *Dallas Morning News,* 28 September 1963.

———. "Town Without Toothaches." *Dallas Morning News,* 16 November 1963.

DUFFAU WELLS (STEPHENS COUNTY)

"Duffau: Land of Good Health and Hearty Crops." *Stephenville Empire-Tribune,* 27 December 1982.
Gibson, Lillie. Letter to author, 31 July 1990.
"Historical Excerpt of Duffau." *Hico News Review,* 23 August 1984.
Perry, H. G. *Grand Ol' Erath: The Saga of a Texas West Cross Timbers County.* Stephenville: Stephenville Printing, 1974.

GEORGETOWN MINERAL WELLS (WILLIAMSON COUNTY)

Scarbrough, Clara Stearns. *Land of Good Water: A Williamson County, Texas, History.* Georgetown: Williamson County Sun, 1973.

GLEN ROSE (SOMERVELL COUNTY)

Carter, Helen M., and Pat B. Randolph, eds. *Legends and Memories of Glen Rose, Texas.* Dallas: Randolph Publishing, 1987.
"Famous Resort Visited on Pleasure Tour." *Dallas Morning News,* 26 June 1938.
Fiedler, Albert G. "Artesian Water in Somervell County Texas." USGS Water Supply Paper 660. Washington, D.C.: GPO, 1934.
"Glen Rose." Marker File, Texas Historical Commission.
Glen Rose Citizen, 1885–86.
Glen Rose Chamber of Commerce. "Glen Rose, Texas: The Famous Health and Pleasure Resort." Pamphlet, 1925. Center for American History, University of Texas at Austin.
"Glen Rose Claims Original Tourists of 10,000,000 B.C." *Dallas Morning News,* 25 July 1937.
"Glen Rose, Texas: 'For Health and Pleasure.'" Pamphlet. N.d. Glen Rose Vertical File, Glen Rose Library.
"Historical Sketch." Inventory of the County Archives of Texas, Somervell County, no. 213. Glen Rose Vertical File, Glen Rose Library.
Martin, Elna. *Glen Rose and Geo. P. Snyder.* Dallas: Bradford Printing, 1927.
Nunn, W. C. *Somerville: Story of a Texas County.* Fort Worth: Texas Christian University Press, 1975.
Sego, Carlie. Glen Rose. Telephone interview, 7 April 1991.
Shelburne, Cephas. "The Hidden City." *Christian Courier,* 18 April 1918. Typewritten copy. Glen Rose Vertical File, Glen Rose Library.
"Snyder Sanitarium." *Somervell County: Centennial, 1875–1975.* Glen Rose: Somervell County Centennial Association, 1975.
"Welcome to Glen Rose, Texas: Home of the Dinosaur and America's Finest Mineral Water." Pamphlet, n.d. Glen Rose Vertical File, Center for American History, University of Texas at Austin.

GONZALES COUNTY'S WATERS

"A Mineral Water from Gonzales." *Texas Sanitarian* 2, no. 1 (1892): 23–24.
Texas Business Directory 1878–79. Austin: Texas Directory, 1878.

GRIMES COUNTY'S WATERS

Advertisement. *Texas Almanac.* Dallas: A. H. Belo, 1859.
Allen, Irene Taylor. *Saga of Anderson.* New York: Greenwich Book Publishers, 1957.
Blessington, J. P. *The Campaigns of Walker's Texas Division.* Austin: Pemberton Press, 1968.
Grimes County Historical Association. *History of Grimes County.* Dallas: Taylor Publishing, 1982.
Houston Weekly Telegraph.
Huntsville Item.

"Kellum Springs, One-Time Famous Health Resort of Grimes County During Era of Civil War, Is Now Practically Forgotten." *Navasota Daily Examiner,* 4 April 1940.

Morford, Betty Houston. "Piedmont Springs Famous as a Health Resort and Social Rendezvous of Generations Past." *Navasota Examiner-Review,* Centennial Edition, 1936.

"Only Ruins of Piedmont Springs, Famous Health Resort, Now Stand." *Navasota Daily Examiner,* 4 April 1940.

"Owls Hoot on Crumbling Buildings of Once Famed Texas Health Resort." *Houston Chronicle,* 9 January 1938.

Phelan, Charlotte. "Piedmont Springs." *Houston Post,* 8 December 1963.

Wilcox, W. T. "History of Piedmont Springs Resort." Typewritten manuscript. Marker File, Texas Historical Commission.

HARRISON COUNTY'S WATERS

Beehn, Mrs. Charles. "Hynson Springs Hotel was Big Enterprise 15 Years." *Marshall News Messenger,* 10 November 1963.

Forrest, Bob. "Historic Hynson Springs Strewn with Debris, Covered by Growth." *Marshall News Messenger,* 9 June 1974.

Hand, Martha. Rosborough Springs. Interview, 7 August 1990.

"History of Harrison County, Texas." *Texas Pioneer Magazine* 5, no. 4 (1880): 224.

Hughes, Inez Hatley. Rosborough Springs. Interview, 7 August 1990.

Inter-State Investment Company. "A Realty Talk." ca. 1905. Typewritten copy. Hynson Vertical File, Marshall Historical Museum Archives.

"Rosborough Springs." *Marshall News Messenger,* August 1897; July 1911. Typewritten copy. Rosborough Springs Vertical File, Marshall Historical Museum Archives.

"Rosborough Springs." *Morning Star,* May 1894. Typewritten copy. Rosborough Springs Vertical File, Marshall Historical Museum Archives.

"Rosborough Springs." WPA Report, n.d. Center for American History, University of Texas at Austin.

"Rosborough Springs: Marshall's Great Health Resort." Pamphlet, n.d. Rosborough Springs Vertical File, Marshall Historical Museum Archives.

Texas Republican, 31 May 1851.

"Two Important Resorts Located Near Marshall." *Marshall News Messenger,* 10 November 1963.

HOT SPRINGS (BREWSTER COUNTY)

Baker, T. Lindsay. *Ghost Towns of Texas.* Norman: University of Oklahoma Press, 1986.

"The Big Bend Country of Texas and Big Bend National Park." Amarillo: O. B. Jarvis, n.d. Big Bend Vertical File, Center for American History, University of Texas at Austin.

Big Bend Natural History Association. "Hot Springs." Pamphlet, n.d. Springs Vertical File, Center for American History, University of Texas at Austin.

Casey, Clifford. *Mirages, Mysteries, and Realities: Brewster County, Texas, The Big Bend of the Rio Grande.* Seagraves, Tex.: Pioneer Book Publishers, 1972.

"The Fountain of Youth." Pamphlet, ca. 1910. Center for American History, University of Texas at Austin.

"Hot Springs." National Register of Historic Places, Nomination Form, 1972. Texas Historical Commission.

Hot Springs' Motel Register. Archives of the Big Bend, Bryan Wildenthal Library. Sul Ross State University, Alpine.

Langford, J. O. "Part I: Childhood Days; Part II: Other Reminiscences of J. O. Langford." Langford Papers, 1954. Center for American History, University of Texas at Austin.

Langford, J. O., and Gipson, Fred. *Big Bend: A Homesteader's Story.* Austin: University of Texas Press, 1952.

Whitaker, Lovie Langford. Interview by Freida Cochran, 27 April 1980. Tape at Archives of the Big Bend, Bryan Wildenthal Library, Sul Ross State University, Alpine.

———. Interview by Teresa Whittington, 30 August 1976. Tape at Archives of the Big Bend, Bryan Wildenthal Library, Sul Ross State University, Alpine.

HOT WELLS (HUDSPETH COUNTY)

Choate, Hattie M. "Hot Wells Editorial," 6 August 1964. Hudspeth County Vertical File, Center for American History, University of Texas at Austin.

Sierra Blanca Mountain Eagle.

HUBBARD (HILL COUNTY)

"Digging of Hubbard Hot Well—Wood's Hospital—-Midwife, Bertha Shanklin." *Hubbard City News,* November 1981.

Hunt, Alan. "Hubbard Keeps Bounding Ahead." *Waco Tribune-Herald,* 23 August 1976.

Marlin Ball.

HUGHES SPRINGS (CASS COUNTY)

Advertisement for Hughes' Springs Hotel. Austin *Statesman,* 1 and 6 July 1882.

"Atlanta, Avinger, and Hughes Springs." *Texas Magazine* 3, no. 4 (1911): 77–78.

Fite, Johnnyrea Luker, ed. *Hughes Springs, Texas, Histories.* Naples: Sesame Literary Club and the Printing Factory, 1986.

Hayes, Robert. "War May Put Etex in Light as Iron Center." *Dallas News,* 20 August 1940.

Tolbert, Frank X. "No 'Fem-iron' Problem at Chalybeate Springs." *Dallas Morning News,* 21 May 1972.

INDIAN HOT SPRINGS (HUDSPETH COUNTY)

Brewer, Steve. "Springs Are No Longer Hot Spot." *Dallas Morning News,* 14 February 1982.

Henry, Christopher. "Geologic Setting and Geochemistry of Thermal Water and Geothermal Assessment, Trans-Pecos Texas and Adjacent Mexico." Bureau of Economic Geology, University of Texas at Austin, 1979.

Lee, Mary. Fort Worth. Interview, 15 March 1989.

———. Fort Worth. Interview, 5 June 1990.

Maltby, William J. *Captain Jeff or Frontier Life in Texas with the Texas Rangers.* Colorado, Tex.: Whipkey, 1906.

O'Neal, James. Telephone interview, Austin, 2 February 1991.

Taylor, Pat Ellis. *Border Healing Woman.* Austin: University of Texas Press, 1981.

———. "Visiting the Mote in Heaven's Eye: An Account of the Cure at Indian Hot Springs." *The God Chaser.* Austin: Slough Press, 1986.

Teague, Olin E. *Congressional Record: Proceedings and Debates of the 90th Congress.* Vol. 114 (8), 1968.

"Testimonials." Private Collection of Mary Lee, Fort Worth.

Tolbert, Frank X. *An Informal History of Texas.* New York: Harper, 1951, 1961.

———. "Journey Through a Happy Wilderness." *Dallas Morning News,* 11 May 1963.

———. "Paved Road to the Springs." *Dallas Morning News,* 24 September 1967.

———. "Not Just Legend at Indian Springs." *Dallas Morning News,* 25 September 1967.

————. "Indian Hot Springs Lures Celebrities." *Dallas Morning News*, 7 March 1968.

————. "Notes on Apaches' 'Fountains of Youth.'" *Dallas Morning News*, 14 May 1970.

————. "Still Some Mystery at Indian Springs." *Dallas Morning News*, 16 May 1970.

KINGSTON HOT SPRINGS (RUIDOSA) (PRESIDIO COUNTY)

Bodine, Dan. "Fountain of Youth? Kingston Hot Springs Promises a Good Time, and More." *Presidio International*, 22 February 1990.

"Kingston Hot Springs Sells to Artist Donald Judd." *Marfa Independent and Big Bend Sentinel*, 5 April 1990.

Paul, Jack, and Bea Paul. Interview, Kingston Hot Springs, March 10, 1990.

Porterfield, Billy. "Texas Springs a Cure for What Ails a Body." *Austin American-Statesman*, 23 September 1991.

"Ruidosa, Ruidoso: Difference Far Greater than Mere 350 Miles." *Houston Post*, 25 November 1988.

Willeford, Glenn. "Closing of Kingston Hot Springs Leaves Public Questioning Its Future." *Presidio International*, 21 June 1990.

LAMPASAS (LAMPASAS COUNTY)

"Arrival of Moses Hughes: Keystone of City's History." *Lampasas Dispatch Record*, 11 April 1985.

Austin Daily Statesman. 1883.

Billingsley, James. "Diary." Center for American History, University of Texas at Austin.

Carhart, J. W. "Lampasas as a Health Resort." *Texas Sanitarian* 3, no. 4 (February 1894): 135–141.

Cole, James P. "A History of Lampasas County: 1882–1895." Master's thesis, Sam Houston State University, 1968.

Cross, F. M. *A Short Sketch-History from Personal Reminiscences of Early Days in Central Texas*. Brownwood, Tex.: Greenwood, 1912.

Elzner, Jonnie Ross. *Lamplights of Lampasas County*. Austin: Firm Foundation, 1951.

Lamity, E. "The Legend of Hanna Springs." Clipping, n.d. Lampasas County Historical Files.

"Lampasas County." *Texas Almanac and State Industrial Guide*. Galveston: A. H. Belo, 1904.

Lampasas Daily Times. 1878.

Lampasas Dispatch. 1877–88.

"Lampasas, Geographical Center." *Texas Magazine* (November 1910): 71.

"Lampasas . . . It Sticks in the Memory." *San Antonio Express Magazine*, 30 August 1951.

Lampasas Leader. 1877–1904.

Lampasas News. 1905.

"Lampasas, Once a Famous Health Resort in Texas, Retains Much of Its Early Day Quaintness." *San Antonio Express*, 5 July 1936.

"Lampasas, Texas: Its Mineral Springs." Reproduction of a ca. 1888 pamphlet by Poole, Chicago, 1972.

Lampasas Weekly News. 1904–5.

Moses, Mrs. W. H. "Park Hotel, Hancock Park Dominated Local Scene in 1898." *Lampasas Record*, 19 December 1963.

"Those Motorists Traveling Highway 66 Will Find it Abounds in Interesting Features and Traditional Hospitality Is Assured to Visitor." *San Antonio Express*, 5 July 1936.

"The Origin of Lampasas Springs." n.p., 17 February 1931. Clipping from local paper. Lampasas County Historical Commission Scrapbook, Lampasas County Courthouse.

Pace, Clint. "Lampasas Thrives upon Soil Prosperity." *Austin American-Statesman*, 8 February 1948.

Penn, W. E. *Life and Labors of Major W. E. Penn: "The Texas Evangelist."* St. Louis: C. B. Woodward, 1896.

Word, John P. Word Papers. Center for American History, 3P51, University of Texas at Austin.

Works Project Administration. "Points of Interest—Lampasas County." Report, ca. 1930. Center for American History, University of Texas at Austin.

LEE COUNTY'S WATERS

Killen, Mrs. James C. et al., eds. *History of Lee County.* Quanah, Tex.: Nortex and Lee County Historical Survey Committee, 1974.

MANGUM (EASTLAND COUNTY)

"Mangum, Once Wide Place in Road, Is Now Thriving Little City; Rapid Growth Predicted." *Fort Worth Star-Telegram,* 3 August 1919. Scrapbook of Mangum, Texas, Centennial Memorial Library, Eastland.

Scrapbook of Mangum, Texas, 1905–1927. Centennial Memorial Library, Eastland.

MARLIN (FALLS COUNTY)

Andress, Evelyn. "The South's Greatest Health Resort." Falls County Scrapbook, ca. 1930. Center for American History, University of Texas at Austin.

Belden, Tom. "Town Taps Past for Modern Cure." *Dallas Morning News,* 5 April 1978.

Berry, Louise MacDonagh. "The Seven Wonders of Marlin." *Texas Magazine* 3, no. 6 (April 1911): 79–80.

"Bonanza in Mineral Water." *Waco Tribune-Herald,* 20 July 1975.

Buie Jr., Neil. Interview, Galveston, 14 June 1990.

Calvin, Grace Catherine. "Marlin Wells: Pride of Brazos Valley." Clipping, ca. 1929. "Texas Cities and Towns." Texas Scrapbook. Houston Public Library.

Carmack, George. "Take Me out to the Well." *San Antonio Express,* 3 November 1984.

Criswell, Mrs. Thomas. Interview, Marlin, 8 April 1989.

Crittenden, Paula. "Little Town of Marlin Thrives as Health Spa." *Dallas Morning News,* 28 June 1963.

Culsaetsa, September. "A World Famed Mineral Water Resort: Marlin, Texas, Famous Mineral Water Discovered by 'Hobo.'" *Texas Magazine* 2 (1910): 80–81.

"Falls County." *The Texas Almanac and State Industrial Guide.* Galveston: A. H. Belo, 1904.

Flanders, Jack. "Marlin's Magic Mineral Water an Attraction." *Waco Tribune-Herald,* 20 July 1974.

"Follow the Road to Good Health." Pamphlet, n.d. Marlin Vertical File, Center for American History, University of Texas at Austin.

Fone, Meg A. "The Pavilion." *Marlin Democrat,* 4 March 1908.

———. "Bathhouse Row." *Marlin Democrat,* 11 March 1908.

Frost, William Schuyler, ed. *Review Marlin.* Quanah, Tex.: Nortex, 1909.

Hale, Leon. "Pitchin' Till You Win at the Harris House." *Houston Post,* 14 April 1971.

Hammond, C. M. "Marlin—Oasis of Health." *Texas Weekly* 8 (October 1932): 7–8.

Harris, Ruby. Interview, Marlin, 6 March 1991.

Houston, Hill. Interview, Marlin, 16 February 1990.

Kreps, Mary Ann. "Austin Architect Extends Option to Buy Marlin's Falls Hotel." *Waco Tribune-Herald,* 5 December 1984.

———. "Architect Plans to Revamp Falls Hotel." *Waco Tribune-Herald,* 17 January 1985.

———. "Falls Hotel Investors File for Bankruptcy." *Waco Tribune-Herald,* 8 January 1986.

———. "Hot Mineral Baths Gaining Steam." *Waco Tribune-Herald,* 30 July 1983.

Lippman, Laura. "Marlin Mineral Baths Spring up Again." *Waco Tribune-Herald,* 9 July 1982.

Marlin Ball. 1903–5.

Marlin Chamber of Commerce. "Marlin: It's in Texas. The Oasis of Health." Pamphlet, n.d. Marlin Vertical File, Center for American History, University of Texas at Austin.

———. "Marlin, Texas: Carlsbad of America." Pamphlet, ca. 1910. Marlin Vertical File, Center for American History, University of Texas at Austin.

———. "Modern Bath Houses, Clinics and Sanitariums." Pamphlet, ca. 1940. Marlin Vertical File, Center for American History, University of Texas at Austin.

———. "Your Spa . . . Marlin." Pamphlet, n.d. Marlin Vertical File, Center for American History, University of Texas at Austin.

Marlin Chamber of Commerce, ed. *Marlin: 1851–1976.* Marlin: Chamber of Commerce and Bicentennial Heritage Committee, 1976.

Marlin Democrat. 1908–11.

"Marlin Ready for Opening of C.C. Meet," 1931. *Dallas Morning News,* April 12.

"Marlin Sings the Siren Song." *East Texas* (April 1959).

"Marlin Spreads the Welcome Mat." *Dallas Morning News,* 19 October 1958.

"Marlin's Artesian Well." *Texas Medical Journal* 10, no. 1 (July 1894): 87.

"Marlin's Mineral Baths, Climate Offer Haven for Health-Seekers." *This Month in Central Texas* (9 September 1948).

"Marlin: The Belle of the Brazos." *Texas Magazine* 1 (1910): 76–77.

McKinnon, Mac. "Putting Marlin on Bath Map Goal of Ex-Rancher Hotelier." *Fort Worth Star-Telegram,* 20 December 1970.

Oltorf, Frank Calvert. Interview, Marlin, 16 February 1990.

Oltorf, Frank Calvert. *The Marlin Compound: Letters from a Singular Family.* Austin: University of Texas Press, 1968.

"Over the Houston and Texas Central." *The Bohemian* 3 (1902): 78–85.

Peacock, Richard. Telephone interview, Bryan, 3 February 1991.

"Plan Proposed for Bathhouse," *Marlin Democrat,* 16 January 1991.

Ryan, Zack. Telephone interview, 4 September 1990.

"Sam Crane on Marlin." *Marlin Democrat,* 29 February 1908.

"Search for Marlin's Hot Mineral Water Progressing." *Waco Tribune-Herald,* 1 June 1979.

Smith, Howard, M.D. "History of the Hot Mineral Water Wells of Marlin." Marker File, Texas Historical Commission, 28 August 1972.

"The Buie Clinic and Hospital." *Private Clinics and Hospitals of Texas* (September/October 1952): 4–5.

"The Hot Well." *Marlin Democrat,* 29 February 1908.

"The Majestic Hotel and Bathhouse Co." Pamphlet, n.d. Center for American History, University of Texas at Austin.

"The Tramp and the Barrel." *Marlin Democrat,* 11 March 1908.

Tolbert, Frank X. "Goddess of Health in Downtown Marlin." *Dallas Morning News,* 15 March 1971.

Torbett, Sr., J. W. *Hot Air Verses from the Hot Water Town.* Marlin: Byrne Color Press, 1914.

———. *The Doctor's Scrapbook.* Dallas: Wilkinson, 1947.

Torbett, Virginia. Interview, Marlin, 13 March, 8 April 1989.

Werlin, Rosella H. "Forever Amber." *Dallas Times Herald,* 9 December 1962.

Williamson, Judy. "Marlin: A Texas Town's Mineral 'Rites.'" *Dallas Morning News,* 12 December 1982.

MIDYETT (PANOLA COUNTY)

LaGrone, Leila B. Letter to Texas Historical Commission. Midyett Marker File, Texas Historical Commission, 8 March 1980.

Nugent, Mrs. R. M. Telephone interview, Carthage, 8 September 1990.

MINEOLA (WOOD COUNTY)

"Mineola." *Texas and Pacific Quarterly* 12, no. 1 (January 1909): 14–15.

Mineola Monitor.

"Mineola Ready When Boom Struck Town." *Dallas Morning News,* 12 January 1941.

Reeves, E. A. "Mineola, Wood County, Texas." *Texas Magazine* 7, no. 5 (March 1913): 459–460.

MINERAL (CITY) (BEE COUNTY)

Fomby, Minnie. "Mineral Once Had High Hopes of Health Resort When the Cure-All Well Was at its Best." *San Antonio Express,* 27 August 1934.

MINERAL WELLS (PALO PINTO COUNTY)

"The Baker . . . a Baker Hotel." Pamphlet, n.d. Rosenberg Library, Galveston.

Baker, J. H. "Diary Excerpts," 1881. *Palo Pinto County Star,* 26 April, 3 May 1940.

"The Baker Hotel." Statement of Significance. National Register of Historic Places Inventory File, Texas Historical Commission.

Baker News, October 1933. Mineral Wells Vertical File, Rosenberg Library, Galveston.

Banks, Harold. "Resort City Opens New Baker Hotel." *Fort Worth Record-Telegram,* 23 November 1929.

Berry, H. M. "A Brief History of Mineral Wells, 1881–1921," n.d. *Palo Pinto County Star,* 12, 17, and 24 April, 1, 8, 22, and 29 May 1942.

"'The Better Way' Mineral Wells Water (Route) to Health." Pamphlet, ca. 1910. Mineral Wells Vertical File, Rosenberg Library, Galveston.

Birdwell, Effie N. "Famous Mineral Water Company." Marker File, Texas Historical Commission, 1989.

Cochran, Mike. "Tourism Well Dry: Town Still Crazy after All These Years." *Fort Worth Star-Telegram,* 16 July 1978.

"Common Sense Concerning Mineral Waters." *Texas State Journal of Medicine* 3 (1907): 206.

Cox, Mamie Wynne. *A Love Story of Mineral Wells.* Mineral Wells, Tex.: Index, 1932.

"Crazy Water: A Pleasant Laxative Mineral Water Distilled in the Laboratory of Nature." Pamphlet, n.d. Mineral Wells Vertical File, Rosenberg Library, Galveston.

Crazy Water Hotel Company. "Here—May You Find All That You Seek of Health, Comfort, and Satisfaction." Pamphlet, 1930. Mineral Wells Vertical File, Rosenberg Library, Galveston.

Daniels, Vernon. Telephone interview, Mineral Wells, 6 June 1990.

Doss, Thelma. Telephone interview, Mineral Wells, 6 June 1990.

Eastland, J. H. "Mineral Wells: Its Climatology and the Therapeutic Value of Its Waters." *Texas State Journal of Medicine* 5 (December 1909): 304–307.

Fiedler, Winnie Beatrice McAnelly. "A History of Mineral Wells, Texas: 1878–1953." Master's thesis, University of Texas at Austin, 1953.

Ford, Robert E. 1972. "Mineral Baths, Thigh Slappers Gone, but Crazy Hotel Still Great Place." *Fort Worth Star-Telegram,* 21 December 1972.

Fowler, Gene, and Bill Crawford. *Border Radio.* Austin: Texas Monthly Press, 1987.

Grothe, Randy Eli. "A Golden Past, and a Broken Present." *Dallas Morning News,* 5 December 1976.

Grove, Larry. "Tax Rule Blamed for Hotel's Woes." *Dallas Morning News,* 12 April 1963.

Hammond. C. M. "Drinking Health at Mineral Wells." *Texas Weekly* 8 (2 April 1932): 9.

Hartman, Sara. "Mineral Wells." *Gulf Messenger* 6 (1893): 292–294.

"Health and Pleasure at Mineral Wells: The Famous Texas Resort." Pamphlet, ca. 1911. Mineral Wells Vertical File, Rosenberg Library, Galveston.

House, Ruby. "Mineral Wells, Then and Now." Palo Pinto County Scrapbook, Center for American History, University of Texas at Austin, n.d.

Jorden, Jay. "Hopes Pinned on 'Crazy Water.'" *Lufkin News,* 9 June 1983.

"Mineral Wells." *Texas Health Journal* 6 (1893): 86.

"Mineral Wells." *Texas and Pacific Quarterly* 10, no. 3 (July 1907): 13–14.

"Mineral Wells Advertising to Be Censored." *Texas State Journal of Medicine* 7 (May 1915): 5–6.

Mineral Wells Board of City Development. "The South's Greatest Health Resort: Mineral Wells Texas." Pamphlet, n.d. Mineral Wells Vertical File, Center for American History, University of Texas at Austin.

Mineral Wells Chamber of Commerce. "Ten Years Younger." Pamphlet, ca. 1916. Mineral Wells Vertical File, Center for American History, University of Texas at Austin.

Mineral Wells Commercial Club. "Hotel Guide of Mineral Wells: The Health Resort of the South." Brochure, n.d. Mineral Wells Vertical File, Center for American History, the University of Texas at Austin.

———. "Hotel Guide for Visitors to Mineral Wells." Brochure, 1909. Mineral Wells Vertical File, Rosenberg Library, Galveston.

———. "Quarterly Guide." Brochure, 1909. Mineral Wells Vertical File, Rosenberg Library, Galveston.

———. "Hotel Guide of Mineral Wells, the Health and Pleasure Resort." Brochure, 1911. Mineral Wells Vertical File, Rosenberg Library, Galveston.

Mineral Wells Daily Index.

Mineral Wells Daily Index. *Health Resort Quarterly,* 19 October 1915. Palo Pinto County Scrapbook, Center for American History, University of Texas at Austin.

"Mineral Wells of Texas." *Texas Health Journal* 5, no. 12 (June 1893): 315.

"Mineral Wells of Texas—The American 'Carlsbad.'" *Texas Health Journal* 8 (July 1890): 45–47.

"Mineral Wells, Palo Pinto County, Texas." *Texas Prairie Flower* 2, no. 3 (September 1883): 116–121.

"Mineral Wells Spot to Do Nothing Best." *Dallas Morning News,* 25 February 1948.

"Mineral Wells, Texas: Where America Drinks Its Way to Health. The New Million-Dollar Crazy Hotel." Pamphlet, n.d. Mineral Wells Vertical File, Center for American History, University of Texas at Austin.

"Mineral Wells, the 'Carlsbad' of Texas." *The Bohemian* 4, no. 4 (1903/1904): 79–83.

Mulé, Lisa. "Mineral Wells' Posh Baker Hotel Once Again Goes on Auction Block." *Fort Worth Star-Telegram,* 7 July 1987.

"New Host of Strangers Invades Mineral Wells." *Dallas Morning News,* 13 August 1967.

Nordyke, Lewis. "That Crazy City: Mineral Wells." *Texas Parade* (March 1952): 20–28.

"The One Water with Analysis on Every Bottle." Pamphlet, n.d. Mineral Wells Vertical File, Rosenberg Library, Galveston.

"Palo Pinto County." *The Texas Almanac and State Industrial Guide.* Galveston: A. H. Belo, 1904.

Palo Pinto County Star. 1940–42.

Pass, Fred. "New Host of Strangers Invades Mineral Wells." *Dallas Morning News,* 13 August 1967.

"Read What Physicians Say about Mineral Wells, Texas: The Famous All-the-Year-Round Health Resort." Pamphlet, ca. 1908. Mineral Wells Vertical File, Rosenberg Library, Galveston.

Register, J. W. "Mineral Wells, Famous Resort." *Texas Magazine* 2, no. 3 (July 1910): 63–64.

Remick, Pat. "Mineral Wells to Celebrate 100th Anniversary Next Week." *Dallas Morning News,* 11 September 1982.

"Texas' Carlsbad." *Texas and Pacific Quarterly* 8, no. 3 (July 1905): 27–35.

Thomas, Les. "Dave Brunswick Serenade Revived in Mineral Wells." *Fort Worth Star-Telegram,* 28 December 1975.

Tolbert, Frank. "Here's Background on 'Home of Crazy.'" *Dallas Morning News,* 22 June 1956.

"The Town of Mineral Wells." *Galveston Daily News,* 4 February 1882.

Turner, Samuel F. *Mineral-Water Supply of the Mineral Wells Area, Texas.* Geological Survey Circular 6. Washington: Department of the Interior, 1934.

Views from the City of Healing Waters. Mineral Wells: Owl Book Company, 1913.

Walker, Bill. "Baker Hotel Revival: Another Miracle?" *Fort Worth Star-Telegram,* 23 August 1981.

"Water that Puts Pepper into Plodders Brought a Bonanza to Mineral Wells." *Dallas Times Herald,* 16 July 1978.

Weaver, A. F. *Time Was in Mineral Wells: A Crazy Story but True . . .* Mineral Wells: Mineral Wells Heritage Society and Houghton-Bennett, 1975.

"What Do You Know about the South's Greatest Resort?" *Mineral Wells Index,* 10 November 1935.

"What Others Say about Mineral Wells Waters: Testimonials (with Analyses)." Pamphlet, ca. 1911. Mineral Wells Vertical File, Rosenberg Library, Galveston.

White, Velva. Interview, Mineral Wells, 6 June 1990.

MYRTLE SPRINGS (VAN ZANDT COUNTY)

Myrtle Springs Herald, 19 November 1891.

NACOGDOCHES COUNTY

Erison, Joe E. "Nacogdoches as a Health Resort? The Story of Aqua Vitae Park." *East Texas Historical Association* 33 (1995): 44–49.

NOLAN COUNTY (GROGAN MINERAL WELLS)

Musgrove, R. A. "Sweetwater and Noland County." *Texas and Pacific Quarterly* 15, no. 4 (October 1912): 65.

"Once Health Center." *Sweetwater Reporter,* 28 January 1968.

Reed, Johnna, and Monte Williams. "Sweetwater: Once Site of Health Center." *Big Country* 3 (1979): 44–45.

"Sweetwater Fast Becoming Famous as a Health Resort." *Sweetwater Weekly Reporter,* 3 April 1914.

ORAN (PALO PINTO COUNTY STAR)

Mineral Wells Daily Index, 6 May 1907.

Palo Pinto County Star, 20 March 1940.

OVERALL (ROBERTSON COUNTY)

Nickelson, Rebecca. Letter to author, 28 March 1990.

PHILLIPS (GREGG COUNTY)

Mayer, Nauty Byrd, ed. *Gladewater, Texas, 1873–1973.* Gladewater, Tex.: N.p., 1973.

Teske, Charlotte. *Longview: From Then . . . Til Now.* Longview: Self-published, 1987.

PUTNAM (CALLAHAN COUNTY)

Abilene Reporter-News, 5 June 1976.

Berry, John. "Mission Hotel at Putnam, Texas." *West Texas Historical Association Yearbook* 39 (1963): 89–92.

Chrisman, Brutus Clay. *Early Days in Callahan County.* Abilene: Abilene Printing, 1966.

Putnam Commercial Club. "Putnam—The Great West Texas Health and Pleasure Resort," prospectus, 1911. Original with Putnam City Secretary, Ida Mae Waddell.

Rutherford, LaVerne. Interview, Putnam, 9 August 1990.

San Antonio Express, 24 August 1986.

RED SPRINGS (DELLWOOD) (TITUS COUNTY)

Jurney, Richard Loyall. *History of Titus County, Texas: 1846 to 1960.* Dallas: Royal Publishing, 1961.

Manley, Perry, et al., eds. *Titus County Celebrates 125 Years.* Mount Pleasant Public Library, 1971.

Russell, Traylor. *History of Titus County, Texas.* Waco: W. M. Morrison, 1965.

RUSK COUNTY'S SPRINGS

"History of Brachfield Recounted." N.p., 27 June 1976. Clipping. Carthage Library, Carthage.

Winfrey, Dorman H. *A History of Rusk County, Texas.* Waco: Texian Press, 1961.

SISTERDALE (KENDALL COUNTY)

Flach, Vera. *A Yankee in German America: Texas Hill Country.* San Antonio: Naylor, 1973.

Geiser, S. W. "Dr. Ernst Kapp, Early Geographer in Texas." *Field and Laboratory* 14 (1946): 16–31.

Kendall County Historical Commission. *A History of Kendall County, Texas.* Dallas: Taylor, 1984.

Lich, Glen E. *The German Texans.* San Antonio: Institute of Texan Cultures, 1981.

Sisterdale, Description of. Texas Historical Commission, Register of Historic Places File.

Wehmeyer, Karl, and Betty Wehmeyer. "Freethinkers on the Frontier." *Austin American-Statesman,* 17 February 1987.

SMITH COUNTY'S WATERS

Clark, Betsy. "Headache Springs." In *Down Country Roads,* edited by Kay Andrews Daphna Lilienstern. Tyler: Tyler Independent School District, 1988.

Davis, Ellis Arthur, and Edwin H. Grobe. "Richard Andrews Riviere." *The New Encyclopedia of Texas,* vol. 2. Dallas: Texas Historical Society, 1930.

Smith County Historical Society. "Tyler Bottles." *Chronicles of Smith County, Texas* 9 (Spring 1970): 54–55.

Tolbert, Frank X. "Headache Springs Park Is Still a 'Headache.'" *Dallas Morning News,* 30 August 1971.

———. "An 'Aspirin Taste' at Headache Springs." *Dallas Morning News,* 24 March 1974.

———. *Tolbert's Texas.* New York: Doubleday, 1983.

SOUR LAKE (HARDIN COUNTY)

Abernethy, Francis E., ed. *Tales from the Big Thicket.* Austin: University of Texas Press, 1967.

Abrams Jr., L. I. *Time and Shadows.* Waco: Davis Brothers, 1971.

Beaumont Journal, 15 July 1955.

Bookman, W. F. "Dramatic Struggle of Nature, Far Underground, Closely Intertwined with History of Sour Lake." *Houston Chronicle,* 21 June 1936.

C.D.M. "Sour Lake Letters." *Galveston Daily News,* 14 July 1857.

Cotner, Robert. *James Stephen Hogg: A Biography.* Austin: University of Texas Press, 1959.

Edmondson, Mrs. E. E. "Sour Lake Was Health Resort." *Beaumont Enterprise,* 30 June 1940.

Hamilton, Jeff. *My Master: The Inside Story of Sam Houston and His Times.* Dallas: Manfred, Van Nort, 1940.

"A History of Sour Lake and Legend of Its Origin." *Houston Daily Post,* 2 July 1903.

Millard, Henry. Letter to Sam Houston, 1 December 1837. Ashbel Smith Papers, Center for American History, University of Texas at Austin.

Morrison, Andrew. "Sour Lake Mineral Springs: The Texas Sanitarium." *City of Houston.* Engelhardt Series: American Cities, 1891.

"The Mud that Once Healed Sick Now Makes Healthy Texans Well-Heeled with Oil." *Houston Press,* 17 October 1951.

Olmsted, Frederick Law. *A Journey Through Texas.* New York: Dix, Edwards, 1857.

O'Quinn, Truman. "Gen. Sam Houston Refused to Pay $4400 for Sour Lake." *Beaumont Enterprise,* 9 December 1928.

Owens, George. "Ruins Tell Colorful History of Sour Lake." *Beaumont Journal,* 15 July 1955.

"Prospectus of the Proposed Sour Lake Springs Company, of Texas," ca. 1898. Sour Lake Vertical File, Rosenberg Library, Galveston.

Rothe, Aline Thompson. "Texas 'Fountain of Youth.'" *Houston Chronicle,* 10 April 1949.

Scurlock, Ruth Garrison. "Sour Lake: Spa of the Big Thicket." In *Tales from the Big Thicket,* edited by Francis E. Abernethy. Austin: University of Texas Press, 1967.

"Sour Lake: One of the Wonders of the World." *Gulf Messenger* 10 (May 1897): 228–233.

"Sour Lake, Texas: Health Resort of the Nineteenth Century." Pamphlet, n.d. Sour Lake Vertical File, Sam Houston Regional Library and Research Center, Liberty, Texas.

"Sour Lake Watering Place, Jefferson County, Texas." *New Orleans Weekly Delta,* 13 October 1851.

Tolbert, Frank X. "Sour Lake Town due to Sink into Earth?" *Dallas Morning News,* 8 February 1973.

Watkins, Mrs. George. "My Experience at Sour Lake Springs." *Oil City Visitor,* 22 December 1928.

Williams, Alfred M. *Sam Houston and the War of Independence in Texas.* Boston: Houghton, Mifflin, 1893.

Ziegler, Jesse. *Wave of the Gulf.* San Antonio: Naylor, 1938.

STOVALL HOT WELLS (YOUNG COUNTY)

Crouch, Carrie J. *A History of Young County, Texas.* Austin: Texas State Historical Association, 1956.

Graham Leader, 29 September 1938.

King, Judy, and Roy King. "Stovall Wells." Flyer, 1989.

———. Letter to author, 4 April 1991.

Mallison, Rodger. "The Well Waters." *Fort Worth Star-Telegram,* 13 April 1989.

WPA. "Stovall Hot Water Well." Report, 1936. Center for American History, University of Texas at Austin.

SULPHUR SPRINGS (HOPKINS COUNTY)

Adams, Florence Chapman. *Hopkins County and Our Heritage.* N.p., 1976.

Brice, Kenneth, and Sidney Brice. *A Century of Memories.* Sulphur Springs: N.p, n.d.

Chamber of Commerce. *Alphabetical Information about Sulphur Springs, Texas.* Pamphlet. Center for American History, University of Texas at Austin, 1915.

SULPHUR SPRINGS (TYLER COUNTY)

Armstrong, Phoebe Young. *From the Forks of Turkey Creek.* Privately printed, 1987.

SUTHERLAND SPRINGS (WILSON COUNTY)

Anderson, Fred, and Mrs. Fred Anderson. Interview, Austin, 16 October 1990.

Fore, Roger W. "Ghost Playground." *San Antonio Express Magazine,* 15 February 1948.

Golson, Josephine Polley. *Bailey's Light: Saga of Brit Bailey and Other Hardy Pioneers.* San Antonio: Naylor, 1950.

Graham, Bill. "Ghost Town—S. Texas Style." *San Antonio Express-News,* 22 August 1971.

McCully, John. "Old Hotel Houses a Family of Five." *San Antonio Light,* 7 May 1939.

Masters, Lillian. Telephone interview, Floresville, 24 February 1991.

Polley, J. B. "Sutherland Springs." *Western Chronicle,* 20 April 1877.

Richardson, T. C. *Autobiography of the Rambling Longhorn.* Oklahoma City: Farmer-Stockman, 1959.

San Antonio Light, 13 October 1969.

Shriber, Gail. Letter to Texas Historical Commission, 18 February 1966. Marker File, Texas Historical Commission.

"Sutherland Springs: The 'Carlsbad of America.'" *San Antonio Express,* 14 June 1909.

Sutherland Springs Development Company. "Why Not Know Why?" Prospectus, ca. 1909. Center for American History, University of Texas at Austin.

Sutherland Springs Health Resort. 1910–14.

Sutherland Springs Western Chronicle. 1877–78.

"Where Healing Waters Flow." Pamphlet, ca. 1911. Texas Collection, Baylor University, Waco.

Wilson County Journal. 1908–10.

THORP'S SPRINGS (HOOD COUNTY)

Ewell, Thomas T. *History of Hood County.* Granbury, Tex.: Frank Gaston, 1895. Reprint, Granbury: Junior Woman's Club, 1956.

Granbury Woman's Club. *Hood County History in Picture and Story.* Fort Worth: Historical Publishers, 1978.

TIOGA (GRAYSON COUNTY)

Cheatham, H. P., Interview, Tioga, 5 June 1990.

Estes, Ross, and Robert Duncan, eds. *I Remember Things: An Informal History of Tioga, Texas.* Quanah, Tex.: Nortex Press, 1977.

Grayson County Frontier Village. *History of Grayson County.* Tioga: Grayson County Frontier Village and Hunter Publishing, 1979.

Kutsky, Diana. "'Magic' Mineral Water Flows in Tioga." *Denton Record Chronicle,* 10 October 1976.

McDonald, W. A. "The Fountain of Youth." *Tioga Herald,* 21 November 1919.

"A New Health Resort." *Texas and Pacific Quarterly* (April 1903): 8.

Pederson, Rena. "Mostly Old, Mostly New." *Dallas Morning News,* 4 October 1975.

Sherman Democrat, 19 September 1948.

Tolleson, Corine. Letter to author, 14 March 1991.

"Tioga, Texas." *Texas and Pacific Quarterly* 15, no. 4 (October 1912): 56–57.

Tolbert, Frank. "Why Tioga Town Isn't Called Autry Springs." *Dallas Morning News,* 26 February 1972.

Williams, Lillian. "Yesteryear: Going, Going, Gone." *Dallas Times Herald,* 13 November 1983.

TRAVIS COUNTY'S WATERS

"Artesian Bath House." *Austin Statesman,* 27 April 1900.

Austin Statesman, 2 February 1882.

"Austin, Texas: A Lone Star in the Galaxy of Southern Resorts." *Texas Sanitarian* 4 (April 1895): 239–240.

"It Isn't the Water, Son, It's the View They Take." N.p., n.d. Capitol Grounds Vertical File, Austin History Center.

Pennock, R. "Capitol Well Smelly: People Keep Coming." *Austin American-Statesman,* 23 September 1973.

Warner, George P. *Something of Interest Concerning Austin, the Great Capital of Texas.* Pamphlet, ca. 1890. St. Louis: Austin Board of Trade and Woodward and Tiernan. Austin History Center.

"Well, Why Not?" *Austin American-Statesman,* n.d. Capitol Grounds Vertical File, Austin History Center.

TUSCALOOSA SPRINGS (WYSER) (WALKER COUNTY)

Baldwin, John W. "An Early History of Walker County, Texas." Master's thesis, Sam Houston State University, 1957.

Crews, D'Anne McAdams, ed. *Huntsville and Walker County, Texas: A Bicentennial History.* Huntsville: Sam Houston State University Press, 1976.

Huntsville Item, 24 July 1858.

WACO (MCLENNAN COUNTY)

General Directory of the City of Waco. Galveston: Morrison and Fourmy, 1898.

McKay, A. F. "Waco: The Geyser City of Texas." *American Climates and Resorts,* 1893. Reprint, *Waco Heritage and History* 3, no. 3 (Fall 1972).

"Waco's Artesian Wells," 1890. *Geyser City Record,* 25 May 1890. Reprint, *Waco Heritage and History* 2, no. 2 (Summer 1971).

WARM SPRINGS (OTTINE) (GONZALES COUNTY)

Gonzales Inquirer, July 19, 1923.

Gonzales Warm Springs Foundation. "Factual Data and History of Your Gonzales Warm Springs Foundation for Crippled Children, Gonzales, Texas." Brochure. Warm Springs Rehabilitation Hospital, Public Relations Office, 1956.

Staton, Dudley. Telephone interview, Ottine, 11 January 1991.

WIZARD WELLS (JACK COUNTY)

Anderson, Lee. "Wizard Wells Springs Again." *Wichita Falls Record News,* 24 May 1975.

Davis, Jim. Telephone interview, 3 November 1990.

Dennis, W. W. "Bill." Letter to Texas Historical Commission, 1979. Marker File, Texas Historical Commission.

Fort Worth Star-Telegram, 8 September 1964.

Horton, Thomas F. *History of Jack County.* Jacksboro: Gazette, 1933. Reprint, by W. W. "Bill" Dennis, 1975.

Huckabay, Ida Lasater. *Ninety-four Years in Jack County.* Austin: Steck, 1949.

Jack County Genealogical Society. *The History of Jack County.* 1985.

Jones, Martha. Telephone interview, Wizard Wells, 8 September 1990.

Peacock, Laura. "A Brief History of Wizard Wells," 19 June 1978. Marker File, Texas Historical Commission.

Stacy, Dennis. "All's Well at Wizard Wells." *Texas Weekly Magazine,* 19 January 1986.

Tolbert, Frank X. "Artists and Deer 'Haunt' the Wells." *Dallas Morning News,* 15 February 1964.

Vineyard City Guide Post 1, no. 5 (27 January 1883). Original in possession of W. W. "Bill" Dennis, Jacksboro.

"Wizard Wells Health and Resort Complex." Report, n.d. Marker File, Texas Historical Commission.

WOOTAN WELLS (ROBERTSON COUNTY)

Allbritton, Fay B. Letter to James Turner. 26 November 1968. Scrapbook of Mrs. Susan Bass, Bremond, Texas.

Baker, J. W. "Wootan Wells, a Cen-Tex Ghost Town." *Waco Tribune Herald,* 23 November 1969.
———. "Wootan Wells." Typewritten copy. Scrapbook of Mrs. Susan Bass, Bremond, Texas.
Cumming, Marion. "Where Society Gathered." *Houston Chronicle Magazine,* 11 June 1950.
Eaves, Flora. Letter to Lottie May Walker, 20 April 1956. Scrapbook of Mrs. Susan Bass, Bremond, Texas.
Eberstadt Papers. Center for American History, University of Texas at Austin.
Etheridge, W. B. "Ghost Towns of Texas: Wootan Wells." *Houston Chronicle,* 27 April 1939.
Florida, Peggy Joyce. "The Swan Song of Wootan Wells." *True West* (January/February 1967): 36–37.
"Historical Marker to Be Unveiled at Wootan Wells." *Bremond Press,* 21 November 1969.
Roberts, John C. Diary excerpts, 1 May, 14 May 1881. Scrapbook of Mrs. Susan Bass, Bremond, Texas.
Tolbert, Frank X. "Cowboys Now in 'Still Life' Cigarette Commercials." *Dallas Morning News,* 1 October 1970.
———. "Cows Wouldn't Drink Wootan Wells Waters." *Dallas Morning News,* 31 October 1970.
Turner, Thomas. "Early Health Resort Lives Only in Memory." *Dallas Morning News,* 17 February 1948.
Wade, Woodie L. Letter to James Turner, 26 May 1967. Scrapbook of Mrs. Susan Bass, Bremond, Texas.
"Wootan Wells." Marker File, Texas Historical Commission.
"Wootan Wells." *Texas Prairie Flower* 2, no. 4 (October 1883): 184–189.
"Wootan's Wells—Analysis of the Water." *Courier-Record of Medicine* 2 (1884): 190.

Maps

Bureau of Economic Geology, University of Texas at Austin, 1982. "Geothermal Resources of Texas."
Colton, J. H. "Colton's New Map of the State of Texas." New York, 1866. Center for American History, University of Texas at Austin.
———. "Colton's New Map of the State of Texas." New York, 1872. Center for American History, University of Texas at Austin.
De Cordova, J. "J. De Cordova's Map of the State of Texas." New York: J. M. Atwood, 1849.
Johnson and Ward. "Johnson's New Map of the State of Texas." 1863. Center for American History, University of Texas at Austin.
Johnson, A. J. "Johnson's Texas." New York: A. J. Johnson, 1870. Center for American History, University of Texas at Austin.
Young, J. H. "New Map of Texas," 1836. Center for American History, University of Texas at Austin.
———. "Map of the State of Texas from the Latest Authorities." Philadelphia: Cowperthwait, de-Silver, and Butler, 1850. Center for American History, University of Texas at Austin.
———. "Map of the State of Texas from the Latest Authorities." Philadelphia: Thomas, Cowperthwait, 1952. Center for American History, University of Texas at Austin.

Index

Printed and bound by CPI Group (UK) Ltd, Croydon, CR0 4YY

09/06/2025

14685840-0003